Successful Cybersecurity Professionals

Successful Cybersecurity Professionals

How To Change Your Behavior to Protect Your Organization

Dr. Steven Brown, CISSP, CCSBP

BEP
BUSINESS EXPERT PRESS
Leader in applied, concise business books

First published in 2020 by
Business Expert Press, LLC
222 East 46th Street, New York, NY 10017
www.businessexpertpress.com

ISBN-13: 978-1-95253-842-1 (paperback)
ISBN-13: 978-1-95253-843-8 (e-book)

Business Expert Press Business Law and Corporate Risk Management Collection

Collection ISSN: 2333-6722 (print)
Collection ISSN: 2333-6730 (electronic)

First edition: 2020

10 9 8 7 6 5 4 3 2 1

Printed in the United States of America.

Dedication for this book goes to my children, Dylan and Jessica. A parent can learn a lot about behavior and psychology watching their kids grow. Asking them for help however, is a completely different story, but they were inspirations nevertheless.

Abstract

What does the New York Statue of Liberty, the famous Brooklyn Bridge, and the iconic Madison Square Garden, where many famous musical bands have played and world champion sporting events have been held, have in common? Well, they've been sold multiple times, to different people, for large amounts of money, and all of it fraudulent. At one point in the mid-1900s, rumor has it that it had gotten so bad that the Brooklyn Bridge was being sold twice a week. So, the New York City Police Department had to place a booth on the bridge to tell the new weekly owners, that the bridge was not sold, and they have been scammed. So, what is this about? Well, behavior. Why we do things, how do we behave, why in the normal course of a day we would never fall for a scam or be persuaded to do something against our better judgment, but in the next instance, we would buy a bridge.

This book looks at behavior from a cybersecurity expert's point of view. And while the cybersecurity expert may not buy a bridge, they may buy a firewall or implement some security solution simply because of persuasion. Due to cognitive complexities, biases, heuristics, and everything else in our environment, we will see how people, even cybersecurity experts, will say they will act one way, but act completely different in a different situation. We will also see, even against their own better judgment, they will change their mind. They will actively work to reach a faulty decision, even knowing that decision is wrong. That is the purpose of this book—to look at and examine our behavior so we make better cybersecurity decisions.

Keywords

Cybersecurity; behavior; context of association; Pavlov's dogs; sextortion; personality traits; deepfakes; theory of cybersecurity; perceptions; hackers; cognitive economy; biases; heuristics; cybersecurity paradox; memory; cognitive dissonance; chain of events; intelligence; cyber maturity; security intelligence; brainjacking; cybersecurity education

Contents

CHAPTER 1

Cybersecurity and Behavior

Introduction

If you were to review the top ten security breaches of 2020, you might see something like the following:

- *Ten million accounts were compromised due to passwords in clear text.*
- *Data leak on government server compromised over 200,000 users' personal information.*
- *Ten million users lost their personal data due to an infected dynamic link library being loaded during a patch upgrade.*
- *Over 130,000 million users lost their personal data due a supplier's vendor, who was a trusted partner, installing new software on one of their servers.*

If you were to review the top ten security breaches of 2019, you might read something like the following:

- *Over 110,000 million users had their personal data stolen due to a server without a password.*
- *Over 200,000 million records were stolen from a company's database whose vendor was allowed to access their data.*
- *A database consisting of over 150 gigabytes of data and over half a million records were stolen by a backup vendor.*

If you were to review the top ten security breaches of 2018, you might see something like the following:

- *Over 37 million customers lost their data due to a lack of response that their equipment was vulnerable.*
- *Over 50 million customers had their data stolen when hackers infected a company's website with malicious code.*
- *Over 90 million users lost their personal data when a company did not verify how its partner was protecting their data.*

We can certainly get a lot more examples, but in all of these, we never learn *why* such things happen!

Why was a password left open? Why was a server left with a default password? Why was a company's vendor never asked about how they secure data? Why did an infected dll get loaded? Why did someone load malicious code on a company's website? We do not need to ask how, because after an investigation we find out how an attack happened, but we seldom know why it happened. Why did we not check the security of that third-party vendor that accesses our customers' data? We certainly check our company's systems for security but not that of a third-party vendor. Was it because we labeled them a trusted host? Well, it turns out it's human nature, and the point of this book. If we ask *why* now, perhaps we can stop the *how* later. By combining human nature, psychology, and cybersecurity aspects, we can begin to wonder about the *why*, and see if we can predict human behavior just a little bit better. Remember, this is not to understand the human behavior of the attacker but our own behavior (i.e., what did we do, what did we not do), what could we have been done to make sure we placed the best possible safeguards, and if we could not, why? This then pushes us to attempt to understand human behavior.

Human Behavior

While research on human behavior dates back to several centuries, research in cyber behavior is very limited, even if almost nonexistent. We try to understand why people commit certain acts, or why people in one circumstance would do one thing, but in another set of circumstances do something completely different. There are fields of psychology that try to explain this, including behaviorism, cognitive psychology, psychotherapy, social psychology, cognitive behavioral therapy, and their many subbranches including conditioned response, psychanalysis, humanism, and conformism, to name just a few. So, with the wisdom of great minds such as Freud, Skinner, Seligman, Loftus, Maslow, Milgram, and Zimbaro, we should have a good body of knowledge to assimilate that could help change the cyber behavior of an individual.

Psychology could be considered a combination of two areas of science: physiology, the physical makeup of the human system, and psychology, which talks about the interconnection between them, and the mental process that guides thoughts, speech, and behavior. Philosophy talks about our thoughts and ideas and psychology talks about how do we even come to have these thoughts and ideas. Could these two bodies of sciences tell us about our workings of our own mind, and if so, could then predict our behavior to some extent? Many early researchers like Ivan Pavlov suggested we could only measure external behavior, not the internal mental state. Researcher Watson looked at interactions with the environment and stimulus–response theory, while Freud examined the psychoanalytic theory, childhood trauma, and the notion of the subconscious in behavior. Then later researchers moved to cognitive psychology, social psychology, and added evolutionary, moral, social, cultural learning. We combined that with the cradle to the grave model, which led to the late 20th-century model of human uniqueness. We even looked at normal and abnormal as being one and the same, just on a scale.

Who could ever forget Mel Brook's movie *Young Frankenstein* and Abby Normal?

Therefore, with this vast amount of accumulated knowledge, I assumed we would have enough information to change behavior. However, after thinking about it for a while, I realized that I haven't stuck to that diet I started, I haven't stopped smoking, I still eat fast food, I don't pay attention as much as I should at times, and the list goes on and on, and then I surmised, if I can't change my own behavior, how can I change that of others? Luckily however, although I still eat fast food, I do eat a lot less, I do exercise a lot more, I do pay closer attention, most of the time anyway. So, perhaps while we may not be able to change someone else's cyber behavior, we can change ours. If even just a little, if we can change our cybersecurity behavior, we can also better protect our organization's security posture. If we, as cybersecurity professionals, can change, or at least modify our own behaviors, we might be able to develop and implement better protective technologies and solutions to protect ourselves, our companies, and our nation.

How then can we do this? If we can understand what went into our cognitive processes during decision making on why we did something in the first place, maybe we may be able to examine our own rationale and try to understand if anything could be clouding our views, so as to change that clouded view, change that behavior, and make better cyber security decisions. This now leads us to our first cognitive problem.

Learned Helplessness

When we examine cybersecurity incidents, many times we wonder why they keep happening as these attacks are very similar. One company gets their data stolen from a system, and we may find later on that perhaps the data was not secured by hashes. So we begin to wonder why. Or we could find out that the usernames and passwords were in clear text and wonder why. Then perhaps data was stored on an off-site without security, and again wonder why. In many cases, we say these are elementary mistakes to make as we should all know better, at least those in charge of security.

But perhaps they just fell into learned helplessness.

We accept a certain outcome by saying this outcome is unavoidable and there is nothing we can do about this outcome. It's important to realize that this can be all in the subconscious. We do not even realize when it is happening, yet our behavior will be directed by this. Maier and Seligman (1976) argued that stimuli impact our judgment. We just learn to accept things, we cannot escape them, and we avoid possible solutions since we believe they will be ineffective. For example, when we are in a meeting and people are talking about some possible outcome, yet in our mind, we argue no, that's not going to work. Or that they do not know what they are talking about, we tried this already, and we put up so many roadblocks. It's very common and very dangerous. But we do not just give up; we subconsciously argue the idea and reject it with force as it's an idea that differs from our cognitive thinking. This manifests itself in many ways. From a global attribution viewpoint, negative events occur across all situations and as regards external attribution, they occur due to external factors. An interesting note is that learned helplessness is a physiological manifestation, and research conducted by Hammack, Cooper, and Lezak (2011) reported that learned helplessness also increased levels of serotonin in post-traumatic stress disorders (PTSD). We come under shock, stress increases, serotonin raises, and eventually the event passes off. In some cases, the damage is done and the increase is much longer and leads to even a furthering of learned helplessness. Again, being subconscious, we may not even realize it's happening and we can go about our daily lives, yet it exists in the background possibly directing some of our behaviors.

As we will see later in this book, people are very easily persuadable, a known fact that marketers have known for at least a century, and current social media companies also know all too well. Some say that people who must be online all the time suffer from low self-esteem, bad self-image, depression, loneliness, and their relationships suffer. However, others say that there are positive aspects, as you can find social groups to do things with, you can find rewarding relationships, and you uncover new ways to be charitable. It would seem then more research is needed, and not everything is in black and white. Black and white as a cognitive economy category will be discussed later in the book.

When I keep writing cyber behavior, I do not say cyberterrorist, cybercriminal, or hacker and cracker as all those are names we have given to certain behaviors of individuals. I do not say cyberterrorist or cyber-criminal because as soon as you see those names, your neural networks kick into overdrive. Everything you can think of, imagine, or see in your head are the results of some neural network associations inside your brain. We learn by these, we remember these, and we can even create new things with these, but as we will see, many of these neural networks are just plain wrong. It is not the neural network associations are wrong, but it's those bits of memory inside that neural network association that have been corrupted. Unfortunately, as we will read, trusting our memory is often wrong.

Let's take for example the following, and fill in the blank with one of the given answers.

A _____ is someone who hacks into an opponent's website to get private e-mails to embarrass them.

Possible answers:

Cyberterrorist

Human rights worker

A _____ is someone who hacks into a farm processing plant to get information on the treatment of the farm animals.

Possible answers:

Cybercriminal

PETA volunteer

Both answers to the questions are correct, but as soon as you see the word "cyberterrorist" or "cybercriminal," what were your thoughts? When you hear the word cyberterrorist on the news, what do you think? We do know from research that our audio and visual cues affect the brain differently, so it is possible that reading this wouldn't have an effect. But hearing something on television from a news anchor, and especially from one we trust, we may react differently. If we volunteer to save animals, we may assume that someone who works with the People for the Ethical Treatment of Animals (PETA) do it for selfless reasons, perhaps love, and that biases our opinion. Nevertheless, in each case, these are the same crimes. This brings up an interesting problem: in the same set of circumstances, what is delivered visually or auditory will have different results depending on the individual, and unfortunately complicating the matter, that individual may react one way, but in a different set of circumstances react completely different.

Let's now rewrite the above example. If we were to change the words a little in the second question to:

A _____ is someone who hacks into a farm processing plant to get information on the treatment of the farm animals to give to state and federal authorities.

When you see the words "to give to state and federal authorities," what did you think? Why would a criminal commit an illegal act and then contact law enforcement? Different problems are evident here. Cyberterrorist—that word just brings up images of bad people doing bad things. Theft, destruction, killings: what do you associate cyberterrorist with? When you hear the words "state and federal authorities," do you have images of law enforcement, protectors of the law, and the common good? A cyberterrorist who hacks into a food processing plant to get information on the on-farm animals. The cyberterrorist again, the bad one. Change it to a PETA volunteer who hacks into a food processing plant to get information on the cruelty of farm animals to release to state and federal authorities. This sounds like a good thing and that it should be done, but basically they are doing the same exact things.

The two issues above are associations and leading, and both guide our behavior.

Associations and Leading

What do you Associate Things With?

There are countless associations in your mind made up of neural networks, and while scientists have tried to put an upper limit on them, they are vast, just like the stars in the social systems. Imagine driving in the United States of America from New York to California and taking any set of roads you see on a road atlas. You can choose any route you like, but just don't choose the wrong route. What's the correct route then? Well, that's the route you chose. Right, your mind would not lie to you. And there are probably thousands of ways to go from New York to California. If they are in your head, they consist of a neural network association, but if you look on a road atlas or a GPS device, you've just learned and recorded in your brain a new association.

Let's turn to leading. Now depending on the placement of a few chosen words, cyberterrorist or PETA, or local and state authorities, or hacktivist, when you lead someone, you can expect the outcome, which is a biased end result. Therefore, when we are working on developing security protocols and procedures to guard against threats, are we guarding against the cyberterrorist or perhaps law enforcement, which has been known to engage in hacking, hopefully with a warrant? We have to be careful because the outcome of our behavioral decision could be different, because our associations were different. If cybersecurity professionals understand that these barriers exist, they can change their security behavior and they can become better at their crafts. We would like to think our behavior or actions should be relatively straightforward: that there is something we want to accomplish and we seek to accomplish that task. It is straightforward for the most part. We do those things we act upon, but the problem is what made us act that way? The thousands of routes that go from New York to California, why did we choose one route over another? Unfortunately, as we will see later on in the book, as we drove from New York to California, we noticed there were road blocks up ahead, but instead of taking a detour, we stayed right on the same course. These will be explained later why our cognitive biases insist we keep following the same route, even though we know it is wrong. We will also see that we make excuses and blame life, as if somehow life got in the way. How come you haven't been to the gym in a while? Life got in the way. How come you didn't stick to that diet? Life got in the way. How come you did not finish that home project you were working on? Life got in the way. It certainly seems that life really gets in the way sometimes.

So how exactly did life get in the way?

Well life is unpredictable. It's full of surprises. Confusing, we are happy, we are sad, we get mad, we are content, and it's crazy. Ever hear someone saying, I would have never guessed that in a million years! Some people say bad things come in threes. I say why be so modest? So when the third bad thing happens to me, I think, wow, maybe one or two more bad things, then I am in for really some good luck. Do you think it was Marie Antoinette who said let them eat cake? Was it Albert Einstein who said insanity is doing the same thing over and over again and expecting different results? Did Niccolò Machiavelli come up with the dictum, the ends justify the means? Well, you would be wrong in all these cases, but if you think they did, then there are some neural network associations going inside your brain that are wired incorrectly. So yes, for the most part life is crazy, and most of the time we believe what we see, which turns out to be another big mistake. We try to take in all of this craziness and create some sense of order. We want to create some way we can handle all this and succeed in our everyday life. The trick is how to do we accomplish this.

When you think of psychology, what do you think of? Does psychology solve mental problems? Is it trying to overcome some character flaw?

Is it crime, drug addiction, hope, despair, or gambling? Stereotyping. What about love, sports, you, me, space aliens, and yes cybersecurity, and yes, everything in between? As you were thinking, what were your associations telling you about psychology? When I mentioned mental problem, were there any leadings going on, that is, did you agree that yes, psychology is all about solving mental problems? With all of this going on as we develop contextual experiences, we make and pass judgments. A big problem with all of these experiences is that we have not prepared ourselves for experiences in the future. Then in order to pass judgments for these future experiences, we have to reply on past experiences. A big problem is we do not have enough past information to make these future judgments and need additional information. When we do not have this additional information, we have to rely on other things to fill in the gaps, like our past experiences, but we do not have these past experiences to help us. But we do have other past experiences and we try to fit them as needed. When we read about heuristics, rules of thumb, and cognitive categories, we will realize we all do this. Further complicating the matter is that we go to extremes, from one end to the other, time of day, time of year, how we are feeling impacts our experiences, which eventually impact our judgments and in turn which eventually impact our behavior. Our future behavior is directed by incomplete past experiences, which are filled with neural network associations from other past experiences, and these associations are not always chosen. We may choose different associations depending on how we feel. All these experiences get stored inside our neural network associations, to be used when needed, even if they are wrong. But they are not wrong. Would our own mind lie to us? We use information from past experiences in order to make judgments on new experiences, even though our past experiences were not correctly registered. Our past information is often wrong, so complicating the problem is that we are making new judgments, and for the most part could be wrong as well. So, with all these choices, it's often amazing that we make any right decisions in the first place, but it turns out we do, not always. But we do. Many of us make the right decision to go to college, and many of us make the right decision to eat better and exercise.

Chaos. We need order and human beings cannot live in chaos. We make order, try to do our best, and make complicated choices. The process repeats itself over and over, and the difference between the real truth and what we perceive as truth are our facts, and we need to narrow that gap. So somewhere along this process, behavior comes in, and we have to do something. Imagine now being a cybersecurity professional whose task it is to protect company assets or develop new technologies that will protect people. We have just seen our choices are biased. So how can we make decisions about critical life-savings matters with all these complications, confusion, and chaos happening. I wish I could say that leading and associations are the only two things that get us into trouble, but as we will see, there are a host of other problems. Can we do anything then? Well, hopefully yes, if we are careful and understand what happens to us when we make choices, we may make better choices in the long run, change our behavior, and for cybersecurity professionals, make better business, technical, and life-saving choices as well.

Counting to Three Is Just Too Hard for Me

Smullyan (1978, 1985) was a master of creating logic jokes. He was also a mathematician, musician, philosopher, and even a magician. He created some of the hardest logic problems ever to be solved. They all had similar leading questions. In one puzzle, take two actors—one who always lied, one who always told the truth—and answers were given in single-syllable responses with da and ja, but, you do not know what da and ja mean. He later expanded his examples to include three actors—one who always lied, one who always told the truth, and one who randomly told the truth. One of his most famous examples is of two cities of knights and knaves, where knights always told the truth, knaves always lied, and knights and knaves often visit each other's cities. The visitor to the city does not know the name, so he asks someone. The first person tells him he is in the city of knaves, but knaves always lie. He still is unsure and decides to ask another person, but he only can ask one more person.

What is the question should he ask?

If he is in a knight city, the knight will answer yes, so too will the knave since knaves always lie. If he is in the knave city, the knight will answer no, but the knave will say yes, since knaves always lie. He developed a god's logic problem—three gods, A, B, and C, and in order we would have true, false, and random. One god always speaks the truth, one god always speaks lies, and one randomly tells the truth or lies. Then you would get three yes or no questions to find out which god tells the truth, which god always lies, and which god randomly tells the truth.

Smullyan seemed to have started with logic problems as a doctoral student. In 1957, he met his future wife, teasing her with a logic problem: I would like to ask you something, and she would reply accordingly:

I am to make a statement. If the statement is true, would you give me your autograph?

If the statement is false, he went on, you don't give me your autograph.

His statement was: You'll give me neither your autograph nor a kiss.

Smullyan got the kiss and his future wife. So, what do gods, knights, and even his wife have in common with security professionals? It was the approach of the person trying to figure out the logic problem. As human beings, we are very narrow thinking and we tend to ask very specific detailed questions, *do you always tell the truth,* when in reality we should be asking, *do you always tell the truth but if and only if you always are in the city of knaves.* It's the third option, and as Boolos (1996) had correctly pointed out, we limit the middle, which he called it the excluded middle. We have the true and the false, but we keep skipping out the middle, this third option. As you go through the chapters of the book and review the material of paradoxes, think about this third option. A very common cybersecurity paradox most often heard is that companies say employees are the weakest link, but instead of investing heavily end-user training, they invest millions of dollars in technical solutions. Therefore, the question might then change from:

Employee's fat fingering is the weakest link.
to
Employee's fat fingering is the weakest link if and only if they have not received the proper training.

Try to understand that perhaps we miss so many security breaches because we just don't understand the other question to ask.

Cybersecurity Implications and Conclusions

Cybersecurity has gone through a lot of name changes. We have security, network security, operations security, Internet security, information security, information assurance, and information assurance and security, and I may be missing some probably. We are now moving to psychology, like cyberpsychology, cybernetics, cyber ethics, cyber behavior, and probably more to come. However, all of them seem to center around do very broad categories:

Protection. The protection of an asset, whether it's data, plants, or people. It's the protection of something tangible.

Psychology. The behavior of people, what they do, why are they doing it, can it be predicted, and can it be minimized.

It seems that in this area, cyber comes into play, as this seems to be growing in the information age, the virtual reality space. Maybe soon we will see a new term in the press, cyber protection, but for now the focus is on the term cyberpsychology. So we can stick with that for now. Cyberpsychology is the connection of the human behavior to computers, usually when online or connected. While the computer–human interface is not new, the influences of social networking, groups, and the influences they exhibit on individuals are a very new and real phenomenon. The Internet has been a great catalyst for the rise of cyberpsychology and will continue to grow. As computers and our dependence on and interaction with them grow, research in this field will continue to progress. If you want to see how much of an impact this has had, go to any airport, and look for a place to plug in your smartphone or computer. On layovers, people seem to sleep right next to a charging plug, just in case. As you go through this book, think about what is happening in the background. What is the message being conveyed in each chapter? Is there any moment that you think, yes, I remember that, I did that once, twice, or a dozen times? That is where we find our psychological bias, our shortcomings, and our own biases we need to overcome to become better at what we do. Since this book is on psychology and cybersecurity, it's assumed you do something along the lines of cybersecurity. So, as you read this book, is the chapter talking about how you view something, how you decide something, what outside factors and stimuli could make you act in a certain way, and not see the big cybersecurity picture? Hopefully, if we can recognize these limitations, we can avoid them and make better cybersecurity decisions, and take that perfect drive from New York to California.

CHAPTER 2

Behaviorism

Introduction

Behaviorism is response to a stimulus. For example, something in our environment changes, something about our circumstance changes, something, somewhere is happening (i.e., a change occurring), and for the most part observable; they may be real or we may simply perceive these as real. I am not walking down that dark street. These ideas in the way we think go back centuries, from Darwin's (1872) expression in man, Watson's (1913) behaviorist manifesto, to Pavlov's (1920s) classical conditioning. Skinner's (1930s) operant conditioning and Tolman's (1948) cognitive maps, to Miller's (1967) biofeedback and beyond, and in between these researchers, we have hundreds, if not thousands of other researchers and scholars.

Up until about the very late 1800s the way we acted was looked through the lens of philosophy, the meaning of man. It was around the early 1900s that psychologists wanted to make psychology stand out as a science, and a different kind of science started to emerge. Bodies of science take on different forms. For example, there is Aristotelian science, which is the classification system we are taught in schools, that is based on observable experiments, hypothesis testing, data collection, and analysis. There is the Newtonian science, which involves laws of gravity and laws of relativity. We cannot see them but accept them as fact. We have Darwinian science, which talks about evolution, pressure to survive, and survival of the fittest. Since this book is about cybersecurity, could its genus be considered information technology science? Since researchers are looking for a theory for cybersecurity and much of that work is based up the sciences of Aristote, think of security models and there is a lot of information and models in information technology.

Perhaps that would be a good place to start. Unfortunately, in reality none of these sciences can easily be applied to cybersecurity. Parts of them can perhaps hold good. Cyberattacks do seem to keep evolving to be successful (i.e., Darwinian). We certainly have a lot of data on attacks, the types of attacks, costs of these attacks (i.e., Aristotelian), and we also have the stress involved, the psychological aspect of these attacks, the influences that people are impacted by, whether to commit these attacks, or be a victim of these attacks (i.e., Newtonian). Perhaps a new field of science will emerge. There is an accepted rule of three. When used in writing, it means things that come in three are more satisfying and easier to remember. There is also a rule of three in marketing, politics, survival, and mathematics. It seems that this rule of three is very popular, so perhaps these three sciences will become a rule of three to explain cybersecurity.

Philosophy and Psychology Diverge

As the branches of philosophy and psychology started to separate, one branch of psychology started looking at conditioned responses. James Watson (1913) who had studied children and conditioned emotional response began researching animals in controlled situations. Then he began to theorize how humans would react to their environment (i.e., the doing and sayings of people) and learned and unlearned tasks that would lead to theories about human behavior.

Some of the earliest researchers in this field were with Ivan Pavlov, and his most notable research is often referred to today as Pavlov's dogs. His studying of a dog's salivation gave rise to his work on stimuli and conditioning, which helped propel the growth of behaviorism. By examining what happens when humans interact to external stimuli, he could then theorize it was the environment that could dictate behavior, often referred to as Stimulated–Response (S-R). Since the mind was not really understood at this point, and no mental tests were available, the concentration was on external stimuli. This approach did lead to many interesting experiments and findings.

Theory of Learning Reinforcement (S-R Learning)

Stimulated–Response learnings, stimuli and response, become stronger each time they are used, and those that are not used are weakened; the more we practice these S-R learnings, the stronger they become, and the easier and faster they are learned. The greater the satisfaction or discomfort effects the strength or the weakness of the bond. Thorndike (1926) believed the more intelligent an animal was, the more capable it was at solving the escape and the quicker its time. He developed the Completion, Arithmetic, Vocabulary, and Directions (CAVD) test and this became a model for future intelligence tests. The test measured mechanical intelligence (i.e., how things work), abstract intelligence (i.e., creative ability), and social intelligence (i.e., interpersonal skills). He also proposed an age idea to these connections. As we tend to think children learn better than adults, he argued it's not that they learn better, they just learn faster (i.e., the speed of learning, not the content).

Pavlov's Dogs

One interesting experiment led to many breakthroughs in psychology, and like many breakthroughs, it wasn't quite what was expected. Ivan Pavlov initially measured how a dog would salivate given some food, but the breakthrough came about when the dogs started to salivate as soon as the researchers walked into the room; it was actually the anticipation of the food. As he continued his experiment, he uncovered it wasn't just the food, or the researchers, or the white lab coats, but it could be conditioned to be any external stimuli. An explanation of his breakthrough research is as follows:

1. An unconditioned stimulus leads to
2. An unconditioned response, add in a
3. Neutral stimulus to the unconditioned stimuli, that leads to a
4. Conditioned response, remove the
5. Unconditioned stimuli and use the neutral stimuli that will lead to
6. Conditioned Response.

A practical example would be:

1. Offer the dog a treat—unconditioned stimuli
2. The dog begins to salivate—unconditioned response
3. Add a bell to the treat—neutral stimuli
4. Give a treat and ring bell together—a conditioned response
5. Remove the treat—unconditioned stimuli
6. Then ring just the bell, neutral stimuli, the dogs begin to salivate, (i.e., conditioned response), even with no treat present.

If Pavlov were to move to another room, the dog would come running and salivate at the same time. Now we have both behavioral and physical factors. Pavlov understood that his experiments weren't just to examine the primitive responses in animals, but more the adaptive learnings in humans. He also uncovered that the neutral stimuli and the unconditioned stimuli had to be close in time. Pavlov's work is very much alive today, especially in marketing, such as food, smell, sounds, all external stimuli that will produce a response and corresponding behavior.

The Behaviorist Manifesto

The behaviorist manifesto by Watson (1913) was a multidecade piece of work that believed that the environment shaped behavior. Through his studies, Watson believed the environment could help with a number of social and human ills. It would be able to predict and control behavior. His work led to other subbranches of behaviorism, such as the radical behaviorist, which was championed by Skinner (1938), and led to his famous use of the Skinner boxes. Skinner believed behavior was a science, not simply a reaction. His belief was that animal behavior could be studied effectively and those teachings can be applied to human behavior. He viewed his work through the stimulus–response lens of operant conditioning, in that the strength of behavior was often viewed by the strength of a corresponding reward or punishment. However, over the long term, other researchers have examined the concept of learned helplessness, which negated this reward–punishment connection to behavior. However, his work did open the field for other researchers to begin exploring behavior due to other factors such as traits, and genetic and intrinsic markers.

Early in the 20th century, it was becoming clear that the human mind could not be studied introspectively, so the conclusion was to start looking at it through the lens of someone's behavior. Watson (1913) attempted to look at behavior from this introspection point of view. Since researchers could not examine the brain, let us then look at the actions of an individual. We can only observe someone's actions from an external viewpoint, which became an experimental branch of natural science. Like most, Watson confined his studies to animals and extrapolated them to humans. He also wanted to study the stimuli–response mechanism and the classical conditioning response. Watson believed there were three stages: fear, rage, and love. He then wanted to see if a person be fooled into feeling one of these in response to some stimuli. His famous lecture in 1913 on behaviorism was later to be called the behaviorist manifesto.

Watson conducted his famous Little Albert study in 1920, and while his experiment would never be allowed today due to its unethical design, key learnings were observed. Watson enlisted the help of a nine-month-old little boy named Albert, with full permission of the mother. The mother was kept apprised of the experiment and the continuing research. His experiment was to see if the notion of classical conditioning could work with a fear stimulus. Basically, if a fear stimulus was present, could he condition a baby to be afraid of an otherwise harmful white rat. During the trials, little Albert was seated and the white rat was introduced. As the experiment proceeded, various objects were placed on the mat, but then at times, with the white rat present, Watson would stand, out of sight and make a big noise with a metal pipe. The baby would then start to cry. Over repeated experiments, Watson hypothesized that the baby would be conditioned to cry whenever he saw the white rat, remembering the loud metal pipe banging noise. This went on for several months and confirmed the classical conditioning approach used by Pavlov. In the terms of classical conditioning, the rat was a neutral stimulus, and the loud noise was an unconditioned stimulus that elicited an unconditioned response. Then after the procedure, the rat became the conditioned stimulus, eliciting the conditioned response.

The effects were worse on little Albert, as the boy projected the response on other non-rat stimuli. The problem became that even after the experiment, as Albert was introduced to other non-rat similar objects, he elicited the same response rages. It became generalized to other objects. This showed the child's fear, anxiety, and everything became conditioned just like Pavlov's dogs, but became generalized and long-lasting. This went beyond Pavlov's experiment in that the elicited responses can become generalized to other objects; they can be modified. Could post-traumatic stress disorder (PTSD) be partially explained by this type of conditioning that still exists in individuals (e.g., soldiers in battle even after they are removed from the field of war)? Watson's work was refuted as cruel, manipulative, and uncaring, and that he only cared about results, instead of the well-being for the child, but he did work on other ways to this fear by working on a method of deconditioning fears. However, his research work was cut short, due to some of his own unique behaviors.

Cognitive Revolution

As researchers began to question the strength of the behaviorist approach, they began to look at other things, such as internal traits, genes, even instinct in animals, or ethology the study of animals. This conflicted head-on with Skinner's approach as it moved away from the reward–punishment connection to internal factors, not easily observed with the naked eye. Edward Tolman was a very early researcher who began to examine perception and cognitions on behavior. This led to the Gestalt movement, which began to look at behavior due to inner workings of the brain. This cognitive revolution led to many famous research studies, one of the most famous being by Ivan Pavlov.

Law of Effect

The law of effect simply states that a behavior will be repeated if it is followed by a pleasant experience, and the behavior will not be repeated if it is followed by a negative experience (Nevin 1999). Edward Thorndike (1926) was a behaviorist psychologist who later expanded into researching operant condition in behaviorism. He was a pioneering researcher in learning environments. Unlike earlier classical conditioning, where we learn from associations between events like stimuli–response, Thorndike championed operant conditioning (i.e., the learning from the consequences of our behavior). We can think of laws and prison, drug addiction, or rewarding a child for good grades in school. Since Thorndike did not have human subjects, he also used animals like in Skinner's experiments.

He placed cats in all kinds of different boxes and shapes, and using different stimuli and devices inside the boxes, timed the results. Eventually the cats were able to tell which results led to escape and a deserving reward, which results did not, and eventually their actions become automatic. Therefore, he proposed a future event is more likely to occur if there is a positive outcome and less likely if there is a negative outcome. Some connection is made between a stimulus (S) and a response (R), and a corresponding neural connection is made in the brain's neural networks. These S–R learnings and connections are stamped into the circuitry of the brain. The concept is that the stronger the stimulus reward, the more the connection if wired in the brain. However, but when the stimulus and reward didn't connect, or was frustrating, the neural connection was very weak. The stronger connections are firmly stamped in, while the weaker ones are still there, but hazy.

Cognitive Maps and Latent Learning

Edward Tolman (1948) was an early advocate of radical behaviorism of psychology, but unlike other scholars, he also looked at aspect of the mental processes, perception, cognition, and motivation aspects. He was a student of the Gestalt psychology and hoped to bridge two ideas. That we not only have automatic responses (i.e., the conditioned movement) but we also have learned responses that we can pick up from our environment. Animals could learn without a reward, or perhaps the reward is intrinsic in nature. He termed his work purposive behaviorism, which was also referred to as cognitive behaviorism.

In his experiments like earlier researchers who used animals, rats would build cognitive maps of their environment. The two types of learning: (i) response learning, where the rat knows from previous testing which route leads to food, and (ii) place learning, where the rat learns to

associate a place with food. In his experiments, the rats that were sub-
jected to place learning learned the correct path much quicker than those
that were tested in the response learning path. In fact, some rats with
response learning never learned the correct path. He argued that humans
also think like rats. So he termed the phrase "latent learning." We build
up all these maps over time, but we really only understand them when we
need to use them.

Think of being a passenger with someone else driving. You've completed a route many times, but it is not until you actually do the driving
yourself do you really understand the route. These cognitive maps and
latent learnings take place, but until needed would stay behind almost
the level of consciousness, thereby tying gestalt and behaviorism fields of
research together. Are hereditary genes causing your behavior? We will
discuss this in a later chapter, but while many people will not admit it,
race does play a part. Muslims, Africans, Chinese, Russians, the United
States—name a country and people will have ill ideas. How can anyone
say that if I do not like Muslims, Africans, Chinese, Russians, and so on.,
that can it be hereditary? Can you say it is not? Are you afraid of people
with red hair, dwarfs, brown skin, someone with warts, how many people
are wary of disabled people? Are these hereditary, conditioned, environment, and learned?

While you may think this has nothing to do with cybersecurity, ask
yourself, is Windows or Unix better? Biases show up everywhere. So,
while researchers have been having these discussions for centuries, it turns
out that it might have been all wrong, or it might have been alright. That's
science. We accept what we know, until we can't accept it anymore, but
that kind of tells you:

We really know nothing.

Richardson (2019) argues that no, it's not really genes that determine us:

So much for my hope I was born with this gift and I am just a natural.

Richardson makes the case that we have not been talking about genes,
but just a crude model of them, and that we all along base our behaviors
upon our assumptions. A lot of applied practical research into genes came

from research studies ages ago, although the genome research currently going on is really opening our eyes even more now. In these older models, we were told we have these genes. They are different, complex, exhibiting different strengths, and the stronger ones rise to the top. This has been repeated throughout history, trying to make the better human being (e.g., the famous Nazi human experiments to make a better soldier), or athlete, scientist, and so on. It was simply in theory; your DNA proteins would lead to the development of your main characteristics. DNA components consist of single-nucleotide polymorphisms that vary among individuals. Let's examine them and see if we can align all these single-nucleotide polymorphisms and relate them to a person's, say, intelligence, or IQ.

However, now it looks like DNA code is just a template. It does not put the proteins together. It's only a roadmap of how they can be put together. Remember that roadmap example earlier from the East Coast to the West Coast of the United States. It's a good template but does not guarantee which route will be taken. Therefore, DNA does not predict gene development but only a path forward. We don't only inherit the genes from our parents, rather we inherit all things about our parents, proteins, amino acids, vitamins, minerals, and when the time comes and we need these, they become available. As a person begins to grow, fertilized eggs start with hundreds of identical cells all communicating with each other and then change into other cells due to instructions. This development could not have been started by just a template. Richardson makes an interesting analogy to a just-in-time inventory system. DNA is a just-in-time delivery system and used as needed. And while, yes, children can inherit the same eye or hair color as their parents, or inherit the same illness from their parents; it's not always the case, (e.g., many children of people with dwarfism grow to be average height of the population). Interestingly the complexity of a human being has less than 20,000 genes, a carrot has about 45,000, the near-microscopic freshwater crustacean Daphnia Pulex (i.e., a water fly) has about 31,000, even a Nematode worm has over 20,200 genes.

So are genes necessary for survival, maybe, but let's hope not for intelligence's sake, as I really don't want to feel dumber than a water fly.

Other Behavioral Approaches

There are many others who have looked at behavioral approaches. Edwin Guthrie (1946) viewed it as simple learning. He argued that reinforcement was not always needed for conditioning to be successful, and that only one experience was enough for the stimulus–response pairing to take effect and make an imprint. He also used experiments and developed the theory of contiguity, whereas a stimulus present with some movement was enough to create an association. If that is repeated, it will be followed by that movement, which was learned from the original stimulus–response association, not behavior. Then in subsequent trails, since the association was already learned, the formation of that act is then considered behavior.

Zing-Yang Kuo (1938) looked at the origins on the formation of behavior. In his famous cat killing rat study, the cat by instinct should kill the rat. However, in his research with varying degrees of kittens being starved and varying degrees of seeing other cats kill and eat rats, also depending on when the kittens and rats were introduced at a young age, the cats would not eat the rats. His conclusions were that kittens can be modified to kill the rats or play with the rats, maybe even love or hate the rats; it just all depends on the kitten's history with the rat. An interesting fact about Kuo's experiment was that he went at length not to interfere in the normal environment (e.g., he did not give the cats extra food). The only factor that he sometimes changed was that he did not allow the young kittens to witness older cats in an act of killing the rats. Just this act does give credence to later researchers who have suggested that it is the environment that gives one motive and lead to his or her behavior. There were some, however appropriately, nine kittens that did indeed kill the rats, without witnessing any older cats killing the rats. Whereas this would give credence to those researchers who suggest behavior is a universal instinct and we cannot change our instinct, most of these experiments showed the opposite.

Moreover, while Pavlov and other behavioralists believed something happened in the brain during conditioning, and this caused chemical or electrical changes in the brain, Karl Lashley (1950) wanted to find where in the brain this was stored. In his research, after the rats learned the maze, he removed different parts of the cerebral cortex. Yet the rats still remembered the maze. Semon (1921), in his search for the engram where a piece of data is stored and activated once a stimulus was placed, was unsuccessful and disproved the notion that memory is local. This led him to believe that there is a mass action, where learning is distributed throughout the brain; it is not localized.

Konrad Lorenz (1937) studied the principle of imprinting and some have affectionally called him the goose man. The act of imprinting is done at an early age. An animal will filter out certain traits (e.g., instinct to bond with another object), even one not of its own species. He stated that perhaps instinctive behavior is also a factor of the environment. Animals have an inner instinctive drive, like bonding with its own kind, but when that early connection is interrupted, animals will engage in non-instinctive behavior (e.g., bonding with a human). Perhaps, it is just the act of bonding that is instinctive, like a self-preservation need, but that actual object of that bonding depends on the environment and time. He also said that this bonding is irreversible and cannot be broken.

Check the Box: A Classic Conditioned Response

While examining security breaches, we can find real-life examples of where behavior may have caused the security incident. We have had Equifax, Target, Marriott, Home Depot, state governments, federal government agencies, for-profit, not-for-profit, military, churches, law enforcement, and many others, hundreds, if not thousands. In many of these examples, companies were indeed diligent in checking off the box. The checkoff box is the attitude toward security and compliance in nature. We had done our due diligence, so we should be safe to go.

Why then did we check off the box? Well, there are compliance and security standards that tell us we must. It's also because of this check off the box mentality, our conditioned response becomes one of confirmatory; we've done what we were told to do, we checked off that box, and now we move on to the next task at hand. Think about compliance efforts such as The Sarbanes -Oxley Act of 2002, The Payment Card Industry Data Security Standard, The Health Insurance Portability and Accountability Act of 1996, The Family Educational Rights and Privacy Act of 1974, or even when you receive calls to participate in standard reviews for potential new and developing standards. It is people who are designing these standards that we are confirming, and to a point, we are confirming their own biases. This is born out of my experience of having been involved in a number of these standard bodies' assessments over the years. A call goes out to numerous people in the field for their expert advice and to provide feedback that will help make these frameworks stronger. This indeed is a valid effort, but these people are working busy professionals, and many times their involvement is one of volunteerism. How much time can possibly be put into these volunteer efforts? It's a great cause indeed, but the reality is that the end result may not be what was intended.

So, in these check-the-box situations, yes, companies did comply, and that was their conditioned response. However, there are those that argue this conditioned response to checking off the box is not appropriate. There are many who argue against this checking off the box (Schwartz 2016; Elmer 2015; Basani 2014; and NeSmith 2018) and others argue just checking off the box is like the conditioned response we are accustomed to and will result in even more security troubles later on.

Cybersecurity Implications and Conclusions

We have examined some of the earliest works on behavior, and how many of the earlier researchers believe behavior is just a conditioned reaction to some stimuli. While some just view it as hereditary, some view it as learned and some view it as being a product of the environment. However, what most of this shows is that behavior cannot be predicted 100 percent of the time. One of the main arguments within cybersecurity is that so much research is static with regard to someone's perception of attacks and someone's motivation why they committed an attack. These are simply one-time snapshots of a person's makeup, but does that makeup change over years? No, it can really change over days. When we think of our own work in cybersecurity and we looked at the conditioned responses, who or what do you believe cause the most problems: kids, terrorists, or terrorist-sponsored states? That's what conditioned means (i.e., are we conditioned to a certain stimulus). Therefore, break that habit—all bearded men are not terrorists, like all blondes are not dumb (we will talk about stereotype in later chapters). Where are all the scary bearded men coming from anyway: the environment, the television, websites, e-mails, politicians? Most likely they are, but be aware of the message. This does not mean any of these studies are necessarily wrong; on the contrary, they could be excellent sources of information. If we keep building on them perhaps, we can fully understand how changes occur in individuals and create better research studies that will lead to a better understanding of cybersecurity.

Later in the book, we will see how you can be so against something but minutes later change your mind. Or you can be so convinced about a topic, and even when presented with irrefutable proof, you will still not change your mind. We will see that even if you state what your motivations are, they are indeed unreliable, and you may not even know what your true motivations are. If cybersecurity relies heavily on a person's psychological and philosophical makeup and that changes, then cybersecurity research cannot exist in a vacuum in these single studies.

As I am writing this book, another attack has been gaining in popularity—sextortion scams. Where a user receives an e-mail, the sender's e-mail address has been spoofed to be the receiver's own e-mail address, which is pretty easy to do, and the subject usually has their password. In the e-mail, it is revealed that this attacker does have your correct username and password of an account you may have used, or still use. In the body of the e-mail, the text is usually, *"hello we installed some secret malware on the router, or in your browser and we have caught you watching porn sites and if you don't pay up soon we will release this on social media,"* and usually followed up by a bitcoin address and a ransom demand. When you get this e-mail for the first time, you really are left in a state of panic. They have your e-mail address, they have your correct password, they claim they have video of you in a compromising situation, and for a moment you are left thinking and panicking what to do.

What is your behavior based upon this stimulus?
This becomes the conditioned response.

This is a real threat. I've been a victim of this, and it's true they do have your correct username and password. Some company I am familiar with, like many of you, I am sure, since it is a major networking social media business: they stored usernames in cleartext and passwords in an unsalted hash. A simple search turned up the company in question, and more research turned up that this successful attack happened in 2016; and yet this company did not notify its users for a long time. Considering the amount of attacks we have seen, and the millions of personal information of users that have been stolen, it would be realistic to believe anyone reading this book has come across this as well. But unlike you or me, the average computer user would not know what to do: would they have paid the ransom? Even in the e-mail, the attacker was nice enough to tell them how bitcoin works. Would the end-user possibly go to a website included in the e-mail and even open up more damage? Who knows, I was taken aback for a minute or two, till my years of training and experience kicked in. I am sure the average accountant does not have my years of experience. However, it does show we cannot always blame someone for something when they don't understand what that something they were supposed to be guarding against, or the case of companies always blaming end users for all the problems.

Maybe it's another reason I do not have a web cam on my computer.

So, now that they have a username and password, and we know these attacks will evolve, so what other data could they possibly get? What data have you shared with your other accounts, banks, credit card companies, social media websites, medical and insurance websites, voting and government websites? Have you ever visited a big theme park and they asked you to swipe your finger for authentication? Are they really deleting your fingerprints?

There is so much data that is out there and since this attack has been successful, we would imagine a lot of people were watching pornography and believe their personal lives were about to be ruined and paid the ransom. So, how does this attack evolve into the next one? Well, perhaps your health insurance company gets attacked, you have some illness or disease you want to keep under cover, but you receive and e-mail saying they are going to release the information. Again, the human emotion, panic, or fear, that's what many attacks focus on, and many are very successful. Unfortunately, this breach has already happened. Quest Diagnostics, a leader in blood testing providers in America, announced in 2019 that almost 12 million customers had their personal, financial, and medical information stolen. You could have guessed by now—it was associated with one of their vendors (Berkowitz 2019). Well, now that they have my blood work results, I better be on the alert for that forthcoming e-mail.

Those examples are very successful stimuli to cause you to action, your conditioned responses. Think of all the data that is being collected besides your username and passwords. Your fingerprints, your DNA, your voice patterns, the way you write, your eye color, facial recognition, everything about you is being recorded, and if it is being stored, expect it to be stolen. Then think what exactly did that data point of yours open? Did my IRIS scan open up a locked door, did my voice pattern open up a lock, did my multifactor biometric data give me access to a website? Well, if that data point about you opened up some portal for you, it can certainly open up a portal for someone else as well if your data gets hacked. Especially since the vast majority of people use the same username and password for multiple accounts.

How do you think scammers will target you when they access your prescription information? Yes, all that is being collected as well. If you go to the National Security Agency (NSA) in the United States, there is a wonderful page on the data they collect on you (*https://nsa.gov1.info/data/*)

- Internet searches
- Websites visited
- E-mails
- Social media activity
- Blogging activity including posts read, written, and commented on
- Videos watched and uploaded
- Photos viewed and uploaded
- Mobile phone GPS-location data
- Mobile phone apps downloaded
- Phone call records
- Text messages sent and received
- Skype video calls
- Online purchases and auction transactions

- Credit card/ debit card transactions
- Financial information
- Legal documents
- Travel documents
- Health records
- Cable television shows watched and recorded
- Commuter tolls
- Electronic bus and subway pass / Smart pass
- Facial recognition data
- Educational records
- Arrest records
- Driver license information
- DNA.

They are kind enough to note that it's only a partial list.

Their main caption is, *Your Data: If You Have Nothing to Hide, You Have Nothing to Fear.*

This was the same slogan an ex-politician used when it became apparent about some wiretapping without a warrant, so it does not inspire trust. As we will read throughout this book, that is not a good slogan to have. People and even some NSA employees generally mistrust governments. This slogan is telling them trust us. However, we may now be feeling some cognitive dissonance (i.e., wanting to believe in something when your mind is telling you not to believe in that something), even this may direct future behavior. To be fair, this NSA policy is one of the most open policies I have ever seen, and they do deserve a lot of credit for being this honest.

But they should change their slogan, to perhaps:

You can run, but you can't hide.
We know when you're alone.
I'd be worried if I were you, or
Relax, we got this.

Because, like we will see throughout this book, at times behavior follows perceptions, within a given stimulus, in a particular circumstance, and that could predict our future behavior (i.e., our conditioned response). Behavior is a very tricky subject, and there is so much disagreement on the subject, that it would be folly to think we could change someone's cyber behavior. It happens even if we are unaware of it happening, behavior follows perceptions within a given stimulus in a particular circumstance, and what we will examine could predict future behavior, but remember in Kuo's experiment, not all the cats ate the rats, and some were good friends.

CHAPTER 3

Traits

Introduction

How many times have we tried to explain someone with an adjective?

Wow, *is he so funny*, or *she is definitely a looker*, or *he must be as dumb as a rock*? Many times, we don't even know that person, or perhaps there might be a very short introductory time before we made that judgment call. Sometimes we just hear something about someone and make a determination. Terms of endearment, gossip, rumors, and so on, and if you really think about them, there are literally thousands of adjectives we use; some researchers have pegged this number at about 18,000.

Luckily however, even with this large a number, over time after consolidation and examination, researchers have narrowed this vast list to around five dimensions. It is also better to think of these as dimensions on an *X*-axis, since he can be crazy as in very dangerous, or crazy as in silly crazy. There is also wide latitude from person to person in these five dimensions, but for the most part, these five dimensions do exist in all. It is important to note in these dimensions that they are also from the viewpoint of what others think. You may think you are not crazy, but others may have a different opinion of you. We also have observable human traits, like hair color, and unobservable human characteristics like kindness, but at the present we are more interested in traits that may predict behavior. They are discussed below.

Conscientiousness

This trait controls our self-discipline, determination, and our organizational skills. Do I carefully plan activities or am I a spur-of-the-moment type of a person? Do I arrive early and say, yes, I can wait, or do I arrive late, and say, well, you were not going to do anything anyway. There is a wide range here; high conscientiousness to some can be taken as stubbornness, whereas low levels of conscientiousness can result in others thinking you are unreliable. An unobservable trait, as I cannot tell how conscientious you are, but through your behavior I can observe your planning, how you act on arrival, your self-discipline, and so on, and I can guess your degree of conscientiousness.

Confidence

Confidence is not to be confused with conscientiousness as it is often mistaken. Is confidence a trait, or really more an ability? For example, I am very confident about my cybersecurity skills, but I would not say it is a trait like being right-handed. It is my years of education or schooling that has made me confident in my abilities; however, I could have underlying traits like openness to learning that allowed my confidence in cybersecurity to mature.

With this confidence, I am more detailed when discussing cybersecurity or have more defined skills, and plan out carefully when doing a cybersecurity assessment. I manage my self-discipline when examining and laying out cybersecurity plans and therefore seem to outsiders as being more conscientious. Another distinction is that confidence can be observable, whereas conscientiousness cannot. However, taking confidence too far can appear to be rude, having a big ego, stubborn, and other things.

Agreeableness

It is the degree of generosity and friendliness we exhibit toward each other, or the reverse. Can you spare any change? Here's two dollars, here's a quarter, or I cannot spare anything. Do I have a trusting nature? Yes, I trust everyone until they prove to me they are untrustworthy, or I do not trust anyone until they prove to me, they are trustworthy. Agreeableness has also been broken down into six subcategories: (1) trust, (2) morality, (3) altruism, (4) cooperation, (5) modesty, and (6) sympathy. Again, these are all on a scale—so I can trust, or not trust; I can show sympathy, or have no sympathy; and I can be somewhere on an *X*-axis of these traits, always fluid and moving.

Each end of a scale has benefits and drawbacks. For example, high levels of agreeableness can make people think you are naïve and easily taken advantage of, whereas low levels of agreeableness might seem to others that you are combative, possibly too difficult to get along with. A longitudinal empirical study by Furnham and Cheng (2016) associated high levels of agreeableness with childhood intelligence, education, occupation, and gender. Family social status affected agreeableness through education and occupation. They also concluded that gender was the strongest predictor of trait agreeableness.

Neuroticism

This relates to how prone one is to psychological stress. Are you nervous all the time, do you lack impulse control, or are you calm? Most often when encountering this, we tend to think of high levels of neuroticism—quick to anger and judge, or compulsive disorders. Some research even suggests these high levels are an indication of more serious psychological disorders, whereas low levels of neuroticism might indicate that you are a very stable person, slow to anger, or think things through. An underlying issue with neuroticism is one's tendency to dwell on the past or their misfortunes. They cannot seem to let go of things that affected them but were outside of their control. They are jealous and envious of others, especially when those people have positions of authority over them. Frustration and anger are often an exhibited behavior. A major self-harming issue is that to extremes individuals with high levels of neuroticism may exhibit this through disturbed behaviors and thoughts since these are associated with their emotional distress. The sub-traits of neuroticism include: (1) anxiety, (2) anger, (3) depression, (4) self-consciousness, (5) immoderation, and (6) vulnerability.

Openness

How willing are you to try new things, experience new cultures, attempt new activities, or does sky diving come to mind? You appreciate art, music, and new experiences. The opposite would be closed off but not always be taken in a rude context. You are closed in that—I am a data-type person; I need to see facts before I judge. I do not have time for new experiences as I am too busy in my life, or seen as being to dogmatic. I prefer to eat the same thing every time I go to a restaurant. I may not like my job, but I am comfortable here, so I will stay. Predictability breeds comfort, so if I can predict something, I will remain in comfort; if I cannot predict something, my discomfort rises and I become nervous or afraid and will start to close off from the outside. The sub-traits of openness include: (1) imagination, (2) artistic interests, (3) emotionality, (4) adventurousness, (5) intellect, and (6) liberalism.

Extroversion

It is the extent to which we enjoy the company of others, how social are we, the tendency to seek stimulation in the company of others. We can be seen as domineering, seeking to control the conversation. The opposite end of this dimension, we sometimes refer to as introversion, a reserved demeanor; sometimes we are characterized as being taken back, self-absorbed. It has been shown that for the most part these traits stay with us for a lifetime, but the placement on the dimension scale may change. We may become less conscientious as we age, less agreeable. So, it is important to not think of these as traits that come and go, but traits that move on a scale (i.e., the X-axis). As we get better educated, perhaps we become less open and need to rely more on data to make our decisions. However, since these traits are typical in everyone and for the most part stable, it has been proven a reliable tool to help us make predictions about ourselves (e.g., careers we may choose).

The Big Five Traits

These five traits we just discussed are often referred to as the Big Five Traits as modeled by Digman (1989). However, even though there is a common set of these five traits for the majority of individuals, some exhibit some other unique characteristic traits, as we see below.

Machiavellianism

This trait is characterized by a person's ability to become unattached or showing a lack of emotions in a certain circumstance. For instance, a horrible airplane crash where hundreds die or a tsunami where thousands die—for some people these tragedies do not bother them. Sometimes these people are referred to as cold-hearted. However, we cannot be quick to judge, for example, an animal getting abused or pictures of whales being slaughtered affects these very same people greatly and they get mad and even cry, so they are not cold-hearted. How many times have you heard someone say, "I prefer the company of dogs over people"?

Machiavellians are very ambitious—those vying for high political office. Originally, high levels of Machiavellianism were coupled with high intelligence, but research has concluded the opposite may be true. Some research suggests that high levels of Machiavellianism may be good in an organization, depending on the position, for example perhaps a high-powered sales position, or a commission-based position. Machiavellianism is also considered one of the three dark trait triads; the other two are narcissism and psychopathy (i.e., antisocial behavior) and due to the malevolent qualities associated within the three. This triad has been used in the fields of law enforcement and applied psychology, and in some cases, cybersecurity.

Authoritarianism

Having this characteristic can either mean someone being absolutely submissive in a role, or the oppression of someone's else role by their commandeering persona. A strong authoritarianism trait can lead someone to having blind loyalty to a cause—a political party or an idea; this unwavering viewpoint must succeed at all costs. They have very strict and defined ideals on what makes up a good person, a good parent, good child, or a good leader. They firmly believe that their work surpasses others' efforts and may inhibit others in their own attempts to be successful. The major problem with an authoritarianism trait is not the trait itself but the aggression that comes with that trait. For the right role, having this trait could be successful, (e.g., a military leader), but in some organizations, for example a person who is very fluid, it may not be beneficial.

Narcissism

Narcissists can indeed be very charming. Very positive, very outgoing, but they also believe that they are superior. Their self-importance is of primary importance and they will let you know they are important. It is important for a person to have self-esteem, but narcissists exaggerate their self-esteem virtues to unhealthy levels. There are studies that have shown that in the short term, narcissists display power and the ability to lead, but over the long term, their shortcomings rise to the surface. Narcissists usually blame someone else for their failures. A narcissist may engage in gaslighting, whereby constant manipulation of someone else leads that person to question their own self-worth. Narcissists are usually good at persuasion and, combined with charm, can lead to social change, but this social change can lead to both good and bad outcomes.

Humor Styles

You may have heard someone saying, *she has a dry sense of humor*, or *he has a warped sense of humor*. There are different types of humor character-istics we display. Researchers agree on mainly four main types. There is the self-defeating style, made famous by Rodney Dangerfield, *"I don't get no respect."* The second is a type of aggressive humor, often characterized by targeting others (e.g., put-downs or stereotyping). The self-enhancing style, comes next, where we try to get everyone to laugh (e.g., at life, kids, work, etc.), and finally, the affiliative style, which is a benevolent style.

It is more the way these styles are applied (e.g., physical humor is an act, like being clumsy, which is a self-defeating style). Dark humor can be an application of self-defeating or aggressive styles. Research does show these different styles could have an impact on the way you behave, and how others behave toward you, and in some cases have been shown to improve workplace cohesiveness.

Achievement Trait

These are the ambitious individuals, self-motivated and open to new chal-lenges. They find enjoyment in solving new challenges. They often exhibit characteristics of taking charge and being reliable. High levels of energy and optimism about an outcome is also noted. Unfortunately, in some cases, their desire to achieve may have a negative effect, in that they are slow to recognize that their current approach to a challenge is not working, and be reluctant to change, and in some cases, even sabotage going backward. Researchers do seem to agree that the higher levels of achievement corresponds to a high level of openness, which might make sense; the more open you are, the more chances you may take, the higher the probability some of those chances will be successful. This is not to apply open to all chances, as some may backfire and result in ruin, but in that you are probably more likely to be open to the idea of new possibilities.

Uncertainty

This is an interesting trait in that it measures the amount of uncertainty someone or some culture will tolerate. In project management literature, it could be compared to the unknown unknowns. In high levels of avoiding uncertainty and high levels of resistance to change, rules and procedures must be adhered. Whereas in lower levels of this trait, being more open to the future and letting things happen as they come is preferred; it is okay to challenge people in higher authority. Some may see this trait as corresponding or complement to risk management; however, these are separate, and avoiding uncertainty is not avoiding risk, and just a set of practices exhibited by an individual or society, although the behavior they eventually practice may be one of risk avoidance.

Other traits exist, for example, cognitive challenges where people want to solve a problem with the goal of just solving the problem: for instance, solving a Rubik's Cube. Once they solve the Rubik's Cube, then their next goal is to solve it in less time. Some individuals believe that people are born naturals, like great athletes, whereas some believe it's conditioning that makes them become special. This trait can cause all kinds of problems, since if we believe people are born naturals, when we deal with these people without really knowing them, we may make assumptions about the results they could achieve that has no basis in reality. Well, he was never going to get that football scholarship anyway, or she really doesn't look like she would make it at Harvard. There is the type A or type B personal theory hypothesis—two polar opposites (Friedman and

Rosenman 1959). Many people may have heard about this theory and have strong opinions on the research as some of the studies were funded by tobacco companies and was meant to look at future heart problems among middle-aged white men. Over time it has also been examined in the light of other activities like driving, motivation, ambition, and so on, and it could be that type A or B are just some of the common characteristics we have mentioned above.

We also have these broadcasting traits, where some might look at us and think *he is a neat freak, she chews like a cow*, or *he has a big national flag so he must be a patriot*, along with other examples. It is a way we make judgment on others, whether they are wrong or right. One final trait, which has some very interesting conclusions, is the delayed gratification trait, also called the marshmallow experiment conducted by Walter Mischel.

The Marshmallow Experiment

This was a simple experiment conducted by Mischel, Ebbesen, and Raskoff (1972) at Stanford University in the early 1960s. A group of children aged four to six were told you can eat one marshmallow now, or you can wait for twenty minutes and have two marshmallows. The marshmallow is just symbolic of the term. There were other treats available, but the method was the same—one now or two in twenty minutes.

It was an interesting experiment because the children did everything they could to avoid the temptation—looking away, covering their eyes, and so on. In the end, only one-third of the children were successful in delaying gratification. The big results of this experiment came years later when Mischel, who had been following up with these children over the later years, announced his observations. The children who were able to delay gratification at the early age did better in school and achieved higher Scholastic Aptitude Test (SAT) scores. Brain scans were done in 2011 and Mischel did find some differences in the different groups' cortex lobes. As with any research experiment, there are always criticisms, some unfounded, but definitely it was an interesting study that threw up some very surprising results. Watts, Duncan, and Quan (2018) expressed serious doubts about the marshmallow test. In their replicated study, they took into account social and economic backgrounds of the participants. In their view, it was the circumstances the children found themselves associated with, not just instant gratification of a sweet treat. Looking back at Mischel's experiment, they pondered could it be the situation the child found themselves in (e.g., perhaps they did not get treats at home coming from poorer families). Can there be any way to predict that if someone has the trait, say conscientiousness, they would be better achievers over the long run? How about—It is certainly worth continuing this area of research. Watts, Duncan, and Quan (2018) did not say Mischel was incorrect, but just that there may be other factors as well to consider.

Self-Control

As with the marshmallow test, does overcoming temptation or better self-control develop overall better habits in an individual? Galla and Duckworth (2015) did a study that identified those who had better self-control also had better structure in their lives. They had a much easier time achieving their goals and perhaps this had to do with planning and structure in their daily lives and therefore were more likely to achieve their goals. Perhaps if I can resist temptation or the rush to make a decision and I practice this as part of my daily life, I will make better decisions overall. They also suggested making something routine would have a better long-term effect. Therefore, perhaps in the world of cybersecurity, the same practice would encourage better security behaviors. While many organizations may send out monthly e-mails to its employees on social engineering attacks and phishing examples, how many cybersecurity professionals practice a similar type of reinforcement strategy?

The interesting results were not that those who showed the most self-control exercised the most self-control; it was the reverse. Those who showed the most self-control actually exercised the least self-control. It is argued the more you enjoy something, the less need for self-control. While it may seem easy to comprehend, eating, exercising, and homework are all considered chores that we do not want to engage in; however, the more we make it part of our daily routing, the less it seems like a chore and the more self-control we have in completing that task.

Dark Trait Triads and the Framing Effect

The set of traits such as (1) Machiavellianism, the ends justify the means, a lack of empathy, and any news is good just as long as it helps to remain in power; (2) narcissism, egoistical, self-image idolization, and self-focus in all relationships, and (3) psychopathy, exhibiting of anti-social behavior, limited remorse, and often associated with the criminal justice system, are seen as a dark triad. There is research looking at others using this dark triad but not within and at ourselves. But how can the dark triad of traits impact cybersecurity professionals, and the answer might lie in its framing effect.

The framing effect is a phenomenon of how someone might behave given a set of outcomes that violates their own expected outcome. Our desire not to lose is so strong that we will make basically the same exact decisions if they are just framed differently (Plous 1993; Tversky and Kahneman 1981). The dark triad is further emphasized by the framing effect. Deutchman and Sullivan (2018) conducted a study with prisoners for testing the framing effect and selfish behaviors. By using contextual cues of gain vs. loss and social vs. non-social conditions, those who exhibited dark trait patterns of psychopathy, narcissism, and Machiavellianism were much more likely to exhibit selfish behaviors. This is a real concern and may contribute to reasons for the psychology of blame that we will examine later.

The old classic game show, *Let's Make a Deal*, also illustrates the framing effect. You have already won a television show; do you want to take a chance and lose it and go for what's behind curtain number one, or would like to go for behind curtain number two and win a new car (i.e., lose television or win car)? Ever pour money into a very old car to fix things up, instead of buying a new car? It's the sunk cost fallacy, and you fear you would have lost that money. Which line is longer, which box is bigger, which person is taller—are all these types of framing effects guide your decision?

What is happening in so many of these cases is that you are using old processing memories as everything you have seen and heard comes into your decision making. In the *Let's Make a Deal* show, it becomes even more apparent since the host Monty Hall would eventually allow individuals to pick two outcomes. For the person who makes the choice of one of the three curtains, Monty Hall would remove the curtain that usually had a can of tuna. Then there are two curtains left, and he would give the contestant another chance to change their decision. The contestants believe that now that there are two curtains left their chance is 50 percent. The problem is in isolation—contestants are looking at all doors being equal instead of as a set. One curtain has the prize—so two curtains, one prize, one not is 66 percent; then the other pair—one prize, one not, another 66 percent pair; this is the Allais paradox, which is sometimes referred to the Monty Hall problem. This framing effect can influence your cybersecurity decisions. When you make a decision to install a new firewall, an antivirus program, or new intrusion detection, are you making that decision in (1) isolation and (2) are you making that decision based on your own understanding of the loss effect?

One thing about all these traits mentioned is that they are on a scale. Even insanity, as we shall see later, is on a scale. Looking at these traits we often judge others, but we do not just do it for ourselves even if we were in the same exact circumstances, as we will rationalize our behavior. Is intelligence a trait? This subject will be touched on later, and as we will see, there is no clear answer. We are designing systems based on our cognitive thinking; we will also see that our cognitive thinking is often wrong. Technology companies are racing to create artificial intelligence, deep learning, and a whole new industry of autonomous commuting and all of this is based our on cognitive abilities.

Prospect Theory

Prospect theory describes the way people choose between alternatives that involve risk, illustrated by the *Let's Make a Deal* framing effect we just spoke about. The framing effect does not examine the outcome but the probability of the outcome, hence the name prospect. What are the prospects on a number of alternatives I can choose from? A major social issue with prospect theory, other than the framing, is that due to human feelings, people can be exploited. Psychologists Tversky and Kahneman (1981) divided prospect theory into two main parts—a value function and a weighted function—and they are not linear. A diagram (Figure 3.1) helps to illustrate this phenomenon.

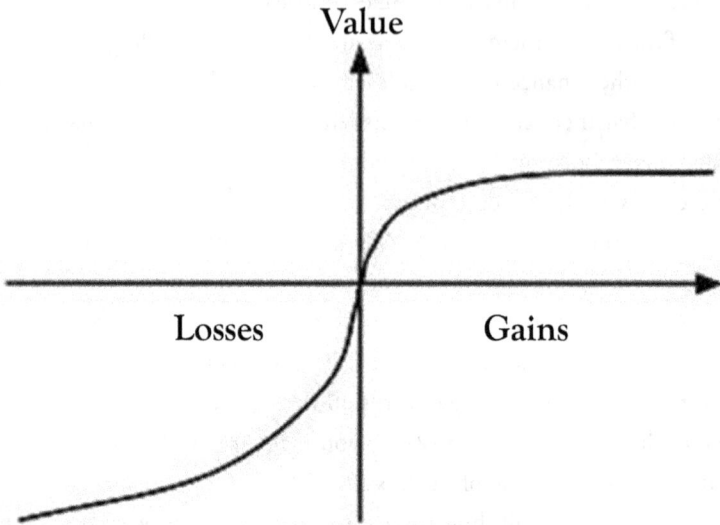

Figure 3.1 Psychologists Tversky and Kahneman value and function curve

If we begin to add values onto the Tversky and Kahneman value and function curve, it really shows the effect (Figure 3.2).

I value losing $50.00 more than I do value gaining $50.00. On the surface it makes sense, as who wants to lose $50.00; however, digging

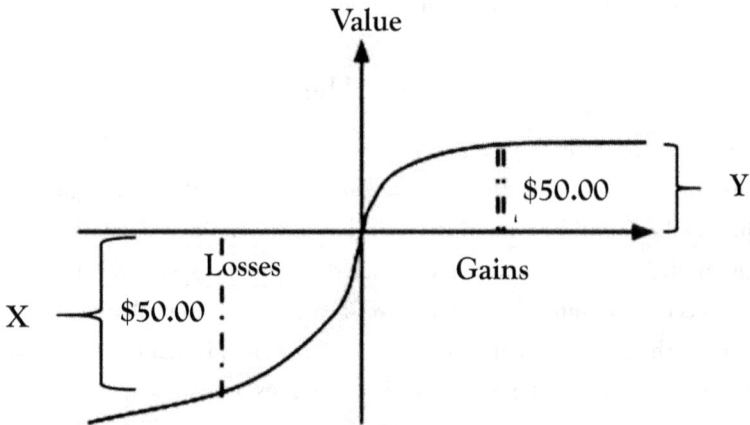

X is greater than Y

Figure 3.2 Value and function curve with shown loses

deeper we have some serious concerns. We prefer to avoid losses much more than achieve gains, which is we like to play it safe, which probably isn't always the best thing to do in cybersecurity. We may become too worried by very little changes in our environment.

Take these examples:

100% chance to win $90, or
90% chance to win $100 or nothing.

The expected value is $90.00 in both cases, and most people will take option (1), a sure thing (i.e., risk-averse) when dealing with gains. Changing the examples around a little, we have:

100% to lose $90, or
90% chance of losing $100 or nothing.

Expected value remains at –$90, but people will now choose option (2) (i.e., risk-seeking) when dealing with losses. Our risk aversion is so great we now become risk takers to take a gamble in the hopes of not losing anything. For a cybersecurity professional, we may put in a security policy since I know it will stop viruses but perhaps not rootkits. That's something different; I do not see the loss of a rootkit attacks, although rootkits could potentially do much more damage. A virus is a sure thing that will happen, a rootkit, well, perhaps not. An infected e-mail gets opened and you rationalize it like the end of the world, but in the overall context of cybersecurity, a virus may be the least of your worries. We are afraid of very small losses, and this does impact our behavior and those cybersecurity solutions chosen. Another problem with this is that how do we decide which is riskier; we use heuristics, which we will discuss later, and mental shortcuts (i.e., rules of thumb) to help us make decisions. Therefore, our use of risk or reward and of mental shortcuts could do more damage to our organization over the long term. You might be able to see why this is such a big problem, and the main reason why social engineering attacks work so well is because they exploit a human frailty (e.g., fear, urgency, scarcity, and watch people's behavior). We make snap decisions—he or she has a vendor uniform on, so he or she must be an authorized vendor. He said on the phone he was a police lieutenant; he must be in law enforcement. Cybersecurity professionals also deal with very large numbers—number of attacks, number of records compromised, number of personal data items stolen, and so on. Unfortunately, humans are bad at a large number. Landy et al. (2013) argued people could distinguish numbers between 800 million and 2 million but confused about 980 million and 2 billion. They seem to imagine a straight-spaced linear line between the words thousand, million, billion, and trillion. We see this a lot in biased reporting, where the scale is modified, or only a very short part of the scale is shown. This problem has a real issue since people may not realize the impact of large numbers, such as political spending, medical expenditures, national debt, or full understanding of personal data points stolen.

Prospect theory is used heavily in cybersecurity and in risk research, and many of the conclusions are the same—people do not always behave rationally and people deviate from a rational consistent viewpoint depending on how the event is framed. The big picture is that in all of these different outcomes, the way the different options are framed will lead to different behavioral decisions. In cybersecurity, we have to make decisions based upon attacks and usually successful attacks. How often do we base our decisions on unsuccessful attacks? We need to guard against successful denial of service attacks, successful phishing attacks, and successful social engineering attacks. The framing effect says we make our decisions based upon on our desire not to lose, and in cybersecurity we do not want to lose.

Cybersecurity Traits

I've reviewed hundreds of websites that mentioned cybersecurity traits. This nonresearch type of primary findings was just to get a sense if there is some consensus of cybersecurity traits. I found many things listed as traits (e.g., technical skills, understanding security weaknesses, soft skills, certifications, leadership skills, communication skills, management skills, black hat skills, hardening skills, and so on), but I did not find a match of any type of human behavioral trait, or if I did, I could count on my fingers those applied to a cybersecurity professional. A dilemma in that is with a lot of information on the topic of behavior and cybersecurity, some ask as these two were intrinsically linked, why were no behavioral traits mentioned? In reviewing the scholarly literature, we found many research studies. Haney and Lutters (2017) mentioned context awareness, which is an understanding of the environment you engage in, along with the groups involved. Later on, we will see how group belonging can contribute to behavior. Haney and Lutters pointed out a good trait not to have was arrogance, or at least the appearance of arrogance, which could describe a Machiavellianism or narcissist type of being and really who wants to work with an arrogant co-worker. If you are designing a new cybersecurity solution, would you think it's better to have a cybersecurity team comprised of only individuals who are shown to be high on openness, or a few on neuroticism, or uncertainty? Like we mentioned already, this isn't necessarily a bad trait, or a yes or no trait, it's just on a scale. Typically, I think of having someone with an analyst's personality, often identified when someone playing a devil's advocate, since it gets others to see their own viewpoints and the soundness of those viewpoints. When we discuss cybersecurity, it is true we can learn from yesterday's attacks to help defend tomorrow's attacks, but we can also learn from the way someone thought about yesterday to what they might think about tomorrow. As research has shown for the most part, our traits will last with us a lifetime; however, where we sit on the scale of those traits will change over our lifetime, so we may use that to our advantage. Research has highlighted individual behaviors from the point of view from someone who might violate policy. For example, Hadlington (2017) points out someone with Internet addiction might lead to an increased chance of bad cybersecurity behaviors. Impulsivity was another key factor mentioned, so there does seem to be some traits that may be a problem. Other researchers pointed to a more focus on the intrinsic individual's side: why would someone open an infected email and why would someone share their passwords? Gratian, Bandi, Cukier, Dykstra and Ginther (2017) reported on research highlighting different human traits and cybersecurity behavioral intentions. They examined four areas: (1) device securement (i.e., passwords and PINs), (2) password generation (i.e., the strength of their passwords), (3) proactive awareness (e.g., spotting fraudulent website URLs), and (4) updating measures (e.g., security patches and up-to-date software). With the use of the Egelman and Peer's (2015) Security Behavior Intention Scale (SeBIS), they correlated it to risk-taking preferences and the various decisions made. Their research was done in a university setting and an involved examining demographics of that population and their susceptibility to phishing attacks. They examined the Big Five traits against weak privacy settings, risk-taking actions with the susceptibility to phishing, and using several decision-making models with susceptibility to phishing attacks and how impulsive decision making may influence mobile security practices. Their results were that the demographics factors for securing the device aligned with those in more a technical nature on the ANOVA analysis, not the regression model. However, they did conclude from the Big Five that those with outgoing personalities were more careful with securing their device. Outgoing individuals are more engaging with others, so it is possible they are more sensitive to locking their devices since they have been exposed to someone else being hacked. Their research did find a correlation between the type of decision making and good device securement. They examined five types of decision-making models: (1) rational, using logic when making decisions, (2) avoidant, the delay of decision making, (3) dependent, relying on others for decision advice, (4) intuitive, instinct-based decision making, and (5) spontaneous, quick decision making. Previous research from Egelman and Peer (2015) supports that impulsive and dependent decision-making approaches were inversely related to those exhibiting good security behaviors. In their research, Gratian et al. (2017) did find that those using rational decision making were better at device securement. It is interesting to note that rational decision making makes use of the top-down approach, which activates our neural network associations. These researchers also reported that in terms of proactive awareness, gender seemed to be significant. Females were reported to have a weaker proactive awareness than males, but that did differ from earlier research and no differences among the business, education, and liberal arts student groups were found. There was also no relationship between ethical risk-taking and updating measures. They suggested that perhaps more security awareness training is needed, that is, cybersecurity is a human behavioral issue, which is constantly repeated throughout this book from research gathered. Matulessy and Humaira (2016) did a review on hackers in comparison to the Big Five Traits, and their study uncovered some interesting results in terms of genetic factors, environmental factors, and gene factors. White hat hackers scored high on agreeableness and in the middle of the other four traits, black hat hackers were higher on openness and centered on the remaining four traits, and the gray hats were tending high on neuroticism, with the other four somewhere in the middle. Their study was done with a small size of six unmarried males aged 19 to 28 who were educated and had an Information Technology background, and an additional 30 subjects were assessed on the Big Five traits, with 10 each representing each hacker hat. The population may not be representative as a whole, but it might highlight some differences between the types, and taking into account the background factors mentioned above, could lead to some more very valuable research. Then, when research was beginning to form around the notion that we think we have the population understood, along comes Henrich, Heine, and Norenzayan (2010) and their study, "The Weirdest People in the World?" For most of the studies done up to this point, researchers have stuck to a small sample of Western, educated, industrialized, rich, and democratic (WEIRD) societies, yet generalized this to the world, but these WEIRD societies do not reflect all the populations in general. When it comes to cybersecurity professionals, perhaps worldwide differences do have an impact, especially on their traits, and ultimately their behavior.

They Bake Bread, Don't They?

Panera, the owners of Panera Bread, disclosed that in 2018 that over 37 million customers had lost their private information, including names, e-mail and physical addresses, birthdays, and the last four digits of the customers' credit card numbers (Houliham 2018; Smith 2018; Hron 2018). Panera apparently was e-mailed by a security researcher warning them about a potential leak of data. Some countermeasures did occur immediately, but the security team failed to correct the vulnerability until eight months later. After the investigation, the results revealed that the data was available in plain text and that Panera was warned about the problem.

While ordering, customers were allowed to set up an account to order food and then go and pick up the food. A weakness in unauthorized API endpoints allowed anyone who had ever signed to become a potential victim of losing their data. This initial leak of the online customer base was small but allowed hackers to use gateways to network over to the commercial division and the remaining 37 million pieces of data.

Isn't this a very common thing currently?
How many supermarkets allow this now—preorder and go pick up?

An interesting point was that when Panera was initially told about this, the one in charge of information security actually thought of this as a scam but stated they were working on a fix. However, eight months later, the site was still unsecured and the way customer data was stored made it very possible for hackers to gather very large amounts of personal data very quickly.

There are, there are two issues here:

Why was data stored in this way?
Why did it take so long to fix?

Considering the vulnerability was fixed when it became evident that, yes, this was a serious problem, number one is no longer the main issue. They finally took the issue seriously and corrected the problem, but why did it take so long to take this issue seriously?

There could be two factors here.

Traits—what was discussed about openness, or the lack thereof? The lack of openness, being closed off, and not being open enough to the potential of a security risk. If I lack openness, I increase my nervous and therefore may just push off what is happening. We all have this cognitive trait; it is just to the extent this may interfere with our incorporating knowledge and new facts. We just spoke about the rush to minimize loss, even a subconscious thought about loss is loss itself. Pushing off subconscious thought about loss can be akin to a positive outcome (i.e., I just pushed the threat off, hopefully to the vendor of that API, it's their problem now).

Conditioned response. We talked about a conditioned response; we are conditioned to respond to some stimuli. In this case, the e-mail was thought to be a hoax; therefore, my conditioned response was to ignore the hoax. However, at the back of my mind, and since action was taken a week later, other stimuli took over to change my behavior but not enough to fully change my behavior until eight months had passed. Not until an abundance of new data would change my cognitive bias that would make me realize, yes, this is a big issue happening and change is needed. This is very important as we will see later, even in an abundance of data, people will still be hesitant to change their behavior.

This was an interesting example, and while we certainly cannot be 100 percent sure, it would stand to reason that conditioned response and traits played a part in the success of this attack. We should also address in general: the thousands of security researchers and the e-mails they send (e.g., we have a message and a receiver). This security researcher did not know Panera or who they would contact. So when sending an e-mail to a company, even a legitimate contact is usually at first suspicious. Once the red flags go up, they are hard to bring back down, so proper channels then may be needed in the future.

Cybersecurity Implications and Conclusions

Since this chapter was on traits, what then could be considered good cybersecurity traits? When we discuss cybersecurity, it is true we can learn from yesterday's attacks to help defend tomorrow's attacks, but can we also learn from the way someone thought about yesterday, to what they might think tomorrow and in the future. As research has shown for the most part, our traits will last with us a lifetime, even though where we sit on the scale of those traits will change over our lifetime, and we may use that to our advantage. Consider all these traits mentioned here—conscientiousness, agreeableness, neuroticism, openness, extroversion, Machiavellianism, authoritarianism, narcissism, humor styles, achievement, avoiding uncertainty, even the marshmallow experiment, and others—and situate yourself somewhere on each of these scales. Realize that we often use these traits to judge others but not necessarily see these traits in ourselves, so unfortunately our judgments are usually wrong. In the world of cybersecurity, where the narrative is often filled with negative words and phrases, agreeableness is often overlooked as being naive and not understanding the real threat. I have met many cybersecurity specialists I would describe as gloom and doom. So, should gloom and doom be stereotyped for cybersecurity professionals? The dark trait triads are negative in nature, the very terms many of us associate cybersecurity with (i.e., viruses, bugs, attacks, etc.). We have two different competing actions, cognitive dissonance happens, and then an internal struggle. If these dark trait triads become dominant, antisocial tendencies will arise and we may not heed some very important information like attacks that were not successful, but that very well could be successful in the future if we don't plan for them now. Would you take up smoking now, probably not, too risky from what you have read? Would you drink and drive, again, and risk legal problems? Would you eat fast food all day? Well, not unless you are a fan of diabetes.

Why?

Fast food, smoking, drinking and driving are all associated in the negative context, and you would not adopt them. Consciously or subconsciously, these negative words, phrases, and factors have an impact on your perception and thus your behavior. Now, try to roll out a cybersecurity program, and you are using these same exact traits, and end-users will not knowingly comply. Again, this is not they will not, but it's the negative association of a threat that they seek to avoid, again, subconsciously. This could all relate to risk factors such as communications. Good risk communications aim to get people to follow good hygiene practices, and bad risk communications get people to not follow good hygiene practices. Haney and Lutters (2017) examined the perceptions of risk communications and the motivations that cybersecurity experts emphasize on dealing with those they must influence to follow good cybersecurity practices. Persuasiveness is a critical factor in overcoming these negative feelings. They reported several important factors that could be helpful: (1) Reputation—credentials of the people doing the persuasion, an official of the company, or a systems administrator no one has heard of before; (2) Knowledge—technical knowledge is very important, but as this book points out, can you explain that knowledge? You cannot expect an end-user's data entry person to know about Crytpowall; (3) Relationships—I as a cybersecurity expert cannot be expected to understand someone doing an accounting database query on payroll, vacation time, sick leave, and so on, and vice versa, but

I can nevertheless develop a relationship of trust and communication. Haney and Lutters (2018) pointed out some other good factors, and it was surprising to note, most of the factors were related to honesty, trust, relationships, empathy, and so on. and not technical factors, which gives support to why cybersecurity needs to move more into understanding human behavior. Where do you situate yourself and then ask this about how each one will impact your decision making? Even decision making is a form of behavior. Are you open to other's opinions, or are you so much on the Machiavellianism scale that only you can create the greatest cybersecurity solution for a company but unfortunately no one can use that solution and the company just wasted millions of dollars? Or to a lesser extent, employees complain so much that they cannot get any work done and management forces you to undo your great cybersecurity solution, but in your zeal to get revenge, you make them weaker, and open the company up to an attack, and be careful, as the motivation for revenge can be subconscious. Remember, skills are not traits, but traits can help you lay a foundation for acquiring and mastering skills, like openness or achievement, or becoming a better cybersecurity professional. Furnham and Cheng (2016) have reported the correlation of childhood intelligence to the trait openness, and openness is also correlated with creativity and intelligence. In addition, given the nature of cybersecurity professionals' work, always adapting to changes, isolating problems, running fault analysis, and so on, they need to be creative.

So, my hypothesis would then be:

Hypothesis: a good cybersecurity professional acts like a little kid.

This is so, I will not be insulted the next time my wife says I act like a 12-year-old.

CHAPTER 4

Perceptions

Introduction

We would like to believe that we have good, or even great perceptions, and that our perceptions would never mislead us. Unfortunately, they cannot be trusted most of the times. Complicating the matter further is that perceptions seem to be biased upon the circumstances we find ourselves at the moment; we touched on this aspect earlier. It seems that Charles Dickens was correct in his famous Christmas fairytale, as *Scrooge* said that with the senses, even an undercooked potato affects them. Our perceptions, even our senses, are not always reliable; we are sure we trust what we see, what we feel, and what we hear. We trust a pie will taste good, until we learn it's a spinach pie, well, for those who do not like spinach. If you think about perceptions, they are just electrical signals that made their way to the brain, get filtered by everything we are sensing at the moment, and then they get lodged into our neural networks, basically your cluttered closet at home. Then they get associated within a neural network, and a mass of other associations take place, some strong, some weak, some make sense, and some do not.

Perception for the most is just a subjective process on our part; it's one part active, one part creative, one part conscious, one part subconscious, one part emotion, and mixed with a number of other parts. Then add in a whole set of sensory information as we mix in those parts. Someone looks at a cow and thinks how cute; later that day the same person might look at the same cow and think McDonald's. Was this second viewing when we were hungry? That means our perceptions are now fluid and changing.

Associations

We touched on associations earlier, and now we will take a close look. Take a word association game, for example. If you are asked to say what is the first word you think of when you hear the word apple, you might say fruit.

Apple
Fruit

You would be correct, well, any word would be correct since there is not a right or wrong answer here. Another person may hear the same word and say dry cleaning bills. How did they end up with dry cleaning bills? Well, following an association, we might have:

Apple
Fruit
Marketing
Fruit of the Loom underwear
Dirty clothes
Laundromat
Dry cleaning bills.

Both associations are correct, the point is simply which of the associations is stronger in a given context. If you are in a supermarket, and thought of an association with apple, you may say fruit. But if you are shopping at a clothes retailer, and thought of that apple association, you may say dry cleaning, or something else associated with the clothing apparel. This gives you a very strong sense of just how much context and circumstances will reveal these associations. Once these electrical signals hit our brain and our neural networks go into action, a magnificent display of associations takes over. We can scratch the surface of these associations or reach into many corners of our mind to uncover deeper level associations.

There is a term in database terminology called "garbage in, garbage out." If the inputs of data into the database are garbage, basically meaning they are incorrect data values, the output will be incorrect data points.

As an example, if on a financial spreadsheet we allow alpha characters to be input into a numeric field containing salaries, we run a report asking for someone's salary, and the output is $45,2p3.23 (i.e., garbage in, garbage out). In the context of the human mind, our perceptions could start with garbage in, we would then have garbage out, but unlike a computer, we add more garbage on top of the garbage that is already there. We do this all the time; we can't help it. Think of any news story you hear—you get a little bit of that news, later on you might get contrasting information from another news source, and later on, still another contradicting news source. So we have garbage in, garbage out, repeat, garbage in, garbage out, repeat and so on.

This happens in our workplaces setting as well, and especially in information technology and cybersecurity. We work on a problem only to the extent we have the correct information, why and how a security vulnerability happened, and the more information we get about that security breach, whether it is accurate or not, is placed upon the existing information we have already learned. In all of these instances, we are perceiving what is happening, we are making interpretations about what we are seeing, and most often, pieces of the picture are missing, and our minds are working overtime filling in missing details. Adding to the chattiness, our brains are just really noisy (Segal 2019). Our perceptions are based upon our situation—are we in a lighted room, crowded street corner, dark alley, even how we feel at a particular moment impacts our perceptions. It is in the context of all this we come to some conclusion, or simply called a context of association. In the context of cybersecurity, are we sitting at our desk, around a conference table, or in a group setting being talked down to by an upper level manager? We sense what is happening, then this data gets encoded into our brains, there is some truth to what is happening, but do not expect it to be an accurate truth.

Context of Association

Our perceptions are always based upon our context. That context can be dependent on several factors, for example, whether an object in question is in the foreground or background. Subtle differences and cues we may not realize will have a profound effect on our perceptions of reality on cause and effect. As Chater (2018) says our brain has no consistency to base our decisions. We base an action on precedent, our past experiences, and our thoughts then can become habit. And we all understand once we get into a habit, it's very hard to break. Our brain, Chater argues, is a master storyteller—we spin answers depending on what we have stored, and unfortunately, our stories can then become fact to us. This phenomenon was a leading research stream during the Gestalt movement. If you stare at something for a while, the brightest of that object depends on the brightness of the background, not the actual brightest of the object in question. Digital cameras highlight this effect easily. Take a picture with a digital camera but hold it for a second or two before taking that picture. The focus is on the main central image inside a small focal point, and outside of that focal point, the images become blurry. But, unlike a simple picture, those blurred outside images get filtered through our eye lens and to our brain. When we are asked to recall those images, they are blurry, so we need to make things up. We do not simply make things up, but rather all our previous associations rattled inside our brains come up with the most logical answer what those blurred images actually were.

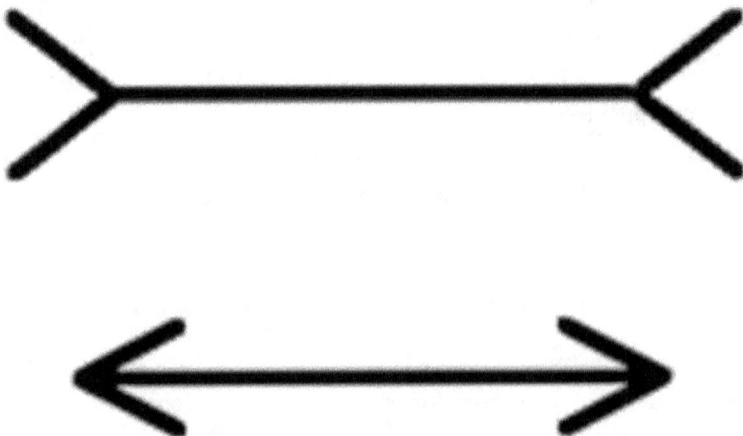

Figure 4.1 Which line is bigger?

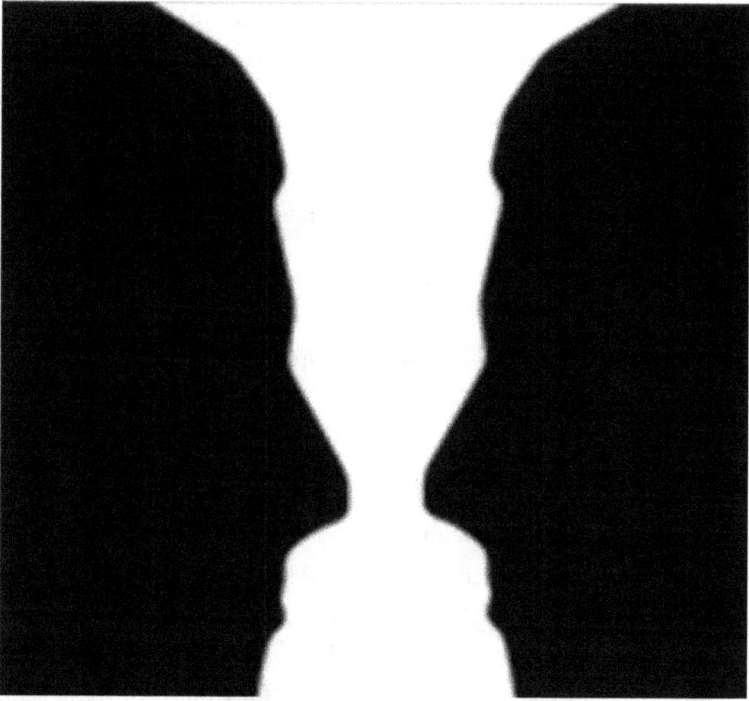

Figure 4.2 Is this picture a vase or a face?

Have you ever come across these simple mind benders, such as?

The problem isn't the person's face, or the length of the line; it was the relationship that existed. These contextual cues will help us to answer a question and then possibly guide our behavior. It was the relationship to the other things in the picture that caused confusion—the arrows points, the room size—what we just call optical illusions. In dealing with this problem, we have to try to find a way to help out perceptions and we use other signals to help us cope, after all, we have to solve this challenge. We use different strategies to fill in the missing information; one common way is to examine between the foreground and the background, and another way is with strategies we've developed over time. Sometimes, these are referred to as Gestalt laws.

Gestalt Laws

The Gestalt laws are founded in Gestalt psychology typically credited to Max Wertheimer, Wolfgang Kohler, and Kurt Koffka (Vezzani, Marino, and Giora 2012). How do people interact within the world, and how certain principles help us interact with the world? How objects interact with one another, from our self of perceptions. This gives ways to five Gestalt laws:

Similarity

Things that are similar in style seem to be appear as grouped together. For example, if we see a set of 30 colored balls—10 red, 10 white, and 10 black—we would see this as three grouping, instead of just the set of 30 balls.

Symmetry

The amount of balance we want to see. For example, picture a seesaw you may have played on as a child in a park. However, in this case, picture only one child on the seesaw and that it is in the up position, meaning the child is up in the air with no other child on the other end countering the other child's weight. Look at an image of this and then try to sense what your brain is doing at the moment. The image is fake, you know it's fake, your brain knows its fake, but part of your brain is trying to make sense of this image.

Proximity

The closer some objects appear, and away from others, the more they form their own unique group. Imagine a piece of paper with 30 circles on it—10 circles drawn on the top, 10 circles drawn in the middle, and 10 circles drawn on the bottom. We would tend to think of these as three individual groups, instead of just one piece of paper with 30 circles.

Closure

Even if something appears not to be closed, we will sense it as being closed. Our mind will fill in the missing details. Our minds prefer closed entities, and even if it is not closed, we will assume it's closed. If we see a piece of paper with a circle or box drawn, but with dotted lines instead of complete solid lines, we would see that as a circle and square respectively. This was illustrated by the figure above, a face or a vase, what closure does it bring you, it has to be one.

Continuity

We see objects on a path, instead of discrete things. Our eyes will tend to follow curves and bends, rather than abrupt lines, like a wall, or a horizontal–vertical break. Take a look at a company logo that has both characteristics: a set of letters and a curve running through that letter. Watch your eye tending to go along the curve, usually to a destination (e.g., a mascot or small image to remember that company). This is a very well-known marketing and advertising campaign; you need to reach a destination. The term "don't leave me hanging" would fit here.

A couple of other properties of Gestalt exist, such as the law of motion (e.g., movement such as athletes) and the law of common fate. Think of a hundred birds all moving in the sky—they are not together, they are all making different adjustments in flight, but to the eye, they are one big dot. Or when you move your mouse to crop a photo on your computer, the movement of your mouse and the cropping seem to be synchronized. Gestalt's properties are a way, a strategy we use to help us solve challenges, fill in the missing pieces. Another way we often hear about is top-down, or bottom-up processing. We are simply trying to fill in the missing pieces, it looks like, it seems to be, it most likely is, our best guess, and unfortunately, our best guesses are many times incorrect.

The Stroop Effect

The Stroop effect (Stroop 1935) is best understood through an example. In the following Figure 4.3, count the number of fruits mentioned and count the number of numbers mentioned.

The answer was 15 in both columns—there are 15 fruits mentioned, and there are 15 numbers mentioned. We can further add to this complexity by using circles with colors. Imagine a number of circles, each one having its own color, but inside the circle the words showing another color, for example, a white circle, with black lettering, indicating the color purple.

Apple	Seven
Pear	Seventy-two
Banana	Five
Grapes	Nine
Raisins	Seventeen
Apricot	Two
Mango	Twenty-two
Melon	Twelve
Lemon	Six
Cherry	Seven
Pineapple	Sixteen
Plum	Thirty-Two
Raspberry	Nineteen
Orange	Seventy-three
Watermelon	Eight

Figure 4.3 Stroop effect

Now examine the Stroop effect in Figures 4.4, 4.5 and 4.6 when colors are used.

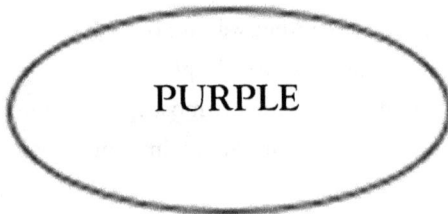

Figure 4.4 Background in red, the word purple is written in gray

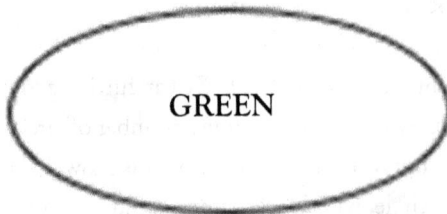

Figure 4.5 Background in yellow, the word green is written in red.

ORANGE

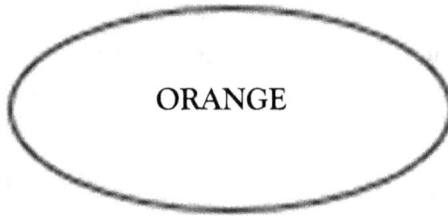

Figure 4.6 Background in blue, the word orange is written in red

These last examples may be a little harder to understand the Stroop effect since this book is in black and white, but if you search the Internet for the Stroop effect, you will be easily spot the confusion. However, even without color trying to make sense of a blue background, with a color, orange, as the orange was written in red, even that can be confusing. Complicating that effect, when you saw orange, did you also think of the fruit orange?

When we look back at our first example, and asked to count, the quickest set to count were the number of fruits mentioned. Fruits, like the word apple, have no relationship to the action on which you were told to do, which was to count. However, when asked to count how many numbers there were in the table, did you count seven as one, or did you count seven as seven, and thought, okay, so that's one. Next, there's a three, but that's two, is it twenty-two or seven? Five, no, that's three, and at each number you stop and pause, so you begin to skip. It gets even more complicated when we are then in the colored circles. We know the color orange, but when orange is written in red, our brain is saying "no, this is not correct." The Stroop effect implies we are on automatic pilot, so apple has no meaning to counting, but 72 has a definite meaning, so we are counting 72 as the number 72, not just the second number listed. This happens with colors as well, or anything that has an associated value with that of which we are being asked to do.

The problems here are twofold.

1. An overabundance of stimuli.
2. We are on automatic pilot.

The overabundance of stimuli hits our eyes, sends back electrical signals, and even though we are just asked to count, our automatic mental processes kick in and start multitasking. Unfortunately, our mental processing often assumes things and things start to break down, and instead of concentrating on the task at hand, we substitute details on what we think to be true.

This impacts our perceptions!

If we can drink coffee and drive, most of us would have no problem, but we cannot text and drive. And while you can drink coffee and drive, you cannot brew coffee and drive. There is just too much stimuli and no matter how hard we try, we can only multitask so much, and we are really not good at that, especially with important matters like driving. Therefore, we have a little attention span spread out over a number of items, or a lot of attention on one or two items, and texting is not one of them.

The Zeigarnik Effect

Our minds want closure, just like the Gestalt laws predict. We want things to finish, and when they are finished, we can put them aside and rest. However, when they are not finished, our minds do not rest. Researcher Zeigarnik (1938) noticed this while in a restaurant. Waiters were able to remember many different orders, just so long as they were not filled yet. I worked with a staff of short-order cooks throughout college. We never had a single waiter or waitress give us a slip with the food order; we just remembered. After the order was finished and taken out of the kitchen, if a waiter or waitress did ever come back and said there might be an error, we would respond, "to what?" The waiter or waitress would say, "to the order I just gave you." Our response: "what order?" As soon as the food order was done and out the kitchen door, it left our memories, and since I worked with five other short-order cooks, who all experienced this phenomenon, this effect is very real.

Consider a project at work, or say you are working on a recipe, a new house project, woodworking, sewing, anything really, but you are missing that one last piece to complete the project. That ingredient, that screw, that last piece of source code: what happens?

Do you just put that task away in the back of your mind, or do bells go off?

It seems to be that, what really happens is:

You begin to focus more on that task.
It nags at you.
You can't help but think about that task.

Where can you obtain that one last piece you need, that one last ingredient? How can you obtain that final thing to finish that project? How, when, and where can I finish that last piece of coding? If you are working on some project over the weekend, and you have a regular job during the week, you will then make plans to get that last piece during some part of the work week; just so you can finish that unfinished project, to bring closure.

Think of any television series you watch:

(a) what was last year's cliffhanger?
(b) A news report that gives only part of the story and then follows with *more news at 10.*
(c) A magician, so what's the trick!
(d) the murderer is ?

Who? The tension is killing us.

You are setting off hundreds of neural networks associations focusing on how to complete that project. You are not just focusing on that last piece; you are focusing on the entire project. This is the Zeigarnik effect, a part of the Gestalt principle of closure.

Why, well it's easier for us.

Our mental processes do not want to work hard; we want to conserve our mental energy (i.e., the principle of conservation of energy). This is not to imply we are lazy, as it could have been an evolutionary trait.

Besides, it makes us feel good.

We are motivated to complete a task; it's a sense of achievement and it satisfies a cognitive dissonance (i.e., to reduce uncertainty). Not completing that task sets off our brain to waste energy into finishing that task, and we simply do not want to do that. If we complete the task, the task is done, closed, it's finished, and I can go rest now. When a task is not completed, we start to fire up those thousands of neural networks to figure out how to complete that task. But in the process, we also learn and increase the strength of associations. Some researchers suggest that is a double copying of the memory. We work on a task, it's stored in working memory, and when it's done, it can be stored in long-term memory. So, when tasks are not completed, they are copied twice or perhaps even multiple times. As the task is going on, it's not being completed, so the brain copies in both working and long-term memory that part of the task. As the task continues incomplete, more parts of that task are again copied in working and long-term memories, and so on. When the task is finally completed, working memory is moved to long-term memory but not just one copy. There are multiple copies now (i.e., via the multiple neural networks associations that get established, and the more associations one has, the quicker the retrieval of that information becomes).

Other Intrusions into Our Perceptions

Several other areas of, well, what some might call weakness or some might call strengths, interfere with our perceptions.

Bottom-Up

Bottom-up is our direct senses—what we know, see, feel, touch. Our reading, training, daily work, all gets fed into our neural networks. Bottom-up design is not bottom-up processing. Bottom-up design is telling upper management what might be needed. Bottom-up processing is our neural networks activating some association to help solve some issue, and many times a top-down directive. These associations become stronger as we practice them, but the reverse is true: the less we practice, the weaker they become and the harder they are at recall. Remember, the problem isn't losing the associations, it's recalling them.

This last note is worth repeating, and as we will see throughout this book, once you learn something, you never really lose it. The problem is recalling that information. How many times has something just popped into your head that you learned about years or even decades ago? If we lost that knowledge, we would never have these moments. These associations are critical to our learning—the more we practice these associations, the stronger they become. However, the same is true for the reverse—the less we practice, the less we can recall. And of course, we do make allowances for natural human aging, trauma, and as we will see, some researchers say the brain is built to forget.

Top-Down

This is our stored data: memories, habits, past experience, what have been told, what have we been shown, and what have we heard (e.g., consumer marketing: effective commercials). The problem isn't that we don't have the data; the problem is we have too much data, and since our mental energy cannot handle all that data, we streamline the data (i.e., the Gestalt laws), and the rest goes to the wastebasket. An issue with this is that when we many times recall an association to solve a current challenge, we may use an association that was stored but built using an older challenge. So does the same association result still hold? On top of that data, we have too many directions (e.g., in security frameworks, compliance, and regulations, management directives, etc.). We pay attention to only a little bit of the information and assume the rest as our attention span is very limited.

To realize just how short our attention span is today, research was conducted by Microsoft Canada in 2000 and the results noted that the average human attention span was 12 seconds, and today it is eight seconds. The average attention span of a goldfish is nine seconds. However, there is much debate to this story: was it serious or meant to be funny? Have humans' attention span not changed since the 1800s? Either way, there is just too much information, and the main point is distractions. There are just too many of them today, so our attention span per data point is limited.

There was an experiment where 100 volunteers were asked to view a video of a nonfatal car crash between a yellow and blue car. At the end of the video, the volunteers were asked, did the red or blue car cause the crash? Half chose the red car, although

There was no RED car.

In another experiment, volunteers were asked to count the number of times a team in a white colored jersey scored a basket. During the experiment, a person in a Gorilla suit walks by. When the experiment was over, and the researcher asked how many baskets were scored. Different answers were given.

However, no one mentioned the Gorilla!

A similar experiment was repeated. People were waiting at an elevator, a Gorilla walks by, and no one mentions a thing. Did they not notice, did they choose to ignore the Gorilla, or did inattentional blindness impact them? How did we miss a simple detail like that? Our senses, even though they are working, may not be aware, we could even be working at not being aware. We saw the gorilla, but did we actively choose to ignore the gorilla? The problem is later on when we need the information again, we may remember the gorilla, but not remember where we saw the gorilla. Where did we see that gorilla, the basketball game, the zoo, by the elevator, on a news report? Some research suggests its due to our visual field, sometimes our eyes. If not interrupted when we are watching a game, we do not see these interruptions. There has been some research that says it could depend on the color (e.g., a person in a black Gorilla suit will be more noticeable than a person in a white Gorilla suit) depending on the colors of the team's jerseys. Some research suggests it's a visual-spatial breakdown that can explain some of the variance. In an experiment conducted with pilots using a flight simulator, putting gauges in front of their field of vision, pilots were quick to notice the gauges, but put a plane in their field of vision, they missed the plane.

How can you miss a plane right in front of you?

How many of us have missed things right in front of us? Ever hear the saying,

Do not put anything right in front of me, I will never find it.

These visual messages, stimuli, or (perceptions of expectations, which is, what happens when we are expecting apple pie but got spinach pie instead). Ever get a call from a friend asking why you ignored them?

When you ask for details, they tell you they saw you, perhaps at a mall or movie, they waved at you, and you were staring right at them, but then turned away. So many times, we are on automatic pilot and therefore we ignore outside influences.

Perception of Information Security

Huang, Rau, and Salvendy (2010) conducted research on people's perception of information security, and although it's over a decade old, it still teaches us a valuable lesson, terminology can change, but perceptions, well, that's another thing. Since terminology changes, can these changes also change someone's perception of threats? Researchers conducted a factor analysis of 21 threats and combined them down into six factors: (1) knowledge, (2) impact, (3) severity, (4) controllability, (5) possibility, and (6) awareness. Then they compared them to the most dangerous threats at that time (i.e., hackers, worms, viruses, Trojan horses, and backdoor programs), and the five least common threats at that time (i.e., spam, pirated software, operational accidents, users' online behavior being recorded and deviation in quality of service). Their result was that there was a significant difference between users' perceptions of information security related to computer experience and the type of loss incurred. Even back in 2004 and earlier it was pointed out that while human factors were being investigated into information security, their perceptions were not. Gonzalez and Sawicka pointed out in 2002 that it was the human factor that was the main cause of information security, its Achilles heel. Security models, protection measures, and implementation models are all dependent on humans, not the other way around. This is very important, even today, since your perceptions about something may eventually guide your behavior, and if your perceptions are incorrect, say about a type of cybersecurity attack, your behavior could lead you into the wrong cybersecurity solution. Perceptions cause behavior, nuclear accidents, driving while driving, and even perceptions on smoking cause a certain behavior. Even if the perception is negative, people will still continue to engage in that heightened risk activity. I know drinking and driving is bad, but I can drive. I know eating junk food is bad for my health, but you only live once.

Huang, Rau, and Salvendy (2010) highlighted some very good categories of threats, and by examining them, now it's clear that perceptions really guide behavior. When you hear a deliberate act of espionage, it sounds very dangerous. How about a password attack? They are the same thing, a category and threat. What about deliberate software attack or a worm? Same idea. While they may not have understood the importance of perceptions during their research, it is much more evident now.

This is an interesting point. What do you hear more of—a virus or a deliberate software attack? The mere exposure effect concurs with Wogalter et al. (1991) who pointed out that familiarity may breed conditioning of reduced risk, yet they are the same, and the only difference are the names. Their work supports the notion that given the different factors (i.e., knowledge, impact, severity, controllability, possibility, and awareness), it impacts the overall severity of the perceived threat. However, since knowledge was defined as a user's knowledge of threats to information security, it could be the "I know about something" (i.e., my knowledge), the more threat of it may or may not impact me (e.g., if I do not use social media, I could perhaps think that social media threats do not impact me), and my risk of them would be minimal. However, have we not seen stories where others have used social media to attack someone else? It happens quite frequently unfortunately.

Here is another perception. Where does your cybersecurity begin, and where does it end? Do you really think you are fully aware of every single component, application, and person you have to protect? Are you fully cognitive of where all your data is—the cloud, the fog, the edge? Do you know who is mining that data—artificial intelligence, machine learning, edge processing? How much of your data is already gone, and you just do not know it as of yet? Just thinking of all this will throw up lots of cognitive conflicts, and rightly so. However, be careful, don't just let them guide your behavior without knowing that these perceptions are guiding your behavior.

How many of us suffer from the action–intention gap (i.e., your New Year's Resolution)? Or if your system gets hacked, and you have to rebuild the system from scratch. Then you decide you are going to make a hashed list of every binary on a system and run it periodically so you can spot early on if a binary gets changed. Well, you never quite get to it, or perhaps I am going to make sure all guest accounts on all devices are deactivated, you never quite get to it. Your company works with hundreds of vendors who come and go and need access into your systems so they can perhaps fix something of theirs (e.g., you work with IBM, and you use Cisco routers, and you give a Cisco engineer credentials to log onto the router). You are planning on removing those credentials, and you never quite get to it. These intentions are stimuli, but sometimes like in Pavlov's experiments, the stimuli are short-lived, so to convert them into actions, they have to be on your mind.

We Sell Hammers

In 2014, Home Depot was hit with a massive cyber-attack that stole over 56 million credit card numbers (Creswell and Perlroth 2014; Nacs 2014). A zero-day vulnerability was installed on a third-party point-of-sale system, allowing malware to be introduced. This then allowed an escalation of privileges, which then allowed data to be compromised over a five-month period. Banjo reported in 2014 that the company may have known about potential weaknesses as far back as 2008 but failed to act. A simple search now will show how this attack occurred, the specifics on how it evolved, the costs and damages, but finding out why Home Depot was slow to react is another matter entirely. Some of the software that was used to protect the network consisted of 2007 Symantec antivirus, irregular monitoring cycles, and not security scanning all stores. A troubling spokesperson comment from Home Depot was that PCI 2009 standards that was used had exceptions from scanning stores vs. corporate stores. In 2012 Home Depot hired a security engineer, who was later sentenced to four years in prison for a computer attack on EnerVest Operating, an oil and gas company, computers. Whether he had or had not deliberately opened Home Depot up to an attack is not clear. A quote in Banjo's article was that when employees told Home Depot managers about security, their managers reply was:

We sell hammers.

Let's forget about the attack—the damage, what was done, but rather why. Was this phrase, we sell hammers, just corporate culture? We have mentioned context of association several times now. Our perceptions are based upon the context we have to make decisions. In the Home Depot case, management's context was probably based upon their competition, not malware, and their decisions would reflect this ideology. To a Home Depot manager, getting enough lawn tractors ordered for the upcoming Spring sales season would bring them much more closure (i.e., remember the Gestalt laws) than some warning about old software running on their company computer systems, especially when they were not the ones responsible for the security of the systems.

If we could imagine the makeup of the Home Depot manager, it was an older male, maybe from the construction industry. Our main concern is closure, we need to get ready for new merchandise, get ready for another season, and Home Depot is very good at logistics. As the Zeigarnik effect has shown, they have been probably dealing with multiple challenges in getting ready for the new season, and they will work on this season's allotment of tractors needed. Ever notice when you go to Home Depot, most times they have what you need. The Zeigarnik effect has been influencing their decisions to get a certain task done as it relates to home improvement, not as it relates to cybersecurity. So, it's very possible that the combination of the Zeigarnik effect and closure set in place a motion for this to occur, or as the employee said, just kicking the can down the road. This can hold true for any organization. Examine some of the latest security breaches, and it turns out many of the attacks were similar. Therefore, instead of focusing on the attacks, let's focus on the reasons, the decisions we made before the attacks, so hopefully we can stop the next one.

Cybersecurity Implications and Conclusions

So, how does a cybersecurity person deal with perceptions?

When security is considered, nonpractitioners often espouse such qualities as dull, confusing, boring, not environmentally aware, and even among security professionals, security has lost some of its glamor. But in some cases, discussing attacks or new models and ways to explore security can be indeed challenging and even enjoyable. However, it is known that a security administrator who is not challenged can soon begin to face boredom. Given what we know about the unique characteristics of foreground and background noise with the laws of similarity, symmetry, proximity, closure, and motion, how effective are the security tasks that we cybersecurity professionals execute every single day? When we are creating a policy, when we are implementing a guideline, and when we are looking at technology solutions, many times we are just looking at similar things we have done in the past.

If we are implementing a set of guidelines for a hotel company according to a national standard such as NICE, NIST, or any other framework, aren't we more inclined to use a model that we have already used for another hotel company? This is not to say any of this is bad; it is just to realize this is happening. If our perceptions based upon our context of association for the last hotel company is a positive one, wouldn't our perceptions be that it would also be positive for future ones? In the bottom-up's processing we discussed the strength of associations. We might see a lot of vulnerabilities like viruses, phishing, social networks, but less on rootkits, and the less we work on rootkits, the weaker the association will become. It is not that we didn't pay attention to rootkits when we learned them, but it is more likely that we didn't know what to pay attention to, and we have to fill in the missing details with our data that was encoded earlier. Everything we experience gets stored—our memories, past experiences, encounters, and the circumstance that were occulting when those experiences happened, and up to and including faulty encoded data. Think now of all the security knowledge we have obtained over the years. What did we encode garbage in with the details? At a conference, struggling to hear what the speaker is saying, or trying to understand a slide on a presentation, we pay attention to only a little bit of the information, and assume the rest.

When examining cybersecurity in light of the Gestalt properties, we might experience the following.

Similarity

Things that are similar in style seem to be appear as grouped together. Perhaps we may use a security policy for one federal agency, but should it be used the same way as a policy for another federal agency. We group similar components of the policy (i.e., the sum) if they are perceived to belong to the whole, regardless of whether they hold or not.

Symmetry

The amount of balance we want to see, so, perhaps the amount of resources we use to develop the last cybersecurity solution should be the same as the level of resources needed to develop a new cybersecurity solution. Just balance the balance, but that balance could be completely wrong.

Proximity

The closer some objects appear, and away from others, the more they form their own unique group. The same physical proximity device key fob will be needed for all access points in a close area. However, if one is compromised, can more be compromised?

Closure

Even if something appears not to be closed, we will sense it as being closed. Our mind will fill in the missing details. Our minds prefer closed entities, and even if it is not closed, we will assume it is (e.g., a finished risk management procedure, a completed flowchart to alerting intrusions, a finished document for testing new security software), the issue is closure. It's completed, I can move on.

Continuity

We see objects on a path, instead of discrete things. Our eyes will tend to follow curves and bends, rather than abrupt lines, like a wall, or a horizontal–vertical break. We see the finished security policy; we see the finished code; we see the finished disaster recovery plan. We see the pieces as on a smooth path to the finished product, but could we have missed some steps along the way? While not in the exact nature of a line or curve, continuity can reference a completed project.

The important thing for cybersecurity personnel then is to realize that our perceptions are based upon our last contextual association (i.e., bottom-up processing), and if those perceptions are good, then we are inclined to use the same methods for the new company, even though things have changed. Our future behavior is guided by past perceptions, but the successful attack a company faces are probably not the old attacks. They are the new evolved ones that our perceptions didn't see coming.

When we work in groups on cybersecurity solutions, all these perceptions and their problems can really impact us. We are sensing, we are interpreting, we are trying to organize all this information with others, and we are trying to do this correctly. We can be in a group and subconsciously not like the person we are working with, and while we may have an outcome, with the outcome be as successful as it could have been. In reality, we are not trusting or not trusting them as a thing, we are actually trusting our own senses, or perceptions about that thing, where our perceptions are true or not, we believe them to be so.

Our perceptions can really play tricks on us. Do you really understand the threats companies face? Do you really understand the details of each and every attack, of every possible system that could be attacked? It seems to be that yes; most of us will believe that for the most part, we are well guarded and understand the landscape. Why are we so confident? Well, just look at the self-confident traits perhaps, and before you search for this self-confident trait, realize it doesn't exist. Self-confidence is also mentioned along with self-esteem, and when you research these, you will find that self-confidence is measured along a set of other traits, like belief about one's own abilities, competitive, accepting, open, and so on, just like some other traits we have mentioned. Then, add in the subconscious traits as well, put that on a scale, sum it all up, and let's just say, well, it's human behavior.

We took a look at the Stroop effect, and while it's often made into a game to teach concepts, like we did with the fruits and numbers, in real life, it is much more dangerous. While the Stroop effect is highlighting cognitive conflicts, it's also about conflict. It is not about colors, or numbers, we are having a conflict in our brain, we see something with our eyes, but our brain is telling us something different. This impacts the anterior cingulate cortex of our brain. Damen, Strick, Taris, and Aarts (2018) and Fritz, Fischer, and Dreisbach (2015) did some very interesting work with the Stroop effect and negativity. Does conflict breed negativity, and is this effect being amplified? First, the Stroop effect is conflict itself, and second, the use of negative word may amplify this effect. Ever hear the saying, you cannot think when you are mad? In this case, think of cybersecurity and all the negative words that are associated (e.g., hackers, cyber terrorists, State sponsored actors, etc.), then add in uncertain, unfinished pieces of data in search of developing a cybersecurity solution. That is why this research was very interesting. It was based not on a complete picture of information, but rather parts of that picture, one that cybersecurity professionals deal with every day, and while their research was not in the cybersecurity area, it should be noted that it is very applicable. You may not know you're mad in the strictest definition, but your brain is in activating that part of the brain. Perhaps knowing the Zeigarnik effect can help the cybersecurity professional.

Cybersecurity professionals work best in small chunks of different individual tasks. Likely because of the nature and breadth of activities a cybersecurity expert must complete. Since cybersecurity experts will have a host of activities they must be responsible for, so a rush through of a task is not beneficial. Therefore, since the Zeigarnik effect is complementing the Gestalt law of closure, so you need to break that closure:

Slow down, Stop, reflect on what you are doing.
Create a to-do list.
Twenty minutes a day activity.

But, it's also critical in that these must be routine, daily, on a semifrequent basis. It has to be part of a normal day's activity.

Therefore, as Larry the Cable guy says just get er done.

However, *don't just get er done,* slow down, stop, move to another project, then come back to unfinished business.

CHAPTER 5

So, How Do We Even Think?

Introduction

Thinking is an interesting concept; when I think that is.

It had to start somewhere. Kind of like that age-old question, which came first? The chicken or the egg? If you think about a car, or a house, or a washing machine, anything really, it's not that difficult to picture that in your brain. When you think about that car, or that house, or that washing machine, they seem actually pretty easy, and most likely you were introduced to them as a young child. But now:

Think about a bear with the feet of a duck.
Then, the bear with the feet of a duck sprouted wings.
Then, the bear with the feet of a duck that sprouted wings starting to play the violin.

Even that is simple enough. We can visualize that.

Now, the bear with the feet of a duck that sprouted wings that started playing the violin suddenly began to grow whatchamacallits and thingamajigs on its back. You think you know what that is, but you can't quite put a name to those whatchamacallits and thingamajigs.

Well, now you're starting to think!

Up until the wings and violin it was just recall. Your previous associations you've built up over your life, but with the whatchamacallits and thingamajigs, it moved from recall to thinking. Now, let's think about something, anything really, that has to do with something else. Again anything really, which has to do with something else, and your mind goes into overdrive. It's trickier when we don't know that something is, but we definitely know (i.e., at least we believe we know what that something is). While we may have experienced those whatchamacallits or thingamajigs, we have not yet experienced that something else quite yet.

Confused? You should be, you're thinking again!
And don't try to think too hard, you'll hurt yourself.

So, where did this all come from? Well, our memory of course, even in thinking it starts from memory. We have this storage of short-term and long-term memory and we are moving data back and forth, desperately trying to fill in some missing pieces (i.e., these whatchamacallits or thingamajigs). We have to remember when we first stored all this data, we encoded it in our memory, but remember the data was faulty (i.e., garbage in garbage out). Further compounding the problem is that even if we are presented with new information that will somehow show us our previous encoding was wrong, and our own cognitive dissonance will prevent us from using this new information. Like we said earlier, we have garbage in, garbage out, and we pile our own garbage on top of the garbage that was placed in our memory.

We are really are own worst enemies sometimes; we refuse to learn.

Researchers have shown that our mental processes are limited. Ever hear the urban legend that we only use 10 percent of our process? However, in reality, we use almost all of our brain power. So, which is more troubling? Seeing all the problems around you, and accepting the myth we only use 10 percent of our brain power, and if perhaps we could use just a little bit more of our brain power, we could solve all of society's problems. Or the fact of seeing all of these problems and realizing that we actually use 100 percent of our brain.

Scary? Perhaps, hopeless, no?

While we are using 100 percent of our brain processing power, we may not be using it effectively, and therefore could we possibly use it more effectively? If we understand our own biases and mental processing states, perhaps we could make much better decisions.

Cognitive Economy

Research shows that our mental processing is limited, and that to save energy we create categories to remember things. They are often called categories, such as mental categories, cognitive categories, cognitive economy, and so on, and we use these to help us decide what our new experience is, what we are sensing, and even these things we have never seen before (i.e., those whatchamacallits and thingamajigs). These categories that we create in our own minds are neither too large nor too small, too big, or too wide, to inclusive, or not inclusive enough. They are just about right size, much like Goldilocks's porridge in her encounter with the three bears. This category of porridge was just the right amount, and we all understand what she meant by just right, since we all have a category called just right.

Take an example. If you were asked to look around and explain the things that you see, you might say you see a house, a tree, or an automobile. You would not say I see a 56 Chevy Bel Air, with a dual four-barrel carb, a 411 engine with 245 Horse Power, followed by the Latin genus of the closest tree. I am sure many people would have no idea what a 56 Chevy Bel Air was anyway, let alone a dual four-barrel carb. Well I do, but then again, I'm ancient as my kids say:

I'm older than history, a boomer. That's the cognitive category they have for me.

What this does show is that categories can be created anytime and for the most part, a large majority of people will understand them. This is the nature of language as we will read later. We create categories for many reasons, and the main one is, well otherwise, it's just too much work. Who wants to work, right? We want to conserve our cognitive energy. Like we mentioned earlier, we are not really lazy as it could have just been an evolutionary trait to ensure survival. We are trying to get the most utility from our limited brain power. We want to save costs. Researchers call this cognitive economy (Hietaranta 2015; Holscher et al. 2011)

So, we are not lazy, just our brain is.

With cognitive economy, we try to squeeze as much as possible into as few of categories as possible, and this way we get the most utility from our brain power. For example, we really only have two main high-level cognitive categories of animals: there are wild animals and there are domesticated animals. We do this with all kinds of things we encounter, but sometimes we also get into a tug of war. How many categories are enough? We need more categories for utility, but we need less categories to conserve effort. We reach that basic steady-state point that we have today. We also have to communicate these categories to others, so our categories not only have to make sense to us, but others as well:

Ok, boomer?

These categories are part of our associations linked by our neural networks, and while we can remember the category (e.g., a dog), we cannot name every breed, and so many times we will say he's a mutt or she's a purebred. We can name a tree, but not its Latin genus. It's an oak tree, but which of the over 600 species of oak trees is that oak tree exactly? Therefore, since these are generalized categories, we can then come up with some definition for a new experience.

In cybersecurity, we will often speak the category of our training, whereas you may know what a computer attack is, you may not know denial of service, drive-by downloads, phishing, man-in-the-middle, SQL injection, malware, birthday, cross-site scripting, and all other kinds of computer attacks. Moreover, even these can be broken down further into smaller categories, but for the most part, we can all understand a computer attack. Hopefully, we can see this as a serious problem for cybersecurity professionals since mistakes can easily be made if we use previous generalized categories to make specific assumptions. Making a birthday attack countermeasure will not work with a man-in-the-middle attack.

An example could be if I say I like chocolate and I like peanut butter, so I will like chocolate and peanut butter. However, I also like shrimp, and I also like French fries, so I might like my shrimp fried. However, fried shrimp will send me to the hospital with an allergic reaction, but what did actually? The shrimp that I like, or the oil I like when they cook my French fries? Something is wrong with my learned associations, and those categories you built about the different attacks and countermeasures are your learned associations you may use to counter new attacks.

Combining categories could cause disastrous results.

Our category making has a lot of work to be done, but it's something we cannot easily do with our mental faculties as there are just too many things in the world to categorize. To further compound the problem, we know when we created these categories, we knew they are not fully descriptive of the thing we are trying to categorize, and we use shortcuts on making these. As we know what gets garbled, the encoded information, and since we can't spend so much time thinking about this, we create mental shortcuts to help us, called heuristics, and can even include more biases.

Heuristic (i.e., Mental Shortcuts)

With the limited amount of mental processing power we are capable of, we generally have two options when we consider new experiences:

Reduce the amount of information on that experience, or
Reduce the amount of time thinking about that experience.

It would be hard to reduce the amount of information out there. Do a simple search on a topic and count the results you might get. I conducted a Web search on the term thingamajig, and received over 800,000 results, and my search on whatchamacallits came back with over two-and-a-half million results. Therefore, if we cannot limit the amount of information on that experience, we have to spend less time thinking about that experience. While this mental energy savings may be efficient, it also biases our judgment (Tversky and Kahneman 1974). Heuristics, in turn, have their own unique categories, so now we are further categorizing categories.

The Availability Heuristic

We are prone to think that if something is easy to remember or commonly used, it is more likely to happen, and therefore we place more importance on that subject. We think a plane crash will happen more often than people slipping in a bathtub. We believe we will be more likely to die being bitten by a shark at the beach than die in a car accident. On average there is one fatal shark attack per year, and on average 40,000 deaths by motor vehicles (National Safety Council 2019). In addition, the easier it is to recall an event occurring, the more likely we are to place significance on that event occurring. These following events are more common to occur: tornadoes, earthquakes, floods, and others. We want to stop smoking because we want to live longer, but sugar kills many more people than smoking. In a study published by Harvard School of Public Health in Boston, Massachusetts, revised in 2017, over 184,000 people die every year due to the effects of sugar (Datz 2019), which is more deaths than the last 40 years of war. The nightly news also has a major impact on our availability heuristic—the more we see a particular news story the more likely we are to estimate the probability of that event occurring. In its essence, it's a shortcut we use to make a decision quickly, which works great for deciding what flavor ice cream we will have with dinner, but not for critical events.

The Anchoring Heuristic

We tend to anchor our decision by something we have heard recently: an initial piece of information offered, what is called the anchor. The television show *The Price is Right* is a very good example. As soon as the first contestant says a dollar amount for their estimated price on a product, the other contestants' offers will be anchored around that first contestant's number. That washing machine is $500.00 according to the first contestant, then the second contestant might say $550.00, the third contestant might say $495.00, and the last contestant might say $600.00. We would not find it likely that the first contestant would suggest $500.00, the second contestant suggests $550.00, the third contestant $495.00, and the last contestant offers a bid of $1,450.00. You might see a commercial for new four-door sedan automobile at $33,000. Then, perhaps in a few months, you went shopping for a new car and looking at a sedan and think that car must be somewhere around $33,000. Think back to that commercial: was it a local commercial for car dealers in the area? Were the local dealers running commercials to anchor this effect into your brain?

We go to a store, see a price tag for $100.00, and notice it's on clearance for $20.00; that's a great buy, and the anchor was the $100.00 tag. Perhaps, you are doing a home project, maybe a new kitchen and you recall your neighbors had theirs done recently for about $20,000. You call a few home remodelers in for quotes, and you get one for $10,000, and think you are getting a great deal. Even though you may have never seen your neighbor's kitchen, you had no idea the materials that were used, or how labor-intensive the construction was. All you just heard was $20,000. This actually brings in two problems: one is the anchor and the other is the availability heuristic, as your neighbor was now the availability anchor. Estimates are good things, and common practice; we just have to be aware where did we get these estimates or anchors from.

The Representativeness Heuristic

The representative heuristic refers to people or events as categories, as in what category does a person belong. It is also the probability of something fitting in the event of an uncertainty. This heuristic is on a scale (i.e., someone with a high level of representativeness would broadly fit into an available category). It's a decision-making process we use to judge someone. Think of movie stars, how should they look and act? If you see someone exhibiting those qualities, do you think that person would make a good actor? Politicians and people of power—do they look to you as they belonged there? Do they fit in? If you call someone a computer nerd, does that mean that they play computer games, or does it mean they are computer engineers or love to design new computer systems? If I tell you that computer nerd also loves science, we may learn that the computer nerd is a computer engineer, and we do all this without even meeting that person. That person is a brain surgeon, he or she must be brilliant, but listening to that person speak, you might be left wondering if there something wrong with that person, and on this scale of representativeness, where to place the brain surgeon?

What about groups of people? You can see different groups of people called by different names daily in the media. This heuristic runs into problems as we are making judgment on an event or person that has no relation to the likeliness that event or person is representative of the population as a whole. While there are more heuristics, we can see that while these heuristics help us in decision making due to the amount of information that is available. These same heuristics are wrong more often than not.

Confirmation Bias

While not a heuristic per se, confirmation bias greatly impacts our decision-making process, similar to using heuristics. In confirmation bias, we are looking for ways to find evidence to support what we believe. We seek out data that helps support our beliefs, notions, ideas, and even hypotheses. With heuristics, we may not actively seek out this information, but we accept it upon learning new information, whereas with confirmation bias, we are actively seeking out to confirm our beliefs, and we could be using confirmation bias to confirm our heuristics. I heard that washing machine was $500.00, so I am going to look for washing machines that cost $500.00, and those that cost, $200, $300, $800, $1200.00, and so on, well, I can ignore them. If we were to use the representativeness heuristic to label an event that is likely to occur, we would then seek out data on that event occurring matching what we believe. We hear about a deadly shark attack and will seek out how many fatal shark attacks are there in a year, and even though you are more likely to die in an automobile crash, that data would not matter since you are confirming your belief in shark attacks.

We take sides in a political discourse when we hear of a person driving a car runs onto a curb and strikes several pedestrians, and we think terrorists. However, many older people, distracted people, and student drivers have also lost control of their cars and jumped a curb. There is a good chance that if even if we did find data to disprove our hypothesis (i.e., this event wasn't caused by terrorists), we will ignore that data. Due to our cognitive dissonance, it conflicts us since this anchoring can impair our association and not based what's under evaluations on any real data.

The real presence of confirmatory information on our biases greatly increases our direction for certain behavioral patterns. When our beliefs are causing us cognitive dissonance, we are in state of panic, whether conscious or subconscious. We are looking for something; it's like a strong addiction, and we need to reach steady state again, or homeostasis. When we find confirmatory information, we will hold on to it longer and believe it more as fact, but that's just the nature of biases. This confirmatory information becomes an illusion of validity (Kahneman and Tversky 1973; Tversky and Kahneman 1974). This is not based upon real data or evidence, but what we believe to be real data or evidence, but it even impacts where we believe the evidence is suspect, it helps us back to equilibrium, and our desire for homeostasis is more of a driving force than external data sets.

Other Biases

While we have examined a few of the more common examples of biases, and whether we called them heuristics or our confirmation, they are still none the less bias. Unfortunately, there's an alphabet soup of biases.

Reward and Punishment Bias

In the reward and punishment bias, people are motivated to do something if they gain from it and avoid doing something if there is a punishment.

The Actor Bias

In the actor bias, we are more forgiving to someone who is good looking and attractive.

The Hate Bias

In the hate bias, I just hate you because I don't know why. I just do, even if that person is the Pope.

The Inconsistency Bias

The inconsistency bias: I've always done things my way and I don't want to change.

Good Things and Bad Things Bias

Good things happen to good people, and bad things happen to bad people.

The Reciprocation Bias

I am going to do something good for you now, because I know you will do something for me in the future.

The Cognitive Dissonance Bias

I am not going to change my opinion, even in the face of facts or real evidence to the contrary.

The Acceptability Bias

The easy acceptability bias is that we over-emphasize what's readily available, rather than taking our time and researching something.

The Blind-Side Bias

We fail to recognize our own biases, but we can easily spot them in others.

The Choice, Sunken-Cost, Bias

I made the right choice, even if this car keeps breaking down. I purchased the right stock, even if it has been going down for months.

The Conservatism Bias

The past holds truth more than the current, when your grandfather starts to say, back in my day we did things differently, and it always came out right.

The Barnum Effect Bias

This is named after the showman P. T. Barnum, in that people will give high accuracy to personal descriptions that can be applied to whole groups of individuals.

The Distinction Bias

You have to have that newer better pricier item in the showroom, but you budget will not allow, so you go for the less expensive item. Yet, when you get home, that lesser priced item seems perfect. You tended to expect much more from the higher priced item, but in reality, the lesser item was perfect. If there was no higher priced item, you would not even experience the distinction.

The Outcome Bias

My decision was successful last time, so my decision this time will be right as well. If you got home safe after a night of drinking last time, you were successful, but does not mean you will be successful next time.

The Zero-Risk Bias

The zero-risk bias is especially applicable for cybersecurity professionals and their organizations. It is the choice of the complete reduction of a risk, even when there are other options that could produce an overall greater reduction of risk. For example, I will never smoke as it will kill me, even as I eat those three donuts. We would rather take an extreme position to reduce a risk to zero (i.e., a terrorist act), and then take a position to reduce other risks (i.e., car deaths, gun violence, health care) when in the long run, the other risks would produce much greater threats. For companies, spending millions more in technical approaches to cybersecurity threats than spending it on human and behavioral approach to cyberthreats may not be right, because in the long run, more threats might be identified and stopped and be less expensive for the organization. If most of the security research we read mention employees mishaps, internal problems, misconfigurations, or phishing as a major problem, yet most of our financial resources are spent on technical solutions, or we are seeking a zero-risk outcome.

I wish I could say that was all, but it's not. Wikipedia has a list of 188 cognitive biases (https://en.wikipedia.org/wiki/List_of_cognitive_biases). It also has a wonderful chart of just how many biases there really are so far, taken from the design work of John Manoogian (see Figure 5.1).

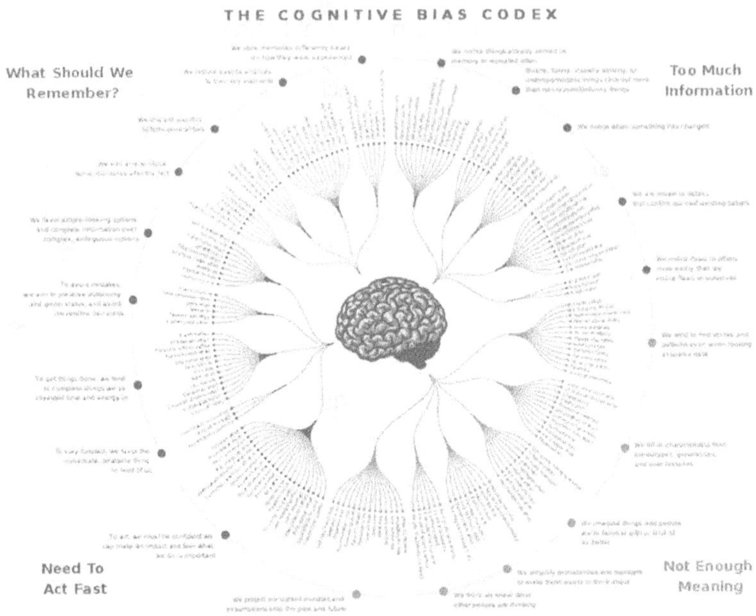

THE COGNITIVE BIAS CODEX

What Should We
Remember?

Too Much
Information

Need To
Act Fast

Not Enough
Meaning

Figure 5.1 The cognitive bias codex

File: Cognitive bias codex en.svg. (April 22, 2020). Retrieved July 03, 2020, from https://commons.wikimedia.org/wiki/File: Cognitive_bias _codex_en.svg

Lost in Translation

While cognitive economy does help, it can also lead us to make bad decisions, and not just from a translation of languages, but from our own translations, our gut feelings, and our intuition that things should go this way. Planning strategies are often a factor—the way we plan something will result in a different planning strategy (e.g., If I believe I know a certain route better, I will follow that route). If I were to look at an online website for directions, I may follow that route, or if I follow a GPS signal on my smartphone I will follow that route, and even though we may get to the same destination, it may not be the same length of time, some may be shorter vs. longer routes, or it may not be the cheapest as some routes may require us to get on a highway with tools. All these scenarios have the same information, the same destination, the same procedure, the same details, but come with different results. This could lead to simply interpretation: the first approach being your brain, and the other two are computer applications, designed by a human, but looking at it as different way of examining things. What this is suggesting, according to Lupyan (2013), is that even well-educated people have real problems placing stimuli into well-defined cognitive categories. This can lead us to the wrong choice, as what we thought was the best was the longer, more costly route. Our brains may not just have the mental power or capacity to compute all the factors this decision requires, given all the alternatives. Judgment and decision are cognitive tasks we all have, and sometimes they are limited, and while getting to the local gas station may not be a problem but developing a new 100-million-dollar cybersecurity system would definitely be a major problem.

There has a lot to do with thinking, or as I like to say, thinking just gets in the way sometimes; and it does.

Sometimes, if we are not careful, thinking will cause a lot of problem (e.g., personalization, you may not think the world resolves around you), but your actions indicate otherwise; someone does not call you back, and you think it must be me, and that person wants nothing to do with me. Your worker is mad, and if you think it is because of something you did, that's personalization. Mindreading—we all do this at times. We know what the other person is thinking, and even though body language and a smile do indicate common patterns of a person's thinking, it does not mean they are thinking that. How many children will smile when they fart at someone? That smile is mischief in the making. Actually, how many adults would do the same thing? We even have emotional thinking, such as when:

My wife would say, I should know what's she's thinking!

In this book we are discussing some of the causes of behavior, and the way we think can also cause that behavior. Could each one of these behaviors be traced to some heuristics, or a combination thereof we mentioned, or our confirmation bias we actively seek out, even our cognitive economy has ways of making us think. During the time when the Conficker attack was prevalent, around 2009, it used basic designs in a very popular operating system network service, and later evolved to include variants that attacked removeable media like flash drives. One of the easiest ways that this virus to spread was the self-running executables installed on many of these smaller removable flash drives. This would require a user run a couple steps to get their flash drive working; however, this simple solution did have an enormous impact on the spread of the virus. It seems this change in the way self-running programs were handled contributed to the condition of infected USB keys. The researcher looking into this issue, Adam Shostack (2017), did not blame the person using the USB flash drive, but rather the system itself. In an interview he gave in 2016, he said people try to explain why a system isn't working, instead of just listening to the person. Systems are designed to support users, not that users are designed to support systems. So if an issue happens, let's examine the system. When examining security breaches, how many of them have been already identified long before the technical recommendation has been accepted. Shostack (2017) argues that technology skills are not as important as those skills that teach us to think.

Mental Models

A model is a representation of something else, perhaps bigger, more complex, even sometimes imaginary. Although most often used in something real world, we do have a model of Santa Claus, the Lock Ness monster, ghosts, and so on. We have to, otherwise how could we model mental illnesses. It is just a way to help us understand something else. It's a simplification of some other phenomenon, real or imaginary. For example, a train model is a model that reflects real-life rail-road cars, just on a much smaller scale. For an airplane model, same concept applies. In inventory control model, the model is a depiction in a formal flowchart, describing how a real-life inventory control model works. A theoretical model reflects various dependent and dependent variables. The solar system you created as a child in grade school to represent the actual universe is a model. Mental models are similar, but it's a mental model of a thought process, much more like in a flowchart, but instead of inputs and outputs, it's a reasoning model. It's based upon people's perceptions, imagination, thought process, and how these mental models eventually help us make a decision. It's a representation of the way things work for us. It illustrates the relationships between what a process is and the resulting behavior, taking into account the perceptions and consequences of those relationships. When they become representations of some external reality, they are now cognitive model (Craik 1943; Forrester 1971). An issue with mental models is that they are impacted by our reasoning skills and the perceptions afforded them. Mental models can be created from perceptions, imagination, and so on., and if our perceptions are based upon faulty neural network associations, what would our eventual corresponding mental models evolve to? In addition, any mental model I could create may not be the same as your mental model created when trying to understand the same phenomenon under consideration. Since mental models are not specific instructions, but rather a generalized conceptually viewpoint of the relationships, how then could they help? Well, it turns out they can help very well if we pay attention to our own cognitive bias when using models. We have discussed models already, but perhaps you did not see it has modeling. Remember Pavlov's dogs? The mental model we used was conditioning.

We are all conditioned to a stimulus. Probably one of the most famous ones was Santa Claus in his big red shit, and while many do not associate Santa Claus with Coca Cola, it was the company that created the condition stimulus. This also shows that over time, conditioned responses can fade. We all probably think of Santa Claus the same way, but not its association to the company, and that's probably because we keep seeing commercials around Christmas depicting the image. Another advantage of these models is that it gets you to think on a much higher plane of thought. Munger (1994) described mental models as they help you move away from simple facts, to more of a lattice model thinking, and that in turn enables the lattice of your neural networks that we have been discussing (i.e., the strengthening of these associations). Many inventors, researchers, and discoverers don't consider themselves experts in any one field but rather generalists in many fields. This allows them to use all their cognitive disciplines and models they know in this lattice approach.

Entropy is another mental model. Most do not know what it means, as it has been used in thermodynamics, computer sciences, mechanical and civil engineering, and so on, and it just describes disorder in a system. The more chaos, the higher the disorder, or randomness, the higher the entropy. We want to reduce this chaos, to use this model, and to make your life less disorderly, take steps to clean up your life, simple small things to make specific things to bring order to your life helps to reduce entropy, and therefore reduce the disorder and chaos in life. Psychologist Steven Pinker (1999) suggests just cleaning up your room helps to reduce entropy since it affects something in our life that we can control.

I did try this with my 12-year-old kids and told them to clean up their room; however, I didn't get the results I expected, so perhaps I need another mental model.

There are indeed many models to choose from, Michael Simmons created a stunning display map of 12 different mental models (see Figure 5.2), and cognitive images that impact them (e.g., our biases, our working memory, social proof, etc.).

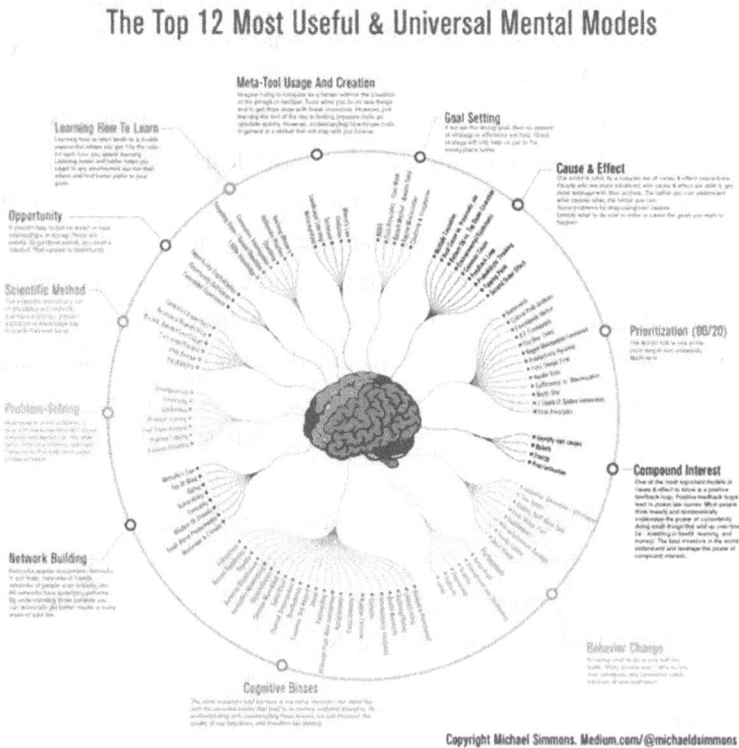

Figure 5.2 *Top 12 most useful and universal mental models*

Simmons, M.D. July 03, 2020. Retrieved July 03, 2020, from http://michaeldsimmons.com/this-is-exactly-how-you-should-train-yourself-to-be-smarter-infographic/

Paradoxes and Mental Models

In understanding these mental models, it's helpful to understand where and how they are applied, and this leads us into the world of game theory and paradoxes.

Game Theory

The theory behind a set of strategic interactions between a set of decision makers, usually based upon a set of mathematical models (Von Neumann and Oskar 1944). In the world of psychology, game theory focuses on how groups of people react in social settings and is usually divided into two categories. In the first cooperative, all players work together for the betterment of the whole, and noncooperative, where players work to achieve their own goals. In cooperative game theory, one can think of cooperatives, like-minded groups, same pollical parties. Noncooperative could be thought of as competing groups, competing political parties, or completing governments. We can break down noncooperative into three similar theoretical areas: (1) a branch of decision theory, (e.g., single player games) and (2) general equilibrium theory, where large number of buyers and sellers with things in equilibrium. We can think of any major government stock market, where we have buyers and sellers and everyone knows all information that is available and (3) mechanism deign theory, where rules can be different. Game theory is used a lot in military research. It seeks to understand how to predict rational behavior and decision making in situations that contain conflict, whereas cooperative seeks to base decisions on satisfying between the rational and self-interested individuals. A noncooperative reveals the problems of social conflicts, and the cooperative tries to solve them. Nash (1949) developed the Nash equilibrium, which was a proposed solution to solving the equilibrium nature of the noncooperative approach. Simply, if I make a decision on what's best for me, and it's based on what you did, we are in equilibrium. If you then make a decision on what's best for you, based upon what I did, we are still in equilibrium. Basically, we cannot make the best decisions in isolation, and we have to know what the other side is doing. This way we are always in equilibrium.

Behavioral Game Theory

While game theory helped us to understand decision making, behavioral game theory expands on those choices by factoring in human emotions and limited processing capabilities such as foresight (Camerer 2003) These game theories models evolved from paradoxes (i.e., a rational explanation leads to irrational responses). Such as the Allais paradox; for example, lotteries, people will choose the lottery with the biggest award, regardless of the odds. With smaller prizes I will take the sure thing, but when prizes become very big, we imagine, well, we aren't going to win it anyway, so let's gamble. What the Allais paradox shows is the following, A risk of 0 percent to 1 percent is the same as the risk from 1 percent to 2 percent, or the risk from 22 percent to 23 percent, or the risk from 99 percent to 100 percent. These are all the same risk levels, and it's just a one-percent difference. We just don't base our decisions rationally. We touched on paradoxes earlier, and let's expand on a couple more:

For example, which one would you choose if given a choice in Tables 5.1 and 5.2?

Table 5.1 *Allais paradox example 1*

Experiment 1	
Choice 1	Choice 2
100% to win 24,000	97% to win 27,000
	3% to win nothing

Most people in example 1 would choose choice 1, for a guaranteed win of 24,000. Let's look at another example, which choice would you pick?

Table 5.2 *Allais paradox example 2*

Experiment 2	
Choice 1	Choice 2
34% to win 24,000	33% to win 27,000
66% to win nothing	67% to win nothing

Most people now would choose choice 2, for a chance at winning 27,000. This is the paradox—in experiment 1, you have an expected outcome. The most utility from choice 1, so by expected utility theory, this would be correct, $E(U)$ of 24,000 (100 percent) is greater than E(U) or 27,000 (97 percent) + 0.00 (3 percent). However, in the second experiment, most people would choose choice 2, which as less expected utility, $E(U)$ of choice 2, 27,000 (33 percent) + 0.00 (67 percent) is less than $E(U)$ choice 1 of 24,000(34 percent) + 0.00 (66 percent).

So, we are choosing in Experiment 2 for less utility, but why?

Well, humans sometimes do not think logically, and researchers suggest that at looking at the numbers, 66 and 67 percent are high numbers, so we may rationalize that you know, I am not going to win anything, so why not gamble it all and go for it all. While these numbers may not be big, if you think of those megamillion lotteries, we use the same exact mindset. We go for the lotteries that have high payoffs, and incredibly low odds, over lower payout lotteries with more favorable odds. The other paradox, the Ellsberg paradox, states that people will choose to base something when they have specific odds, instead of a choice with odds that are completely ambiguous. A classic example Ellsberg uses is of urns with both black and white colored marbles. Both urns are covered, and you are told the first urn has 50 black marbles and 50 white marbles, the second urn you are told has 100 marbles in total with no breakdown on colors. Now you are asked to pick a black marble and you win a prize, you get one chance and can pick from either urn. As this study has been repeated many times with different prizes, people always pick the one with the 50–50 ratio of black marbles to white marbles. After the contest, you could even find the second urn actually had 99 black marbles and 1 white marble, the researcher could have explained to you the nature of the paradox, yet people would still choose the first urn.

Why, it simply reduces the ambiguity of not knowing.

Paradoxes can and do exist in cybersecurity decision making. How much money are companies investing in cybersecurity solutions for the chance of a high payoff (e.g. instead of investing in human training, where there could be a very high expected utility return, they invest more money in technical solutions to stop all and every attack), but yet, so many of these attacks seem to be the same types of attacks, so the response. Let's throw more money at the problem. There is also discussion that perhaps the cybersecurity paradox is on privacy vs. security paradox, but isn't that decision? Do you want more security, less privacy, or less security, more privacy? A privacy vs. security paradox would be you have two choices to make, and in one choice you choose (Choice 1: more security, less privacy), and in the second choice you choose (Choice 2: less security, more privacy).

1. *More security, less privacy*
2. *Less security, more privacy*

But if you advocate for (i.e., more security, less privacy), that would be the paradox. You want the maximum utility, but your decision does not reflect your desire (i.e., less security, more privacy). In many surveys, respondents have been asked, where does your company spend most of its cybersecurity investments? Lets consider these new choices in Tables 5.3 and 5.4.

Table 5.3 Cybersecurity paradox example 1

Experiment 1	
Choice 1	**Choice 2**
Technical Solutions	Human behavioral Solutions

Typically, they would select choice 1. Technical solutions are where they spend the most money. Given another experiment, where do you think the biggest problems in cybersecurity are?

Table 5.4 Cybersecurity paradox example 2

Experiment 2	
Choice 1	**Choice 2**
Cybersecurity problems are caused by technology	Cybersecurity problems are caused by humans

Most of the respondents who chose (experiment 1, choice 1) now choose (experiment 2, choice 2). This is very similar to the Allais paradox (i.e., picking less expected utility or value). This is not to blame anyone—in a car crash, is it the automobile, or the driver the cause of the crash? In a truck crash, plane crash, and so on., most often a set of events that should have been caught were missed, so when someone fat-fingers an e-mail, remember, there was a chain of events that led to that fat-fingering. Look up the great electrical blackout of 2003 when the U.S. East Coast went dark; it was traced back to a fuse. The nonmalicious end-user was not the problem; the end-user was just unlucky enough to be at the end of the chain of events. So, the cybersecurity paradox is not that we are throwing money and resources at a problem. Mankind has done this for centuries; we always throw money at the problem. The cybersecurity paradox is irrationally selecting a choice when a rational choice is more appropriate.

Can we somehow explain this paradox, possibly?

One reason could be as with the Allais and Ellsberg paradoxes, that human just think irrationally, we let emotions interfere, and when given choices we mix them. If we are given a set of choices to make, we sometimes assume they are all related and have to look at them as a whole (i.e., like the Gestalt laws we discussed earlier). When in reality they are all mutually exclusive and we have to step back and judge one independently.

Cybersecurity Investments: Another Big Paradox

According to the chronology of data breaches at Privacy Rights Clearinghouse, 2015 saw over 500 publicly acknowledged successful breaches and over 300 million records compromised. The year 2016 saw over 826 publicly acknowledged successful breaches and over 4 billion records compromised, and 2017 saw over 862 publicly acknowledged successful breaches and over 2 billion records compromised. The year 2018 saw over 700 publicly acknowledged successful breaches and over 1.3 billion records compromised (https://privacyrights.org/data-breaches). Now we have to be careful about reading anything into someone's data points (e.g., 2018 saw only 1 billion records compromised, but we've recently had a major hospitality breach suggesting over 500,000 million records exposed). So, depending how they are announced, when they are announced, and so on, can change the reporting, but we definitely have a cybersecurity paradox. As the amount of cybersecurity investments went up, so do the amount of records breached. Rational thinking would say, as the amount of cybersecurity investments go up, the amount of records breached should go down. Shouldn't our behavior tell us something is not right, and this shouldn't be happening? Why are we still investing heavily in cybersecurity then? Investments in cybersecurity are akin to the old car you have. You have so much invested and you don't want to lose your investment, so you keep investing (i.e., the sunk cost fallacy). This fallacy, this belief, this way of doing things guides our behavior and we will see, there are just so many things that impact our beliefs that, yes, we will keep investing in something as long as our beliefs guide us. Unfortunately, and as we will see, even when our beliefs tell us something is wrong, many of us will still choose to follow that behavior that we know is wrong. Why? Maybe we are just looking at cybersecurity investments incorrectly, maybe we are just not getting our money's worth, or a million other reasons. We did mention earlier companies seem to blame the end-users a lot, but in the case of many successful breaches, end-users would not have had any privileges to interact with those systems. Pixel tracking, another type of attack, views the image, and hackers now have information. Can anyone really expect the end-user who gets an e-mail and doesn't open the e-mail? It's just in their inbox, but if the image shows, information is then sent back to the attacker. How many examples of these kinds of instances can end-users really understand?

WannaCry, WannaCrypt, WannaBet

So, what do all these have in common? Simple. Malware, more specifically ransomware, and considering we just looked at mental models, wannabet some of these attacks are successful because we use the same faulty mental models that we are using the same mental models we created. Malware is one of the most successful attacks that have plagued computer systems for decades (Langde 2017; Washburn 2019; Lemos 2013; Siwicki 2017). A simple attack that keeps changing, adapting, evolving, and for the most part, unstoppable and successful for two simple reasons: (1) trust, and not just people, but trust relationship of vendor to vendor and (2) technology getting old, outdated and for the most part dying, as in no longer supported. Trust relationships exist at all levels of computer systems. Think of any retailer and their suppliers. Trust relationships are set up to facilitate business, they have to be. Can you imagine a supermarket having to call in their supplier when a gallon of milk is needed? A point of sale register salesperson having to call the credit card company up to each time a person wants to buy something on their credit or debit card. Imagine operating system getting to end of useful life. Pick any current operating system in an organization and think about all the previous versions of the same operating system (e.g., while many organizations may have the latest Windows 10 operating systems, you will most likely find Windows XP Service Pack 3 running as well). When patches are released the latest operating system will be covered, but what if earlier releases are not, what if the vendor doesn't even support the earliest versions anymore. These are not technical problems. These are mental model problems. Technical solutions cannot fix our mental processing errors. Think about the discussion on cognitive economy and the availability heuristic. A new ransomware malware is out, and we have to update our operating systems. Our cognitive economy will force us to update our companies operating systems, what operating system is the manager in charge running, most likely the latest.

Our available information and our cognitive economy tell us to update the latest operating system (e.g., Windows 10); however, our available information is not on our Windows 10 operating system, but on our Windows 7 operating system, Windows XP operating system, and Windows 2000 operating system, and even older medical machines, as recently as February 2018 are still on Windows 95 operating systems. So, as we are thinking about our computer systems, we have to remember, it's not a patch to an operating system. These are patches to an organization. Think about of all the security breaches you read about. Our limitations were not technical; they were trust and coupled with the anchoring heuristic it's who or what we trust. In the paradoxes we discussed, we paradoxically choose for technical solutions, yet we advocate that employees are the biggest threat. We are anchoring in technology, yet the issue is trust. Trusted relationships are abundant in successful cybersecurity breaches. We trust software, computer applications, and interconnected devices, but we do not trust humans. That is why we make extremely difficult password requirements, yet let vendors install software in our companies' systems. Managers and decision makers can certainly understand bad passwords (i.e., availability heuristic), but cannot understand zero-day attacks, or an Apache Struts vulnerability. Further enflaming the problem is when we are getting answers to these potential problems, and those giving those answers could be falling into confirmation bias, since it will most likely be something that they have read or believed in that contributed to the problem.

Cybersecurity Implications and Conclusions

Michaelidis (2018) makes a very good point, that the road to cybersecurity is paved with extraordinarily basic things. That the things that are preached like better passwords are extraordinarily basic things, yet we fail to deliver on extraordinarily basic things. Will newer and more complexity make this better? Has it done so far? If we do an extraordinarily basic thing like just opening up an infected email, or missing a patch announcement, why wouldn't an extraordinarily basic thing help to solve that extraordinarily basic problem. Perhaps it's just the perception of the problem. That humans are incapable and technology is the answer. Given that the cybersecurity literature is littered with terms that are negative, like viruses, or bad actors, cyberterrorists only worsens our perceptions of the problem.

Looking at cybersecurity spending, 90 percent of it is on technical solutions. That's another cybersecurity paradox. We spend so much more money on technical solutions, when we know it's a people issue, and unfortunately the conditioned response of you will be fired if you violate some policy simply does not work anymore. And if we believe all employees are the problem, then you may as well close the business as it's hopeless. So, once we move to understand all the paradoxes, we moved to game theory and behavioral game theory for possible answers. It's a strategic cat-and-mouse game trying to outwit our opponents to figure out their next move (i.e., their behavior). But if it is anything that this book has highlighted it is that we cannot predict someone's behavior, let alone ourselves.

Think in any of your decision making with cybersecurity, any ambiguity or uncertainty pops up. Well, I am not sure of this attack, I do know when the next attack will occur, I am not sure of this technology, and so on. Cybersecurity unfortunately is filled with nothing but ambiguity. In addition, companies better brace themselves for even more misery. There was a lawsuit against Fiat-Chrysler's Jeep Cherokee (Greenbergm 2015) for a vulnerability in the automobile. Researchers were able to demonstrate to the court they were able to take over the Jeep remotely by hacking into the entertainment system and controlling the cars speed and direction. Luckily, no one was ever killed, but in January 2019, the Supreme Court rejected the automobile manufacturer's argument that they should not be liable since no one ever got hurt. The plaintiff's argument was that they would have never purchased the automobile had they known of the vulnerability. This showcases two really important points. First, in the chain of events, which will be discussed later in the text, basically the control of the car was just the last line in the chain of events. It could have been started way before the car was ever built when the decision about what type of entrainment system to offer. Second, companies better brace themselves since if this case does succeed and Fiat-Chrysler is forced to pay damages, any company may now be vulnerable to legal recourse due to the extent of a successful cybersecurity attack. Another major disaster that had been developing during the writing of this textbook was that of the Boeing Corporation's 736 MAX aircraft. Two deadly crashes happened and the cause of fault seems to be isolated in the Maneuvering Characteristics Augmentation System (MCAS) of the aircraft, which is used to help nudge the nose of the aircraft during some specific maneuvers to help avoid stalls. The cause of the crash is not the purpose here, but what is problematic was reported by Nicas et al. (2019) as to some of the statements made. Employees made statements such as, "That's nuts," I'm shocked," "To me, it seems like somebody didn't understand what they were doing," "It doesn't make any sense," "I wish I had the full story" (p. 19). Looking back on this chapter and the discussion on biases, can you see how any of them could be attributed to the reward and punishment bias, the inconsistency bias, the cognitive dissonance bias, the blind-side bias, or the outcome bias? These biases can guide our thinking, and eventual behavior. What about implanted medical devices that are becoming more normal, or microchips? Something out of a Hollywood movie, I'm afraid not. A company implants microchips, with the employees' consent, so that these employees can buy food in the cafeteria, walk into the building's entrance, use resources, and so on. Sounds great, no more badges to carry, no more pocket change needed. This has also now expanded for security reasons, to better protect employees. Even in the United States, we are getting close to allowing parents to get their children implanted with GPS in case of abduction. All for security sake, and while all this sounds like a good cause. A child gets abducted, use your cell phone. An Alzheimer's patient gets lost, use your cell phone. But just how far can we extend this? There is no doubt computer–human integration is coming. We would have to be very naive to think otherwise. We will never be able to disconnect from the grid. However, all this data goes somewhere, it will be stored somewhere, and the closer this technology gets to interacting with one's own nervous system, or brain functions, how much more valuable will that data become to some authoritarian government wishing to control a protest, or possible some hacker discovering a vulnerability in the latest microchip?

So finally, back to how do we learn to think. In the classic 1960s comedy *Hogan's Heroes*, the German lovable bumbling guard Sergeant Hans Schultz played by actor John Banner would go around saying his famous line, we have ways of making you talk:

Well, talk yes, think no.

However, this line did not originate from *Hogan's Heroes*. It came from an older Gary Cooper's 1935 move, *the Lives of a Bengal Lancer*, and what I did there was introduce an anchoring heuristic. It wasn't a lie, as when I originally thought of the line, I attributed it to *Hogan Heroes*, and when I went to research it, I found it was from a Cary Cooper movie, so now my confirmation bias is causing a cognitive dissonance headache. And all this leads my behavior. So, to teach a lesson that I should remember, is that:

maybe I shouldn't think too much.

CHAPTER 6

Memory

Introduction

Our memory, for an easy analogy, is basically a living computer hard drive. A place to store data points and then retrieve those data points when needed. All these individual data points are connected by neural associations, and it is in these neural networks where we experience our perceptions, emotions, relationships, and dreams. The problem we have is that when these data points go into memory, it is often encoded by current experiences and current circumstances, and we often do not get the whole complete picture; we miss details of the event. In a computer, the input one plus one would reveal a result of two, but in our brain, an input of one plus one could reveal a result of red. Why? Well, our brains are just too noisy. In a computer, we have a data bus where a bit of information gets sent down that bus and picked up at the receiving end. However, in our brain the analogy would be of a real bus. As we are going to our final destination, people get on and off the bus. The stimuli are abundant. Noise, colors, movements, all affect our various cortexes dependent on that stimuli. An important note is that our visual cortex does not need visual cues (e.g., our bus could be driving through, at least what we believe, is a bad area, and yes, our visual cortex becomes active on what we think we might encounter). Therefore, when we need to remember these events, we fill in the details about what we think happened. However, there are no data points here. So what happened and how do we fill in the missing data points? It is then we use previous memories to fill in these missing details. Not all of this is incorrect necessarily. It is just our experiences we are relying on. We could actually have correct facts, but in the wrong order, the wrong time, the wrong order of steps, or we could think we have the correct facts.

Where you ever told when you were younger not to go swimming right after eating, or do not drink more than two or three cups of coffee a day. So, at times the data may not be technically incorrect, but it could have been technically incorrect at that moment in time it was encoded. We talked about cognitive categories earlier. Well, we also have categories of memory. We can refer to topographic, or space memory, as we are able to orient ourselves (e.g., in space, familiar places, traveling, following an itinerary, etc.). There is the term "flashbulb memory." These are very detailed and specific episodic memories of emotional events. This was described by Roger Brown and Kulik (1977) and it's the ability to recall very specific details during certain unforgettable events (e.g., the first moon landing)—people can recall where they were, who they were with, what they were doing. Although some researchers have since argued, certain details are very vivid, but in many cases, very incorrect. We are so sure we can see, feel, touch, and even smell those vivid past memories, but most often they are incorrect. Baddeley (1986) suggested that we have an inner voice to assist us, a multi-store model. One of the greatest examples is of Tommy Tutone's and Jenny's phone number, 8675309, a hit song from the 1980s. However, now, we are crossing into long-term memory. We also have an inner whiteboard where we can draw internal pictures and places. We have the declarative or semantic memory, which is more the conscious memory, from where facts and figures can be easily, and often, retrieved. This is important as it implies work. The more we work at these neural associations, the stronger the memories are, and the more often we will get those data points correct. There is a procedural memory, where over time we have learned to do many things instinctively, like walking, talking, riding a bike, and so on. It's a subcategory of another type of memory, called implicit memory, where we have used past experiences enough that we do not need to really think about them anymore. We have an easier time remembering a set of distinctly different sounding words than a set of similar sounding words. It is also harder to remember a string of similar sounding letters than distinctly different ones. But, it's also easier for us to listen to someone who is talking and drawing (e.g., a teacher giving a presentation) than to listen to that same teacher and take notes ourselves. Once we have something and think we will need this later, we then encode that and store this data to long-term memory.

Caution is noted however; these categories of memory do not necessarily translate into learning. We may have these categories of memories to help us recall data, but it does not mean we learned that way. A metanalysis research study done by Willingham, Hughes, and Dobolyi (2015) who looked at different ways in which people actually learned found no significance. This was further backed up by Rogowsky, Calhoun, and Tallal (2020) who observed that it could be that people think they learn better (e.g., by picture) and will try to use visual stimuli whenever possible. So, in essence, people's cognitive beliefs tell them they will learn better by hearing, so will tend to auditory learning materials.

Short-Term Memory

Short-term memory is continually working and continually changing. What should I be doing, what do I want to watch, where am I going, what was I thinking again? Who am I, where am I, and so on? This could be somewhat analogous to how short-term memory of a computer system works. This is the short-term Random-Access Memory (RAM), which is the fast memory the CPU accesses first. But unlike a computer where RAM memory is written to hard drive once calculations are complete, the human brain is continually moving these data bits back and forth, even before calculations are complete, even before the correct answer has been achieved. Because of this, unfortunately, the human brain will transfer all kinds of data points, regardless of the quality of that data back to storage. To make things even more complicated, it is not just our senses that are inputs, our thoughts, dreams, and emotions are all inputs to our memory. Therefore it is memory feeding memory. In contrast, the computer usage of memory will transfer the correct data to long-term storage assuming the programming was done correctly. Complicating the matter is that short-term memory is always working, and because of this there is a limit what it can process. Remember what we said about the limited processing power of the brain earlier.

Research has suggested that for the average person, we can juggle about seven different pieces of data at a time. So, what happens when we need to juggle more? To help us manage this problem, we use other techniques. For example, you may have heard when we have to remember a set of things, we create acronyms using words or sentences where each letter in the acronym has a wider more applicable meaning. We used to remember the planets in our solar system using *My Very Educated Mother Just Served Us Noodles (or Nachos)*. Growing up when we understood Pluto to be a planet, so we used another acronym *My Very Educated Mother Just Showed Us Nine Planets*. At the time our correct data said there were indeed nine planets, and it was encoded as such.

Another example is if I asked you to name 47 types of automobiles, now that's a pretty hard task, but let's break it into categories, can you name any?

Sports cars
Sedans
Pickups
Station wagons
Electric cars
SUVs
Four-wheel drive
Convertibles
Four-door cars
Two-door cars

While this is still a task, we actually can complete this task of naming 47 automobiles we can even use more categories to break this down further.

Pickups:

Toyota Tundra
Ford F150
Chevrolet Silverado
Dodge Ram Charger
Honda Ridgeline
GMC Sierra
Ford Ranger
Toyota Tacoma
Nissan Titan
I remembered all these, and I take a train to work.

You could then repeat this process with another category of automobiles (e.g., sedans). It's the categorial process that makes this easier. Looking back at cognitive economy, we talked about the need to conserve mental energy. The next step is to convert short-term memory into long-term memory correctly.

Long-Term Memory

Long-term memory is where data is sent from short-term memory once it is done. However, it is not simply as once I am done in short-term memory, it will store in long-term memory, as these two are constantly working together, and in some cases these two memories are fighting each other (e.g., in cognitive dissonance). Some like to think of long-term memory as all the stuff you knew, then forgot, but called up as needed, which I believe highly respected researchers would greatly argue against that simplistic usage. As data is stored in long-term memory, we encode this data with details, which are often incorrect. Then later, we need to look up this information, but the ingoing details were encoded incorrectly, and research as shown as we pull data out of long-term memory, it is often modified to fit our current circumstances. It is a very interesting phenomenon—we have encoded data, mixed it with our experiences, and stored that data. However, when we now pull out that data, it gets combined and influenced by our current environment, and that end result is completely different data. You may have heard the phrases *facts, alt-facts, truths, half-truths, multiple truths,* and so on. Well, it seems depending on your encoded data and the circumstances you find yourself in when you need that data. There might be something to these multiple truths. Of course, it's from that person's point of view, a different person, given the same inputs and outputs in the same set of circumstances can have a different set of multiple truths. Our neural network associations are affecting these details. The unfortunate part about this current recall in our current environment is that things can be easily manipulated by leading and associations, as we shared examples of this earlier.

When people who are trained memory athletes are asked how they remember so many details, they usually say it is because they add other cues, like a person's face, physical stature, build, and so on. This may imply the more connections you make about an event or item, the more neural network associations you create, and the easier it becomes to recall these events. Many memory athletes will utilize the *Memory Palace*, also known as the *Method of loci*, which was used by the ancient Greeks and Romans. This procedure utilized certain familiar layouts like a building to create discrete points (i.e., loci, and create an association between that particular loci and the item that needs to be remembered). This should point out that to remember something, the best way is to actually add more information about that bit of information, not less. So instead of deciding to study this one concept over and over till it's in long-term memory where it might be harder to find later, the best technique is to add more data points. A fruit that is red, juicy, pit, leaf, Jonny comes out to apple. This red, juicy, pit, leaf, Jonny are associations and we just made a bunch of these associations in our neural networks. These neural networks are plentiful; on average, researchers suggest the human brain has over 100 billon neurons, with each one connecting to somewhere between 7,000 to over 10,000 other neurons, creating the ability of a vast network of associations where data can be stored. Researchers from Johns Hopkins University do seem to agree with this memory technique. They argue if you practice or review the same concept in the same way you are trying to store this content, you may not learn it as effectively, and in fact you may worsen your memory recall. They suggest attacking this concepts from different angles, for example, practice this concept you are trying to remember, possibly faster or slower, break this concept into smaller pieces, use a different area to review, and as you continue keep modifying these extraneous factors surround us (Johns Hopkins Medicine 2016). The brain toggles between focus and unfocused. The brain uses energy differently between these focused and unfocused events. However, it's not like the brain isn't doing anything in this unfocused state; it's looking back at its stored memories, shuffling data back and forth, and it's actually helping you find information in your conscious. Too much focus temporarily uses all these focus circuits and you begin to make bad decisions. A conclusion reported is that the brain uses more energy in this unfocused state compared to the focus state, further suggesting the brain in the unfocused state is using more energy trying to examine the issue at hand (Long et al. 2016). Another study showing that, indeed, too much studying can actually interfere with our ability to remember. Think of a computer's RAM, that short-term fast memory allocation of data. Now, instead of the computer writing that data in RAM to long-term memory, it now overwrites the RAM memory and erases what was previously stored. Shibata et al. (2017) have shown that brains are flexible, moving in and out, and if you train on another task right after you trained on the previous task, the previous task is lost. They say in this instance, the brain is in what they termed a plastic state. However, after you learned a skill, then took a break, and then do a similar task, the results are long-lasting. They label this as retrograde interference, and during magnetic resonance spectroscopy examinations, they identified higher amounts of glutamate-dominate excitatory, which helps the brain at learning. Overlearning decreases the amount of glutamate-dominate excitatory. So, this overloading can help, and has been suggested, overload by similar stimuli, like a different area of the subject, a different starting point, and so on. This study seems to agree with the research done by Pageaux et al. (2014; 2015) that mental fatigue (i.e., too much cognitive activity) can be caused by an increase of adenosine in the brain, which reduces neurotransmitters, such as dopamine. The increase in adenosine was caused because too much cognitive activity burns up glucose, a building block of energy. Further, Pastuzyn et al. (2017) suggest that neuronal plasticity structural changes are needed so that memories are to remain. They report that the Arc protein and its interaction within plastic changes in neurons helps in memory formation, which seems to mimic a virus structure, and that while the proteins needed for long-term memory do not remain, nevertheless, the actual memory does.

Priming

Implicit memory is memory we use a lot. It's the subconscious effort based upon past experiences. Examples are riding a bike, walking, driving a car, and so on. Decision making can be based upon implicit memory, and we often use the priming effect to reach our decisions. In priming there is a deliberate effort to activate some stimuli, which in turn will activate other stimuli to help in memory retrieval. Priming is very important, because while we have conscious memory, it is not always available, and sometimes other stimuli needs to be primed in order to get to that bit of memory we are seeking. We do this quite frequently. We just did an example earlier with the 47 automobiles; if we started with just one automobile category, we began to prime our brain and made recalling the other automobiles easier. As you are heading out the door and you can't find your car keys, you naturally think back to what was the last thing you were doing, where were you—in the garage, at the neighbors, upstairs, the kitchen—so that all these priming stimuli will help you to eventually find that one bit of memory—where you left your keys. Priming is also subconscious; as soon as we see something, hear something, taste something, and smell something, you flash back to a measurable or tragic event that has some consequence to you. If you did not hear that sound, or smell that food (i.e., the prime), you would not have been brought back to another event. It does not mean you never go back to that event outside of the prime, or even if you if you smell or hear that sound again, you will recall that event. It's just in this moment in time that prime brought back an event.

As with the different types of memory, there are different types of priming. Negative priming, perceptual priming, conceptual priming, associative priming, repetition priming, and so on, but they all work on a principle of some stimuli acting upon another stimuli. Remember with these neural networks. These billons of networks can become very complicated. The good news is the more you remember, the more you actually remember. Hard work also counts here.

Deep Brain Stimulation

There is a lot of work that goes on with neural networks and chip implants. Deep brain stimulation (DBS) is a priming technique that uses a small device to send electrical currents to point in the brain. Current research is looking for ways to treat debilitating diseases like Parkinson's and epilepsy. Some of these early Defense Advanced Research Projects Agency (DARPA)-funded studies do seem to indicate real results in manipulating the mind's memory and increase short-term performance in recall. And unless there is physical damage to the brain, it is not the memory that is the issue, it's the recall of memory. This research has been around for decades. You may have heard of cardiac pacemaker where a pacemaker helps the heart beat at regular intervals, DBS tries to help the brain in similar ways, by injecting a simulation by means of an electrode to areas of the brain that cause these neurological dysfunctions. Another method is of transcranial alternating current stimulation (TACS), which stimulates key areas of the brain and has shown progress in helping memory deficits (e.g., dementia, injuries or other brain-related issues) (Reinhart and Nguyen 2019). However, even with this progress, we have examined if this circuit be hijacked. If you think not, some of the protocols developed are over Bluetooth, not the strongest security protocol we have. Even if this research can just mimic the priming effect, it is possible that indeed we can use recall memory better. That does not mean we will listen and follow our memories, as many of us have said that in the case of evidence, you know, looking back, it wasn't one of my greatest moments, I should have known better. But like everything else, there is a downside, even to priming, and it's called retrieval-induced forgetting.

Retrieval-Induced Forgetting

Too much remembering some information tends to lead us to forget previously remembered information, and while there is a lot of debate on what causes retrieval-induced forgetting, the phenomenon exists. There was a fictional television comedy sitcom in the 1990s called *Married with Children*. In one episode, in order to get his sister Kelly Bundy to be able to compete on a Sports Trivia game show, the brother Bud Bundy kept filling his sister's head with facts about sports. Day and night, facts, more facts, night and day, and still more facts. During one of these study sessions, the doorbell rang, and Kelly Bundy asked:

Bud, What's that?
That's retrieval-induced forgetting.

Our mental associations, those neural networks that help us to remember things and help us to guide our behavior, need to be practiced. You've heard the phrase practice makes perfect. It turns out, yes, the more we practice, the better we become. Experiments have been done with students, where after giving all the students the same material, they would be separated into two groups. One group would be given practice exams covering part of the material, and the other group would be given extra time to study all the material. It turns out in the short term both are statically tied, but the group that used the extra time to study did slightly better than the group that just used practice exams. However, over the longer term, the extra time study group did lose a lot of the material, which researchers expected. The group that used the practice exams did slightly lower than the extra time study group, but they remembered more over the long-term.

But only the material on the practice exams.

They lost the memory of the material that was not on the practice exams, even though the material was important and both groups were initially presented with the same material. One could think of those certification cram exams many have used for helping in passing a security certification. We did not really lose that information; we just cannot find it when needed. We study taking these certification tests on some material, but only certain areas of the material. The more we practice one set of associations, they become stronger, but the other associations less practiced become weaker. Again, you do not actually lose the unpracticed associations, it's just that they are much harder to locate and retrieve when needed. The more we practice with a set of neural network associations, the more harder to recall those areas we didn't practice as much. I have an older friend who has Alzheimer's, who cannot go into a grocery store today for fear of getting lost, but this 94-year-old man leads me around Brooklyn, New York, telling me about all the different places, where everything was, and what has changed since 1924. So, these subtle cues about some past experiences open the floodgate to a whole set of emotions.

So, should we trust just our memories?
Well, in checkers yes, nowhere else.

Everyone Loves Memes, Don't You?

So, who doesn't love a good meme? Memes are cute, funny, entertaining, and very dangerous. Just ask some users of Facebook, Google, Twitter, WhatsApp, or any other app that have had infected memes installed.

Memes, or memetics, are a way cultural information spreads. These concepts, beliefs, and practices that spread through word of mouth (Dawkins 1976) recently have now spread online. Internet memes, a subset of memes, include some of the more familiar ones such as *distracted boyfriend, ice bucket challenge, miss me yet, Gangnam style, and grumpy cat.* Some are referred to as a gene that can spread from person to person, but in that case, I would suggest some memes are more like viruses that are airborne, and there are very bad memes, the dark memes as they are called. One recent bad one was the tide pod challenge. Since they are spreadable from person to person and can incorporate aspects of culture, it in turn can lead to stereotyping and groupthink. Hackers were able to exploit WhatsApp's messaging system to get people to click on sites that installed malware and keystroke collecting software from their other social media accounts (Kaufman 2018). Lately, even hidden messages have been hidden behind these memes. The movie *Matrix* and the meme, what if I told you, contains malware that will steal data.

So why do we keep falling for these—e-mails we open, web pages we visit, memes we run, after all, who doesn't like cute cat gifs? Perhaps it is related to retrieval-induced forgetting; there is just too much new stimuli, too much new information upon us, so by letting our guards down, we open ourselves up to be victims, and perhaps that is where we can learn. As cybersecurity professionals, we know people are curious, but we also know people forget and we know people will go around system barriers to get their work done. Therefore, what solutions can we use? Continued training and enhancing these neural network associations, absolutely. The issue is timing—with too much training, we tend to ignore things, too little, we forget. Luckily, we do have some research to help us. The German psychologist Ebbinghaus developed his forgetting curve that illustrates most people will tend to lose about 90 percent of what they learned within a week (Ebbinghaus 1913). That's correct. In 1913, over a century ago, it was argued that people will forget over 90 percent of what they were taught within a week, yet, only recently, within the last decade or so we have taken security training and awareness and making is practice. So, if we teach something, we need to understand it, create something, challenge ourselves to create an instance of a learning agent that sets off and codifies hundreds, if not thousands of neural network associations. Dale's

(1946) works agrees with Ebbinghaus's premises that if we teach someone a skill, that training further helps us in remembering and recalling that information. Therefore, perhaps the next time you want to teach your staff about a security issue, ask someone in that department to create a learning resource, and check your results, you could be amazed.

Cybersecurity Implications and Conclusions

We've mentioned how humans use categories to help us remember. Lets' take a look at this cognitive economy in the application of passwords. Password reuse is one of the most common user problems security administrators have to address. But let's think about it from an end-user's perception. It is not that I can't remember a password with 8 to 12 characters and that it must contain an upper and lower alphabetical letter and it must contain a number and a special character. I can remember that, and yes, if I have to change my password, I could probably remember the new one. But I can't remember this password for 10 different systems that change once a month, my expertise is in human resources, and I am not a memory mind Jedi. What eventually happens is reuse work-around. What happens, is that we use the same password all the time, but just change one character, for example

Happy12, then
Happy13, then
Happy14, then
Happy15, then
Happy16, then
Happy17, then back to
Happy12

This is for those systems that do not allow you to use the last three or four passwords, or one that has been used in three months. The bigger problem I see is that we use the same passwords for all accounts: I have Happy12 here, and a Happy12 there, and a Happy12 somewhere else as well. Yes, we can use password manager programs and many of them work well, but like anything else, technology changes, browsers get updated, mobile devices, and so on, password manager programs run into issues and again, we are back to Happy12. So, the question would then become can we get an individual to remember seven different passwords at the same time, and most likely we could, because:

Why 7? Simple, it's 7 ± 2, well, it's 5 or 9 really.

Miller (1956) suggested that our memory is limited and that our working memory only has a limited capacity, and his research shows that for the most part, people can hold in memory seven plus or minus two data points. Miller's experiments show a human's uncanny ability to juggle seven plus or minus two things, whether they were numbers, songs, tunes, patterns, people's facial expressions, and so on. Remember the categories about the automobiles we discussed earlier. He made a remarkable point about one of the most famous words ever mentioned in a 1964 movie titled *Mary Poppins—supercalifragilisticexpialidocious.* If we use too much stimuli our brain comes up with a chunking mechanism, breaking things down into smaller chucks, that is:

Supercalifragilisticexpialidocious can be broken down into
Super cali fragi listic expi ali docious = 7 categories

Miller's work has been repeated and validated by other researchers. It has also been questioned by others that perhaps it's only four pieces of data we can hold. Is it possible then we can use some of this magical number seven plus or minus two and chunking to come up with a better way to remember passwords? By chunking, we can now even break this down further, I have to go to Supercalifragilisticexpialidocious, the supermarket (Super) and pick up coffee and apples (CA li), and French toast and cereal (F RASIN BRAN agi), and some meat (F Frankfurter ragi), then I need to run to the bank to deposit a check to pay some bills (expi), and so on. Hopefully, you get the point, we are allowed 7 ± 2 and then we can chunk it down further.

I wonder, have we ever asked any end-users about 7 ± 2?
All I remember is always writing my passwords down.

Now that we have examined short-term and long-term memory, how can we apply that to security? Do these different types of memories help us in any way? Remember the discussion we just had on cramming vs. having extra time to study the material. The result is that yes, practice does take hard work; however, if you only build up certain mental associations, you lose other ones. Remember research has shown it's not the actual forgetting of the material, it's the retrieval of that material that is the problem. And like all research, there are opposing viewpoints—some researchers say, yes, we can forget and some even suggest the brain is designed to forget (Davis 2011; Hardt et al. 2014; Richards and Frankland 2017). An argument is made that with too much information our brains would be working too hard with so many empty memories, those memories that do not contribute to something at hand. We are working on a problem and we remember, yesterday, it was warm, the day before it was warmer, the day before that, not so warm, the day before that, a little cooler. So, how would all these empty memories help us? It's not clear-cut, but if we use the analogy of our brain to the largest hard drive ever created, all these memories could be stored since we would not need them until recall, but much more research is needed in this area. Recently in 2018, the largest organ in the human body was identified—the interstitium. So perhaps we may find in the future other areas where we store data.

Let's look at another example. What if I asked the following question?

> Tell me about the last cybersecurity attack you head about?

Figure 6.1 Skimming effect

There is nothing wrong with your eyes, and by the end of the book, you will probably remember this question.

Oppenheimer, Diemand-Yauman, and Vaughan (2012) conducted a study using two random fictional facts about two random animals, a pangerish and the norgletti. The only thing different was the font used. There was an easy to read 16-point Arial font used for the fictional animal norgletti, and a much harder 12-point Comic Sans font for the fictional animal pangerish. At the end of the study, the participants were able to recall more of the fictional facts on the norgletti. This would on the face of it, be counterintuitive, since the pangerish was using a much harder font to read the facts. However, after studying the phenomenon, it might make sense. While using a blurred text does take more time, it also reduces the skimming effect, where we just skim over words trying to fill in what we think we see in figure 6.1. Remember, earlier we saw that we want to save cognitive energy, so what better way to save than skimming. The phenomenon puts a brake on the skimming. It is not as simple as skimming. These researchers also suggested maybe it's confidence. Since I can't read these words, I am beginning to lose confidence in my abilities, and therefore I will try harder. The question is also conceptual in nature. It is asking you to (1) recall an incident—the when, where, how, who—and (2) heard about—was it from the news, a website, an e-mail, and so on. These types of conceptual questions set off hundreds, if not thousands, of neural network associations looking for the answer, and in doing so, strengthen the recall of this memory incident.

Perry (2001) looks at this thinking as a two-step process. We can see all the information in a nonblurry image. We recognize it from our associations, and perhaps even more. In the blurry text, and even though the details are hazy, over time they come into focus. This blurry text is still hazy, but it's cleared and focused in our minds, and perhaps it's one of the types of memory we discussed earlier. All of our neural network associations are working together to come up with a complete image of what is being displayed, and the more neural network associations we have working, the better our memory and recall of specific events. Cybersecurity hands-on experts are indeed experienced with this. Have a cybersecurity expert who has a lot of hands-on experience with attacking tools, network sniffers, hexadecimal viewers, and so on. Have them read a 40-page security incident report, and then review and write up a report on what they have read. Then have the same expert write up a report but just on the technical hands-on experience with the actual protocol packets and details on the attack vectors. Some may ask, was this the same person, as most likely the writings will be very different from each other. It is simply what have chosen to focus on, and what's inside our brain's neural network connections.

However, there is hope for us mere mortals who need to remember these important data facts. Dresler et al. (2017) have worked with memory athletes, those individuals who compete in memory contests and must remember hundreds of names, numbers, colors, and so on. They noticed these memory athletes exhibit unique brain connectivity patterns. Then they applied some behavioral tests and techniques to nonmemory athletes, and after a while, they found out that these nonmemory athletes exhibited some of the same brain connectivity patterns of these memory athletes, thereby suggesting with the correct amount of training, memory recall could be improved.

CHAPTER 7

How Are We Motivated

Introduction

Many researchers have looked at motivation to understand behavior, from the earliest behavioral researchers who focused on stimuli–response, to later ones that focused on suppressed memories, to those who looked at social needs and so on. In a simple sense, if we can understand motivation, we might then be able to then predict behavior, and if we can predict behavior, we might be able to solve someone's ills, or stop them before they do something of bad consequences. We can think of motivation as a force as an analogy to electricity or water; the larger the electrical current, or larger the amount of water, the more pressure will be exerted on wiring and pipes. The larger the motivation force, the more pressure will be placed upon an individual to exhibit some type of behavior. Many early researchers studied motivation and one of the most famous ones was Abraham Maslow (1943).

Maslow's Hierarchy of Needs

Prior to Maslow, researchers looked at two basic needs that might guide our behavior. They were self-preservation needs, such as hunger, food, housing. These needs would direct our behavior to accomplish those things to sustain life. Then other researchers looked at higher abstract philosophical questions like why are we here, what is the meaning of life, and what is our destiny. Maslow had issues with both approaches as they were missing other important details (i.e., you might question what is my purpose, but you still have to eat to survive). In his world all of these are important, and so he created a classification of needs that cover the larger human experience with the need to survive.

Maslow's hierarchy of needs is often depicted as a triangle, starting with physiological needs on the bottom, then once these needs are satisfied, we move up to the next level of safety needs (i.e., safety needs). Once this level of needs is met, we move up to the next level to belonging or love, then to esteem, and then to self-actualization. In Maslow's hierarchy of needs, we start at the foundation, (i.e., food, the basis of life that guides our behavior) to self-actualization, and the question, why are we here, to finally reach our maximum potential. As each layer is satisfied, we then tend to seek to achieve the next higher layer. Once we are satisfied with a layer, we move up the hierarchy. However, a main problem is that we do not just live with the lower order needs, but we actually prioritize over them, and in a sense let the lower ones suffer. Food is a perfect need, a foundation for survival, but we make many excuses for not eating, such as fasting, dieting, low carb, low fat, and fast food is bad. On the face of his model and that of a basic need, none of this should matter since the foundation is survival, not the type of food for survival. Another criticism of the basic foundational need is that just by changing a label (e.g., less salt, no artificial sugars), it seems that if the need is due to a hormonal hunger signal, the force becomes much stronger. Again, at the basic need for survival, none of this should matter. Many experiments have been done with food such as smaller plates, different colored plates, different shaped plates, different smells, and different distances to the food, as food is such a great attribute to work with to see just how basic needs can be modified. In some experiments, as long as food servers were still putting food on our plates or soda in our cup, subjects kept eating and drinking. Therefore, this foundational level might need some more research. Finally, once we cover our basic motivation for survival, we then move up to more abstract needs, which are even harder to understand and manage than just the basic Maslow's needs.

Other Factors of Motivations

Motivations are also based on outside influences. The term *keeping up with the Jones*, as they have a new car, so we need one as well, or she is so cool that I need to hang out with her and I can be cool as well. Our motivations, therefore, could be extrinsically linked (i.e., to gain some external reward or perhaps to even avoid external punishments). They can be linked to conflicting influences as well. If I pay someone by the hour to do a job, they may work slower, whereas if I pay them a fixed price, they may work faster but possibly cut corners. These outside factors can influence our motivations, and therefore our behavior, and even though there is not a clear sign they will, it's important to understand they exist. Many other influences can also impact our motivation–behavior connection (e.g., you pay your kids for doing chores), but what happens if you stop paying, or what happens if they just no longer care about that momentary reward, perhaps they think it is not worth the effort. We can even have negative motivation that we enjoy, as in I like to live dangerously, I like to live to the extremes. Our motivations influence us to pay for a privilege. Two decades ago, many of us would have never thought about paying for water in a bottle. Now, not only are we paying for water in a bottle, we are paying huge sums of money for the privilege of specialty bottle water, or just look how much a gallon of oat milk costs. Currently, at the time of the writing this book, there are shortages of oat milk, and quarts are going for about $20.00, and they are selling out, compared that to a quart of regular milk that goes for around one U.S. dollar. We also pay for a fast pass at many amusement parks for the privilege of skipping to the front of the line. In all these instances, we need to realize that while Maslow and other researchers contributed to our understanding of motivations, there is still a lot more to understand, and like other human factors we have encountered, it could be just that motivations are fluid and will continually change as we are introduced to new stimuli (i.e., new factors that will motivate us or the same factors in different circumstances), as we have spoken about earlier, everything in context.

Goals in Motivation and Motion

It's not hard to understand the rationale of using step goals in motivation. I may not be able to accomplish a major goal, but perhaps I can accomplish a number of smaller goals on my way to the much larger goal. If I am writing a 400-page novel as my main goal, then maybe I will write five pages a day (i.e., minor goals). If I want to lose 100 pounds of weight, again my major goal, I may try to drop two pounds per week, my minor goal. A lot of research has been done on goal theory and how they may motivate us, and generally this has divided them into two broad categories: performance goals and mastery goals (Locke and Gary 2002). A performance goal could be that I want to build 7,000 cars in a month, or cook 1,000 turkeys for a Thanksgiving feast. A mastery goal is I want to create only one automobile, but the best automatable there is, or I want to create the best turkey cooking recipe. Therefore, both of these could be related, but the corresponding behavior would be different. There are the drawbacks to these goals, as I can build 3,000 different pieces for the U.S. space shuttle program, but if I am asked to design one critical piece in particular that might be used for a mission to Mars, I may not have the expertise. Or if I am only making one prototype for the best car in the world, however, what happens if that prototype never leaves the design phase. Our goals were not fully aligned with our expertise.

An important look at these goals reveals more intriguing results. Why would I want to build 7,000 cars? Who for: my manager, my company, my board of directors? These are external rewards, otherwise called performance goals. In contrast to an internal reward, a mastery goal, I want to be better than myself: strong, smarter, faster. The drive is strong, but also unfortunately this drive can push us to make really bad business decisions to be the master. Even more so, our goals change, and people's goals change, so we have to adapt to both their goals and our goals, and the more we analyze performance goals, we may decide to analyze mastery goals as well, so our goals are also in motion.

Goal Gradient Hypothesis

The goal gradient hypothesis, developed by Hull (1932), postulated that we become more monotonically motivated to accomplish a goal from the start of that goal to the closer we get to that goal. Our motivations become stronger and drive greater the closer we get to completing that goal (i.e., we want the reward we worked so hard for). We see this a lot in marketing and in loyalty programs (e.g., for free travel miles). We go to our favorite restaurant and they stamp a card each time we go. They might offer a discount—buy 10 lunches, get one free. As we get close to some reward, we will make more of an effort to reach that goal. However, it has been shown repeatedly we put more effort into this, even if it's just an illusion. Nunes and Drze (2006) conducted an experiment where they gave out 300 loyalty cards to car wash patrons. Each time you buy a car wash, you get a stamp on your loyalty card, buy eight car washes, and you get a free car wash. They handed out 300 cards loyalty cards in all, but the only difference was that on half the cards, 150 of them, there were 10 places for stamps, but two were already stamped. The remaining group of 150 cards have 8 places for eventual punch stamps.

Group 1: 150 cards, 10 places, 2 already stamped, 8 more a free car wash
Group 2: 150 cards, 8 places, 0 already stamped, 8 more a free car wash

These two groups had basically the same deal—wash the car eight more times and you get a free car wash, but the result was that the group that had the card with two stamps already placed on their card filled the remaining eight slots quicker than the group that had to fill out just the eight stamps. The group that had the loyalty card with two stamps already placed on the card were closer to their eventual goal, even though both groups just needed eight stamps each, showing support for monotonically linked motivation to the eventual end goal. Goals can also be categorized as want-to goals vs. have-to goals. We want to lose weight, we want to quit smoking—we want to. However, if we have must-to goals, we just have-to lose weight, we just have-to quit smoking—we just have to. These goals are much harder to obtain since we have-to succeed and this causes a loss of motivation.

The Means–End Chain and Laddering Goals

Means–end chains have been used in understanding motivation and goals in many studies. It is through a mean-end chain that a hierarchy of value is revealed and may induce someone to act in a certain way, to achieve that goal. Means–end chains as defined by Gutman (1982, 1997) describes a series of linkages from someone's (1) attributes to (2) consequences to (3) goals.

1. *Attribute*: You place a value on a product's or service's attributes. Attributes are facets that make up a product or service. Color, material, return policy, and both tangible and nontangible items are considered attributes. We place some value on these (even if have never experienced this product or service before). Remember all our neural network associations and top-down processing, something, somewhere is giving us a perception of value.

2. *Consequence*: We begin to place a value on that attribute. Is the color fading, is the material too hot, cold, starting to tear, is their return policy so cumbersome that we just do not bother to send it back? This step is important, because this is the step that we really are making judgments on will we achieve our eventual goal.

3. *Goal*: Did we end up achieving what we wanted when we started out. For example, did this product keep me warm? Did the product last? Did this product help me to keep up with my neighbors' image, which in turn reflects my own image?

A very simple means–end chain could look like that shown in Figure 7.1.

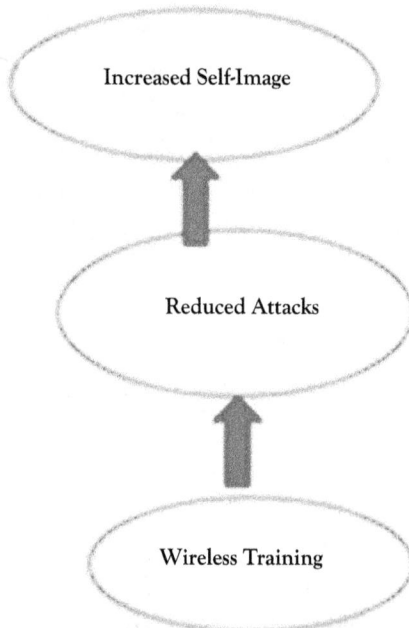

Figure 7.1 Means–end chain

In the above example, an attribute of wireless training could lead to reduced attacks in a company, which could lead to an improved self-image of an information technology administrator. We may want to think the reduced attacks is the end goal, but really, it's not, it's a means to an end. You do not install an alarm system in your house for the end goal of setting off an alarm if someone tries to break into your house. Your end goal is safety for you and your family; the alarm system you installed, the attribute, would lead to a consequence of sounding that alarm, which would then lead to an alarm going off. The one trying to enter may run away, and your goal of safety has been realized for now. Goals, like we saw earlier, are higher level abstractions. The way we obtain this means–end chain is through a use of a laddering qualitative design, by asking individuals what they want to achieve, their end goal, and then work backward, as an example:

What *would be a goal for your family in a new house? Safety, the goal. How would you obtain that safety? If I had an alarm in case someone tried to enter, the alarm would make a loud noise, the consequence. How would you get something to give off a loud alarm? An alarm system, the attribute.*

It's important to note, this is not a one for one, for example, we may have (Figure 7.2):

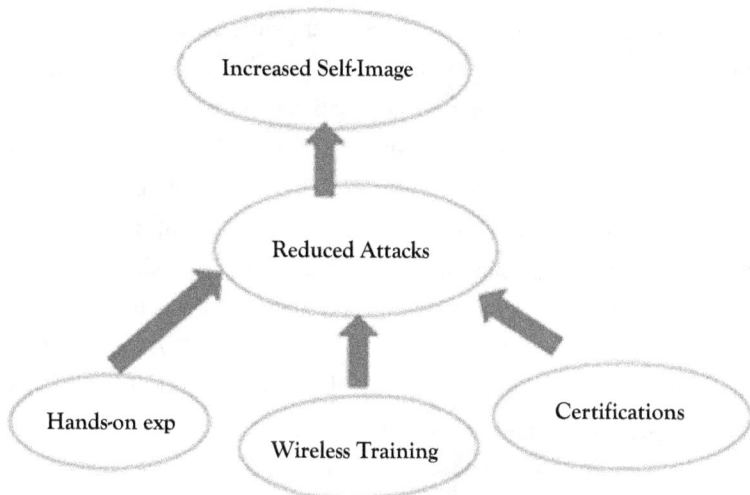

Figure 7.2 Multiple attribute means–end chain

In this case, I could several attributes—my wireless training, my hands-on experience, and my wireless certifications.

I could also have more (Figure 7.3):

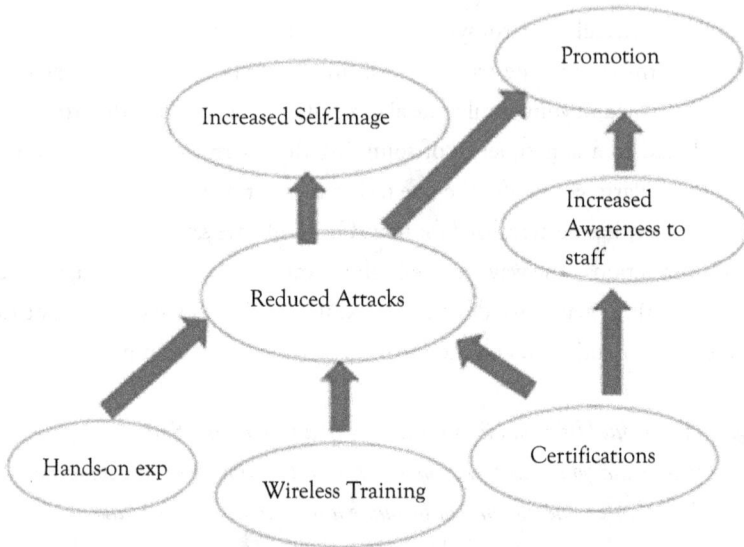

Figure 7.3 Multiple attribute, multiple consequences, multiple goals, means–end chain

In this case, my attributes of wireless training, my hands-on experience, and my wireless certifications could lead to both the number of reduced attacks, and the ability to share with others in my organization increased self-awareness of wireless attacks. Then it may lead to me improving my self-image in the company and possible promotions. As you may be able to tell, this can get very complicated. In a previous book I wrote, *the Value Matrix Approach*, I looked at eight dimensions of electronic commerce, and in one of those dimensions, information technology infrastructure, a map similar to Figure 7.4 appeared.

It's not important to understand the actual meanings, but rather the linkages that are created, as this one was done in B2B electronic commerce. The goals are just generic goals that anyone would have, such as increased sales, convenience, and others were less upgrades, costs savings, and less downtime (all denoted by G1, G3, G7, etc.). Consequences were

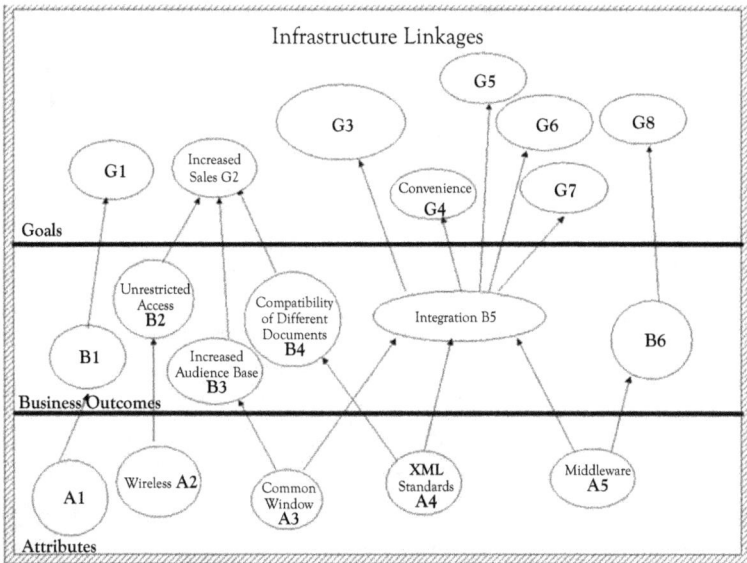

Figure 7.4 Advanced means–end chain.

unrestricted access, integration, and compatibility of different documents, followed by attributes, such as wireless, XLM standards, and Middleware.

The important thing to remember is that goals typically will not change, because if they did, modern manufacturing could not exist. Your desire for a certain type of goal may change, but not the goal itself. Imagine people wanting an automobile with four wheels, and then six months later, wanting an automobile with only three wheels. Manufacturing could not exist for building a four-wheel automobile one month, only to have it not being sold a few months later. Therefore, automobile safety would always be a goal. Consequences are somewhat stable and will change over time. Instead of a consequence of an airbag inflating in front of me from the dashboard, it now inflates to the side of me, protecting my head. Finally, the attributes will change a lot—an airbag installed in the steering wheel vs. an airbag installed in the top of side door.

At the end of creating all the linkages among the attributes, values and goals across categories, a value chain matrix is typically drawn (Figure 7.5).

The Value Matrix							
If Your Firm's Goals Include:	You Should Use These Dimensions:						
	Infrastructure	Process	Assessment	Media	Procurement	Delivery	Collaboration	Electronic Markets
Better Business Pleanning				X	X			
Better Purchasing Decisions		X				X		
Better Relationships					X		X	X
Better Resource Allocation		X						X
Centralized Place for Information				X			X	
Compete Qulickly		X						X
Creating a Better Strategy		X					X	
Faster Internet B2B Presence								X
Gain Competitive Advantages	X		X	X			X	
Improved Pricing Strategy			X	X	X			X
Improved Revenue Stream Prediction			X					
Increased Liquidity of Products						X		X
Increased Benefits To Company			X	X				X
Increased Convenience for Organization	X			X				
Increased Customer Satisfaction		X						
Increased Global Opportunities							X	X
Increased levels of Turst								
Increased Probability of Future Business		X	X	X		X		
Increased Productivity	X	X		X	X	X		X
Increased Resources for Other Programs		X						
Increased Sales	X	X		X		X	X	X
Increased Sales Per Employee				X	X			
Increased Understanding of Your business			X					
Increased Market Share		X			X			
Keeping Investment in Older Systems	X							
Keeping Distributors in Business							X	
		X						
Monitoring Across the B2B Enterprise	X	X					X	
No Unforseen Issues						X		X
No Vested Interests								X
Optimum Amonunt of Personnel		X						
Partners Acting Quickly to Help							X	
Potentila Customer's Bookmark Page	X			X				
Push Technology					X	X		
Reduce Costs on Purchasing and Labor					X			
Reduce Fradulent Charges		X			X			
Reduce Inventory Costs					X	X		X
Reduce Legal Exposure					X			
Redundancy of Systems	X							
Sense of Belonging							X	X
Staying in Business						X		X
Tailored Customer Pricing				X				

Figure 7.5 Value matrix map

After all the chains are developed, a value matrix is drawn. Across the top are just dimensions of B2B electronic commerce, and down the left side are goals mentioned. As we have discussed in this chapter, motivations and goals may drive our behavior, and the value matrix and means–end chain may show factors of motivation. In this last section on means–end chain and laddering, we stated that goals will not change; otherwise modern manufacturing could not exist. A little earlier, we said our goals are also in motion. So, do they change or are they stable? We cannot really answer this question because it is not clear-cut; if it were, we would understand motivation, and then be able to predict behavior. Researchers have noted that challenging goals are much better than specific goals up to a point of specificity. We therefore break a reachable goal into smaller parts, always keeping the end in sight, and if that end is too far away, we will just abandon the goal. Our self-awareness also comes into play—I do not want to fail, and I will do everything to avoid that end goal, including sabotage if I think I will fail. There are many things about goals that motivate us and have been broken down into all kinds of goals including generic goals, specific goals, challenging goals, and simple goals. It seems we have all kinds of goals, and each one can motivate us differently and guide our behavior. However, it is clear from the bigger picture that goals may change, but may change slowly over time, and not days or weeks, but years and decades, so perhaps both views are correct.

Legitimate or Illegitimate, the DNC Hack of 2016, and the Rest Is History

Probably, one of the most famous cyberattack that will live in history is that of the Democratic National Committee (DNC) attack of 2016 (Lipton, Sanger, and Shane 2016). A simple phishing attack, attributed by U.S. intelligent agencies to a hacking group with ties to Russia, led to incredible turmoil in the 2016 U.S. presidential elections. This attack, like most successful attacks started months before, and as we have seen throughout this book, these attacks do not suddenly come on. There were warnings, and even the DNC was alerted in 2015 of potential breaches. In the event of the DNC attacks, this was only a starting point, as the attackers jumped off the DNC networks to attack outside targets whose information they gleaned from the DNC computer servers to be able to continue their attack.

Think of the details of what was happening. Candidate Hillary Clinton is running against Donald Trump. While Ms. Clinton was battling Congressional hearings on the use of a private e-mail server, the DNC was allegedly favoring Ms. Clinton over challenger Bernard Sanders from Vermont for the Democratic nomination. The DNC has to be in chaos battling these fires and not wanting any bad press to get out. As the same time the FBI field office was telling DNC staffers that there were intrusions going on, but unfortunately for the DNC, the FBI was being clandestine in its communications with the DNC since they did not want to tip off the Russians hackers. All this led to confusion on the part of all the staff of the DNC, and we can surmise chatter among individuals in the

DNC who were caught between the current campaign and the Russian intrusion.

So, how where they motivated?
The goal gradient hypothesis may lead to a possible answer.

We work harder the closer we get to achieving a goal; for the DNC staffers, that goal was the election, not the hack. Everyone's emphasis was on winning the election, not the day-in, day-out of running the computer systems. So, when the dreadful day that an e-mail landed on Mr. Podesta to change his password, it was not from a simple e-mail, but from a trusted source inside the DNC who made a typo in an e-mail, from illegitimate to legitimate and once that link was clicked, the rest is political history.

The goal gradient hypothesis tells us the closer we get to a goal, the harder we work at that goal and the more accelerate toward that goal. The other issue at hand we discussed is that we have limited brain processing power, so when we are racing toward a goal, any goal, we concentrate on that goal, and forsake other cognitive reasonings, and then coupled with Mr. Podesta receiving change your password from a trusted friend (i.e., the compliance bias), the situational constraints of Mr. Podesta may have led him to be in conformity with that fateful e-mail to change his password (i.e., this is a legitimate e-mail).

Cybersecurity Implications and Conclusions

Motivations are wonderful to get us. Well, motivated, they get us moving, aspiring, reaching for that goal. We are in the reach of something special, or so we hope, but motivations hurt us as well. We looked at some theories that might help us explain motivation but there are many more (e.g., piece rate theory; I will pay you more per unit of something you create), the Hawthorne effect (Landsberger 1958), originally designed for better working conditions, but the result was more socio-psychological significance in that simple observing individuals proved more effective, Maslow's hierarchy needs, Theory X, Theory Y, and many more, but all these seem to motivate us, not inhibit us, which at times might seem the realistic course to take. However, it turns out there may be research that can help us answer this dilemma. Woody and Szechtman (2013) suggest we may have a hard-wired gene (i.e., a brain circuit), similar to a security motivation system that helps us and warns us against threats (e.g., walking down a dark alley, parking near security cameras, and lights at night). Humans may have developed this from an animal's instinct to protect themselves from predators, whereas humans are cognitive of their environment as well. An issue here further developed by Brown et al. (1993), and Wingfield et al. (1998) suggests that even with weak cues we become very vigilant, and once turned on, this defense mechanism takes a long time to shut off, which in turn may drive behavior. These weak cues will kick the security motivation system in high alert, even without further confirmation. In the case of a physical threat, we might be able to see what is in front of us and the threat, but in cybersecurity, the threat could be illusionary, which even make us more prone to act in such a way. We do not want to act without full information, but the nature of cybersecurity contradicts this. A result of this is that in this system and in the light of threats, activation causes the security motivation system to engage in some behavior. These activities are then used as a condition to eventually terminate the motivation and those behaviors. As an example, we find an infected e-mail, and our security motivation guard becomes active. We then seek to clean and remove the virus from the system. After which, we install antivirus protection, and these actions shut down our security motivation guard, and the initial motivations that led to this action. It's an interesting study, since the unknown variable is the subject who is exhibiting the security motivation guard. In their study they were concerned with human ailments such as anxiety, obsessive-compulsive disorders, not cybersecurity, but their proposition of a hard-wired system, which could be of great benefit in the cybersecurity field since the proposed hard-wired system does have roots in one's biology and traits. In regards to this and our understanding of motivation, do our self-protection mechanisms prevent ourselves from developing the best cybersecurity solutions we can in lieu of the threat faced? Is the threat from my manager if I do not finish in time, will I be fired? Is the threat real or imaginary? What if I do this, what if I don't finish this, what if this, what if that, and so on, and we continue to build upon what-ifs. Woody and Szechtman suggest that within these threats there are two kinds of systems: a feelings-based system and a rational based system. It is not always evident, even to us, which one is primary and in control. Therefore, in the condition of partial cues, which one is dominant or in the condition of major incidents which one will become dominant. Are we more monotonically motivated to accomplish a goal such as meeting a deadline to finish a cybersecurity goal? In all of these scenarios, our motivations, either consciously or subconsciously, are driving our behavior, and we have to be aware.

CHAPTER 8

Social Influence

Introduction

Many of our behaviors are shaped by the circumstances we find ourselves in (e.g., think road rage). Sometimes we are calm and relaxed while driving, but other times we get behind an automobile steering wheel and get very angry; we may have seen others exhibit the same behavior. An interesting thing to remember is that we don't judge others as we would judge ourselves in the same instance. For example, we may have read a news report about someone driving a car down a highway over 100 miles per hour and think there is something wrong with that person: are they looking to hurt someone? However, if the driver was rushing someone to the hospital because he or she was just in a horrible accident at home, we might think differently. The actions we may or may not deem as wrong, but our motives of their underlying behavior would change. We still might assume there could have been other options that person could have taken, but we are less to assume that person was doing something on purpose to hurt someone. If we were driving at 100 miles per hour due to those same exact circumstances (i.e., saving the life of your child who just got into that horrible accident at home), how you rate your behavior? If your reasonings are different due to the driver, then what would cause our different reactions to the same set of circumstances?

Field Theory

In the 1920s Kurt Lewin believed that behavior was a function of the individual and the environment they found themselves in at the present time (i.e., the field). It is the psychological environment of the individual or a group's collective reasoning at any point in time. It's the totality of both that contribute to behavior. We can have helpful forces and hindering forces, like if someone in a group goes against the group's collective rationale for a decision the group is leaning toward. These forces are dynamic, the tensions are real and since the individual and environment change, so does this fluid nature, and so too will behavior change.

Later Lewin (1951) understood the body of research on change, and the reluctance of people to change, which is important since if we are affected by this field, we must change this field to motivate us to change behavior. He developed a model of three steps to change: (1) unfreeze, get individuals to understand the issues that are happening, (2) explain the need for upcoming change for survival and make the actual change, and (3) freeze that change. This model has been used in many organizations and is often used in project management when change is needed. A notable problem with this is that if taken to extremes, these decisions can cause some serious judgment errors that will cloud our corresponding behavior, like rushing to build a multimillion-dollar information technology project only to witness its failure.

Fundamental Attribution Error

We seem to ignore the circumstances that contributed to the behavior we deem objectionable. What led that person to drive 100 miles per hour, or whatever action it was we objected to, even though we might find ourselves in the same situation and would not consider it objectionable behavior. How many of us would not hesitate to break speeding laws to drive a loved one to a hospital? It is our belief that people act in the way they are, rather than the circumstance, or how we judge ourselves in the same circumstance. For example, you are late to a movie, a concert, a meeting, and you say, traffic was horrible, I had an important phone call, and so on. Someone else arrives late to the same venue, and you think, they are really rude, why didn't they leave earlier. The issue in this is that when we do something that might be offensive to others, we tend to blame the circumstances, but when others do the same thing, circumstances and situations are ignored and that person is to blame (Jones and Harris 1967). So, just how do circumstances dictate our behavior, and why are two behaviors that are identical are viewed differently depending on our point of view (i.e., we did we commit that behavior or did someone else commit the same exact behavior). There seems to be a few common ways we all engage that could help shed light on this phenomenon.

Conformity

I find no better example of this other than in the 1980s Television show Mash. When a character nicknamed Hawkeye (played by Alan Alda) asked Major Frank Buns (played by Larry Linville), what about individuality? Major Burns response was, "individually is fine, as long as we all do it together." That's conformity.

What people wear, how they act, how they vote, and what music they like. I remember hearing from my grandfather "why are you listening to that junk music, in my day we listened to real music." The issue can get really heated not only if we disagree with someone, but when we expect that someone to act in the same way we do, or the group we belong too. Groupthink is a classic example of conformity. In so much that we will choose the wrong answer, even if we know the answer to be wrong, just as long as we assume the rest of the group thinks it's the correct answer, when in reality, several others in the group could also agree with you, but our assumption is they do not.

Asch (1951) discovered that very few people are immured from groupthink, whether consciously or subconsciously. In his Asch conformity experiments, as typical in many experiments, there were individuals who were informed of the nature of the experiment and those who were unknowing participants. The test was very simple, there were three straight lines A, B, and C, and a target line. The test was to simply state which of the lines A, B, or C was closest in length to the target line.

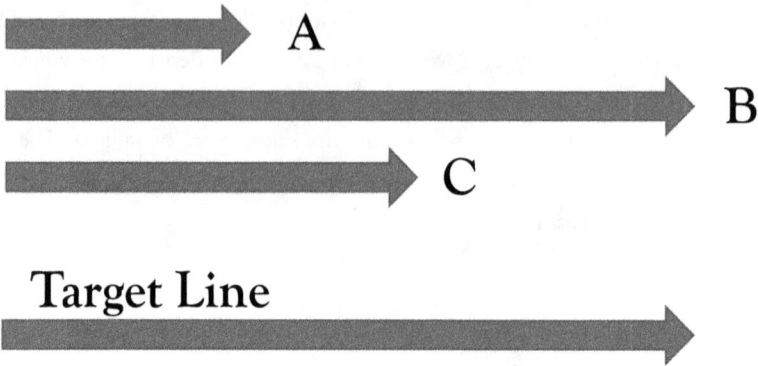

Figure 8.1 Which line is longer

The informed group was told to choose the wrong answer. There were no tricks on the lines like arrows pointing in different directions, just very simple straight lines. What was interesting was that after even knowing about the details of the experiment, people made an incorrect answer, while the other unknowing participants followed along with the group and agreed with the incorrect answer. When Asch conducted follow-up interviews with the unknowing group, they even admitted they knew they gave the wrong answer, they just wanted to go along with the group, to conform. So, even though they knew better, they wanted to conform to the rest of the group.

Compliance

Humans respect authority, even to levels that are unsafe. We trust them even more if they are introduced from a trusted person. For example, a person calls into an office building and gets the receptionist and tells the receptionist they need to speak to someone in billing and identifies themselves as a police officer. The receptionist would then contact someone in the billing department and tell them that a police officer is on the phone and needs to talk to someone. That person in billing may now take the word of that receptionist that the person on the call is a police officer, and trust this person more, even without identification.

Milgram's (1963) shock experiment showed that people will continue to hurt people, just as long as they have been told to do so, and even if they believe they are hurting that person. There is a chilling 2012 movie called *Compliance* by Craig Zobel. It goes beyond cruelty what some did to another person in the mistaken belief of authority. Yet, it only took one person to not to fall into compliance to stop the behavior. As the ending credits rolled, this was not an isolated incident and happens more than people would imagine. Can you see the real-world consequences of this behavior, and coupled with conformity?

This is a reason why social engineering attacks work so well, just like the sextortion attacks happening. Attacks that play on basic human conditions and traits are more successful. There are several different types of social engineering attacks; some include authority intimidation, consensus, or social proof, obtaining small amounts of information, impersonation, scarcity description, urgency description, trust description, all effecting some small trait.

As another example, social attackers will call up a company and tell the receptionist who answers the phone that they forgot the name of a person in legal and need that person to help them. After the receptionist gives the name of that person, the attacker thanks them and hangs up. A few weeks later, they will call up and identify themselves as a Police Lieutenant and that they need to speak to a person; of course, they will give the name of that person they found out a few weeks ago. The receptionist will now pass the phone call through, and if the attacker is lucky, the receptionist will tell that person in legal, "I have a Police Lieutenant who wishes to speak to you on an urgent matter." It's a simple trick in removing so many barriers. We have authority intimidation; Police Lieutenant, we have social proof; the receptionist concurs and affirms that this is Police Lieutenant; and we have impersonation and urgency description. Social engineering is not that complicated to correct, as there are no technical controls, but changing behavior is another thing all together.

The name social engineering is almost synonymous with probably the one who put the concept of social engineering attacks in everyone's vocabulary, and that was Kevin Mitnick. Mitnick understood early on the intricacies of technical knowledge with an understanding of human behavior. I do not necessarily think Mitnick was not a psychologist by training, but he did understand how people would react, and in his mischief days of the 1980s and 1990s, he caused a lot of companies' grief.

Mitnick was a magician, and we all know, people love magic tricks, and he pulled off a number of magical feats. We can be grateful these days Mitnick has turned his life around and runs a very successful computer security business. One of the greatest things we learned from Mitnick *was that we learned*. He shared with us his secrets and we have now developed better social engineering training, and more checks and balances in verifying people who claim they are.

Play Your Part

A very interesting and very horrific experiment was done in a prison setting using non-prisoners and non-guards to see just how much participants would follow instructions from authorities, in the infamous Stanford Prison Study. The Stanford Prison Study (Haney, Banks, and Zimbardo 1973) helped to show just how much in character people will become and stay depending on conditions.

It was not a psychological thriller movie but was a psychological reality experiment that was going incredibly wrong, so much so that the experiment had to be stopped due to the abuse of the actors playing a part. People you could laugh with, have lunch with, joke with, and so on, took on the role of play guards in a make-believe prison setting and unleashed terror on the play acting of another group of individuals pretending to be inmates. At the beginning everything was fine, but those playing guards took on a new life in playing the part of guards in correcting those playing the roles of inmates, and taking directions from those running the experiment. Even when the inmates and guards themselves were raising concerns about the experiments, the researchers kept pushing them to continue the role of the guard, and as such they grew more and more into this role, and began to exhibit more negative behavior they were already exhibiting. While there has been a lot of criticisms on the part of the experiment, there is enough evidence to show that people will play a role, will cause pain in that role, and continue to do so upon continued instructions.

Situational Constraints

During certain situations, if someone is told to do something, they will forgo everything else to get that thing done. I need certain supplies to get a task accomplished, but if time to procure those supplies are prohibitive, I will forgo the normal process to get that task accomplished. I will bend the rules to suit my circumstances and what I deem important. Therefore, depending on my circumstances and situations I find myself in, my behavior will be different. One being rushed makes one overlook things they normally would not. They would also display tendencies in one place where these tendencies would not be shown in another. For example, I may be timid because of my boss, but at home, I consider myself king and everyone will bow to me.

Persuasion

We can normally be predicted to act in a certain way, but we can also be persuaded to act in a completely different way. We can be persuaded to act against our own beliefs, attitudes, intentions, and motivations, and it is usually not hard or difficult. New information, or an emergency, an interesting sales pitch, or a sense of danger will all factor into our thinking and change our behavior. Physical appearances play a role—the more attractive a person is, the more appealing that person may appear to be, and the more likely we will change our personality and agree with that person.

Erving Groffman (1959) argues that impression management plays a role in the way we try to manipulate the way others see us. Personality is the sum of roles in everyday life, and all of them, teachers, workers, management, lovers, friends, rolled up into one. He does suggest this works better if others also believe you belong in this role. If you go to a movie and see an actor or actress, you expect them to live and present themselves a certain way, and therefore they should live up to that part and present themselves that way. Wardrobe, hair, shoes, all the props of movie stars. When you think of a computer hacker, what impression do they give off? Is there any specific traits you can identify? Impressions can also be names, such as the hacker group Anonymous. What do you sense when you hear that name? Persuasion certainly effects our buying, forcing us to buy something we would never buy, but the store is going out of business, or the item is the last one on clearance, and only a few boxes left on the shelf, so it offers buy one get one free. This will make people behave in ways you would never imagined, including themselves.

What happens to some people on Black Friday?

Reciprocity

You probably have heard the saying, if you scratch my back, I'll scratch yours.

It's usually the result of positive kind actions, if you do something positive for me, I will do a beneficially thing for you, although not always verbalized, but always implied. The need is to be weighed against negative reciprocity and against gaining someone's unwilling compliance. If we give a token of something before the request for reciprocity is made, it is more positive that the request will be fulfilled. Negative reciprocity sometimes is called revenge—an evil act committed on someone will result in an evil act in return. There is also the rejection-retreat reciprocity, where the first attempt to ask for something big, then back off and ask for something smaller (e.g., a smaller donation at first), then come back after a time to ask again for a larger donation. There are also other ways we are persuaded to do, or buy something we would not normally do—we are given offers, or offered some concessions, as in the act of bargaining and promotions. Moreover, in many of these types of persuading techniques, we will often see a number stated, like 45 percent of the population recycles, 76 percent of people back national health care, and 34 percent of people are against trophy hunting. Just by the introduction of a number, real or not, can help, or trick, into persuading people. That is why persuasion, advertising, marketing, and so on, are so effective, because we change our behavior by persuasion. This is why companies selling us things will not always try to sell us a big item, but instead a smaller item (e.g., an add-on package to an existing product or service) you have. It's much easier selling that, because we purchased that smaller add-on. We might then be persuaded to buy something much bigger, a brand-new phone with a new two-year contract later on.

An interesting thing about persuasion is that people who have been successfully persuaded and went against how they would normally act is that they would later say, I would have never done that in 100 years. As we have examined our neural network associations, these associations have informed us this wasn't a good idea, but we ignored them anyway and did exactly what we said we would never do. We then compound our own internal reasoning by way of confirmation bias, well, perhaps it really wasn't that bad of a deal, or perhaps I can get some good use out of this. Perhaps, just say I fell for the sales pressure, and hopefully I can learn from it the next time it happens and you can probably be sure, another sales tactic is right around the corner.

Mere Exposure Effect

Another very interesting phenomenon is the mere exposure effect. After a while of just being exposed to something makes that something more acceptable (i.e., the more you see it, the more you like it). While you may not like it, you are less disposed to do something about it. The more familiarity becomes, the more attitude changes, and the more familiarity with the changes, the faster the attitude changes, and quite possibly on a subconscious level, preferences and affection change as well.

Zajonc (1980) argued that preferences could be based on exposure, not beliefs or attitudes directly. Our feelings and thoughts are very independent of each other, but many times we make decision with force (i.e., impulse, fast, instinctive, without information). In the context of social facilitation, it is possible that higher cognitive processes are just not primaries and often used in social personation. This happens in relationships, where a man and woman for the most part would mate with someone they know or knew for a while and is in a close proximal distance. Also, to the effect of empathy, where old people tend to look similar in features.

Psychology of Blame

Was your coffee cold this morning? Did you get stuck behind a slow driver? Did you arrive late to work? All of us have had days like that, but some individuals take it to the extreme and blame others. The company that made the coffee machine makes horrible products; even though you made the same coffee yesterday and the day before. You were late work even though you left later than normal for work and that person wasn't going slower, but you were just going faster trying to make up for leaving late. Can you ever recall why you had that bad day at the office, and the only thing you can remember is it was someone else's fault? Some people even just blame themselves. Your two coworkers are fighting and somehow it's your fault. You see someone slip on a piece of garbage that you saw a few moments ago and did not pick up. That person could have simply not been paying attention, and you could blame them for not paying attention, or perhaps you blame yourself for not picking up that piece of garbage. Well, it's the psychology of blame (Alicke 2000; Burger 1981; Shaver 1970). Blaming others or yourself is a psychology of attribution—you blame yourself or others for things that happen; after all, someone always has to be responsible. But, do you blame equally? For example, consider two cars speeding down the road, where one gets into an accident and the other does not. Are they both equally guilty? Was their intent just to speed that caused the accident? We have to blame someone, or maybe I will blame myself as I saw them speeding but did not call the police in time.

Blame has some real challenges, as it helps our cognitive defenses: (1) it's convenient—you were there, you saw what happened, so it's great for my defense; (2) an attack countermeasure—don't blame me for that, even if I caused the problem, after all, they made me do that, I was told to; (3) behavior is illusive—I have no idea why they did that, or even why I did that, so you know it's just their fault, and (4) just lie—maybe they won't find out it was really me.

Psychology of blame is a self-serving bias, and many times we may see someone take credit for good things that happen, yet blame others when bad things happen. If you pass a test, it's because you studied very hard and deserved passing, but if you failed, the test was at fault; there were things on that test that were not on the study material, or I was feeling sick that day. Do you think this just happens to one individual? You would be surprised that a majority of people blame others for anything and everything that happens. I would never walk down a dark alley; she was asking to get robbed. I would never invest my money just because I see their ads on television; he deserved to lose all his money. He deserved to get laid off; he was doing a lousy job anyway. Besides I know I will save enough money in case that happens to me. The concept of blaming others may be an important trait, or condition. It's a lack of self-awareness, it's a form of psychological projection, and we are projecting undesirable feelings, emotions, and opinions on others. While blaming others can affect behavior, one of the most serious conditions of blaming others is the contagious impact it has. It is a socially contagious phenomenon that can really hinder an organization's collective posture, putting others in bad moods, ineffective teamwork, and by legitimizing your own actions by blaming others contributes to an overall ineffective organizational culture, and one that should not exist in any, especially in a cybersecurity culture, where there is more than enough blame to go around.

Cognitive Dissonance

When circumstances force us to change our behavior, *we will also change our attitudes toward that behavior.*

It's important to read those words again, as they are deeply troubling. We will also change our attitudes toward that behavior. Our beliefs clash with our actions, or what we believe to be true. Even with irrefutable evidence, we go against our better judgments and accept the alternative. The anti-vaccine arguments, flat-earth believers, Holocaust deniers. It gets to a point where someone will do everything they can to find evidence to support their belief that the earth is flat, or vaccinations kill, and ignore all other evidence. A major issue here is not the belief itself, but the behavior that follows, as some will go out of their way to convince others of their own belief to satisfy their own internal discord and that behavior could result in harmful action to others. If a person has cognitive dissonance, he or she sees the world to be round as they would in a typical educational upbringing (e.g., the moon landing photos, photos from satellites, NASA images, etc.), but believes they are all lies and the earth is really flat; so then how could they function in the real world. Not all start out with cognitive dissonance; many anti-vaxxers were originally pro-vaccine, but due to something they read or heard about—a newspaper article, a meeting they attended, hearing the illness of some child who got a vaccine when they were a baby—they changed their belief. Coronel et al. (2020) reported that people may even purposely misremember information to match their beliefs. Given accurate information about a subject, people will misremember key data points if it does not match their beliefs. Further, when giving others information on a subject that conflicts with one's beliefs, the data gets even further from the truth.

This is why dis-information is so destructive; it spreads and can spread rapidly.

Festinger and Carlsmith (1959) did a very interesting experiment on cognitive dissonance and forced compliance theory by conducting a very boring experiment of turning some yarn spools, and then recording participants reactions to an imposter actor of the experiment to convince them the study was fun. Two groups of participants were awarded, each either $1.00 or $20.00, but the $1.00 group also had the imposter. As expected, the $1.00 group rated the experiment more highly than the $20.00 group. The experiment was very boring, but the $1.00 group had to internalize and experienced cognitive dissonance between what was real and what they were led to believe. There are other social influence experiments that have an impact on how we can be persuaded. Moscovici (2000) stated it could arise from curiosity; we want to know other things, engage with others, and join the conversation. The more we converse, the more our value systems will merge, and as a collective set of common senses, but not in the sense to advance any knowledge. Recall, we spoke about the mere exposure effect earlier. Glasser's (1998) choice theory states that while we are driven by needs like food and clothing (e.g., Maslow's hierarchy of needs), but we are also driven by many of the ills we face that are by choice (i.e., our own makings). We want to increase pleasure, we want to decrease pain, we want to feel love and belongings, and therefore we will make choices to reach those needs. Lerner and Simmons (1966) proposed the *just world theory* that good things happen to good people, and bad things happen to bad people. That we want to believe we live in a just world, and if something bad happens to a good person, somehow, they deserved that. Think back to the psychology of blame.

After the horrendous Kent State college shooting in 1970, people wanted to believe that military reserve officers would never shoot unarmed students. So, rumors were started saying the college students engaged in action that resulted in their own deaths. This may not have been with malicious intent, in that people wanted to believe in a just world, and could not believe police officers would kill people (i.e., cognitive dissonance). This can happen in a doctor's office, when a doctor would say you are causing your own problems, or you hear about a woman getting raped in a dark parking lot, and you rationalize that you would never be the victim of such an incident, since you know better than to be in such a dark and lonely place. Aronson (1972) even argued we are all somewhere on the line of sane to insane, just we differ on the spot we sit. Sane people do crazy things, and if we are unaware of social circumstances that engaged them, we may label them as crazy.

Life Is Short, Have an Affair

What a slogan, and a very interesting business. This was the slogan of Adult FriendFinder, which unfortunately was the victim of a successful attack in May 2015 (Ragan 2015; Peterson 2019; Whittaker 2016; Staff 2016). I am not sure if we can imagine what was going on in the minds of the security personnel at Adult FriendFinder after it was revealed that over three million records were uncovered. Apparently, the damage could have been much higher if the original claim of the entire 60 million records that Adult FriendFinder claims to have were compromised. But it seems after initial reports of three million accounts hacked, it turned out to be much worse in that over 400 million accounts were hacked. Even deleted accounts attacks were uncovered, as Adult FriendFinder and affiliated company FriendFinder was targeted.

Was it three million, 60 million, 400 million? Not sure if we will ever know, but it's probably safe to assume millions of records were compromised. It was probably very difficult to pinpoint an exact number since the data went back 20 years. Older accounts were not removed—people who quit the service, people who deleted their accounts. It turned out their deleted accounts weren't actually deleted. People who may have just quit or perhaps died, so we will probably never know an exact number. Still, it still was a massive attack, and unfortunately, the credentials of clients of Ashley Madison are still at risk. More recent research shows that those stolen credentials are now used in sextortion schemes (Fazzini 2020).

So, what happened, what caused this to occur?

It seems this attack was one of revenge. Adult FriendFinder owed someone money, a ransom was then demanded, it wasn't paid, and the successful attack occurred. An investigation revealed a local file inclusion attack. Basically it allows a file to be included into another application (e.g., an image can be infected to then run an application), and the output of that application can grant access, display an image, and so on, but in this case instead of displaying pornography, it displayed account numbers. With this access, user names, e-mail addresses, and passwords were retrieved. There are many issues here, but just looking at the reasons, could it rest on social influence? Pornography has always had an impact on social activity and pressures, infidelity as well, but to acknowledge, not all these accounts are the infidelity kind as there were also many single consenting adults. And we are not even discussing why local file inclusion would be an issue. The real reason is why was this allowed to happen in the first place? Why was over 20 years of data still stored on data. In another instance, another site associated with the pornography industry, PussyCash, announced a breach of one of their Amazon storage data buckets. PussyCash acted as an affiliate to paying pornography sites, and as such, had a lot of personal data to verify clients, like passports, driver licenses, credit card numbers, and so on, Luckily, the breach was detected by a security team who alerted the company. But the reason they were successful was that the data was unsecured and unencrypted. PussyCash response was that the data was from 2013, and the data was eventually secured the same day they were notified (vpnMentor 2020).

So, could some of the answers here lie in the psychology of blame? We blame others and we extort others. If you gamble and lose your home, it's your fault. If you walk down a darkened alley and get robbed, it's your fault. If you choose to be associated with a company where affairs are encouraged, again, it's your fault. Could the management of the company itself even use this excuse: hey, if you use this site, it's your own fault for cheating, don't blame us if you get caught. Very limited details are on the actual breach, but I do hope medical companies are safeguarding patient information, as we can see very similar scenarios; you smoke and have lung cancer—your fault; you are overweight and have diabetes—your fault; you have HIV—again your fault. The psychology of blame can really influence our behavior, or lack thereof.

Cybersecurity Implications and Conclusions

Are cybersecurity professionals fully aware of the threats companies face? Are they sure of their skills? Are they in denial of just how many threats are out there? During a panel discussion at an event hosted by Artic Wolf Networks in 2016, there was a discussion on cyber dissonance—what we believe and what is reality. As in many cyber research studies, managers and security professionals were overly optimistic on how they believe their companies cybersecurity positions were vs. reality in what the role of cybersecurity even means.

Putting it another way, I am sure I know I am guarding against threats well enough; I just don't know what threats I am guarding against. Confusing, right, or put another way, I will figure it out later.

Which in reality is the standard course of the majority of businesses. After an attack, get back up online, restore backups, get everyone working again, and then, when we have time to investigate what happened, we will. The next time comes; it's a different attack and we start the cycle anew. This describes the reality of cybersecurity—just how is the role defined, what areas are a cybersecurity professional responsible for, what is the meaning of a cybersecurity professional's life. Could it be like this chapter describes, social pressure and affiliations? If you are a member of a router group, will all your cybersecurity solution be primarily to routers, and if this vendor's product works with routers well enough, their solution to viruses should work well enough. Trust has been shown to cloud our judgments, so the closer we are to a social group, the more we may fall vulnerable (Tetri and Vuorinen 2013). Ever go to the National Security Agency's (NSA) yearly conference on cybersecurity, or any of the other security conferences held every year across the world? In a sense, these are social groups and their influence is present. If you are a member of a Windows working group, will all your cybersecurity solution be primary to Windows? Any group, Linux, Blockchain, social media, and BYOD, does your group affiliation direct your behavior to put in more safeguards for that group's position, and less from another group's position? Will the conformity and compliance pressures from your group direct your behaviors to get along with that group, even if you know things to be incorrect? You know things could be incorrect (i.e., your beliefs), but you want to comply (i.e., pressure), and an internal fight within yourself begins (i.e., dissonance). You start to change your beliefs (i.e., social influence), and then you look for evidence that aligns with your new beliefs (i.e., confirmation bias).

Have you noticed we always hear that the employee is the weakest link in the cybersecurity chain? But as we look at all areas, we have to understand there a number of things that direct employee's behavior—persuasion, conditions, traits, among others. If we don't examine the connections, sure a company could get rid of an employee, but the social pressure is still there and affecting everyone else. Some researchers want to examine what is called social cybersecurity to help others become better aware of threats. Based upon Cialdini's 1984 work on social proof, people tend to copy those around them to participate in the same forms of behavior. It's the act of social influence where people emulate others to take the appropriate form of behavior. Social proof is a type of conformity, but we have just seen earlier, conformity can be a bad thing to occur. But perhaps social proof as a type of conformity could be also a benefit to a company. This could be, and a very worthwhile look at individual's behaviors on a social connection level if we believe the employee is the weakest link. However, this book is not on the end-user employee's behavior, it's on the cybersecurity behavior. So, in this case, the social influence that might cause our actions would not be our friends getting their accounts hacked, but rather the social influences we see and read about the latest attacks, and possible remediation measures. Remember, social influences have a great impact on your potential eventual dissonance.

CHAPTER 9

Stereotypes

Introduction

We discussed cognitive economy earlier, where we group things together to help us save mental energy, for example, dogs, cars, trees, and so on. We also do this with people as well, and it's called stereotyping. If you think about it just a little bit, you might realize we have a lot of categories, and many of them are even derogatory categories for all kinds of people.

Stereotyping

Stereotyping is just another example of a neural network association we have about people's race, color, political leaning, jobs, ethnicity, and so on. Whatever the group, we have an association for that group. In some limited sense, stereotyping is fine as it helps us to function. If I am making a lesson plan for French people, I am going to assume (i.e., stereotype, they speak French). If I am making a meal for people of Mediterranean origin, I might make something according to a Mediterranean diet, like fish and nuts. If I am creating an advanced class on behavioral security, I am going to assume (i.e., stereotype) that they know some of the basics of security. This does not means it's correct in the group as a whole but generalizable, and it could also be incorrect (e.g., the French group could have been a group that has been in America for the last 20 years and speak English well), and they want the course to be in English, so in this case more information was needed. This is also the basis for many scholarly PhD dissertations. We want to generalize it to a much larger population, another example of stereotype. The small specific sample we used can be generalized and then stereotyped to the larger specific population as a whole. We conduct medical tests on groups of people: sometimes different ethnicity, sometimes different genders, sometimes different ages. After our results, if acceptable, we then generalize it to a larger population of that same ethnicity, gender, or age group. However, in a scholarly dissertation, we normalize the population, meaning we expect the overall larger population to have the same characteristics as our sample group, but it is a stereotype. That specific population will have those same characteristics as our sample should respond the same way given the same procedure. Unfortunately, while there are exceptions where stereotyping is useful, as a practical matter it is almost always wrong. French people like bread and wine so they must be fat. Search for images of French people, and it seems that bread and wine can actually make one skinny, a contradiction. But that itself, bread and wine can make French people skinny, is a stereotype. Short people have a problem reaching high things so we shouldn't trust them, yes, there are people who believe dwarfs are untrustworthy. Many Middle Eastern men have beards, and the terrorists I've seen also have beards, so anyone having a beard is a terrorist.

So, after all these years, we find out Santa Clause was a terrorist.

Wearing a fur coat, black hat, white dress, painted toenails on a man, tattoos on a woman, his name is Boris, he's from Russia, his name is Guido, definitely in the Italian mob. You name it, we have a stereotype. A very bad behavior we exhibit is that even in the face of evidence, our stereotyping still exists, and we will not change them. Remember our neural network associations are very strong, and like we have read, they have to align with what we think we believe. We do not want to be in conflict, so up acts our cognitive dissonance. While we normally believe vaccines are good, if I am an anti-vaxxer, all doctors are evil since they push vaccines on innocent children. Our associations, our experiences, everything we have seen and learned through life help us to deal with new situations. Stereotypes persist in the face of evidence, and groups help to amplify the effect and misunderstandings. We reinforce stereotypes by talking about them, and our top-down thinking further influences what we see.

Stereotypes and Priming

We discussed the priming effect earlier; it also works with stereotyping. We start with something small, and let our associations influence the stereotype. Let me tell you about this Italian Godfather; wait, tell me no more, I can finish the story. He was such a handsome boy, wait, my Jewish grandmother always says that about me. In bad cases of stereotyping, Italian godfathers are not associated with the mob. Groups further interact and strengthen this link (i.e., the rumor mill)—or tell a story to one person, he tells the story to the next person, she tells it to another girl, then to another guy and so on, and eventually it comes back around, and nothing like the original story. In each iteration of the telling of the story pieces are missing, but what is then filled in is each own person's associations and stereotypes. It's what helps us function in society.

Insidious Social Repercussions

Sometimes we tell little white lies, but then they turn into really big lies and we get caught. But sometimes they work in reverse, as when a teacher tells a student, "I expect great things from you," and sometimes the student will actually improve. We could say, "you will never amount to anything," or "you are useless," and if it comes from a trusted authority, that person may actually believe and act in that manner. When we believe what other people think about, or tell us, can reflect in our own behavior, so these negative stereotyping can lead to self-fulfilling prophecies. Feedback stereotyping loop can also occur. The police officer is watching me, he makes me nervous. The police officer thinks that person is acting nervous so he must have done something. There is also the racist and ethnic negative stereotypes, where just belonging to a certain group makes one believe you are more likely to commit a crime. A negative stereotype directed at you can undermine your own performance. Poor people are dumb because they never really worked at improving themselves (e.g., by going to college). Since I am poor, therefore I am dumb and I should accept that since so many people say I am dumb. You cannot spell, so you are really stupid. Well, since I can't spell, maybe they are right and I am really stupid, and perhaps I won't even learn how to be a better speller.

In research conducted by Schrader and Hall (2014), they reported that black students did worse on an achievement test when they were told the test measured intelligence. However, when black students were presented with the same test, but this time told it was a problem-solving test, they did much better. So, what was the negative stereotyping that may have been prevalent in these black students' lives concerning the word intelligence? You say to your kids you are going to end up behind bars. The child might think, well, since I will end up in prison anyway, why try to change myself. Unfortunately, it takes a very strong positive personality to overcome all these stereotyping directed at someone. It is not all bad as many of these stereotyping can be overcome by associations with groups and by familiarity with the object of the stereotype in question. Common interest groups, goals, religious affiliations, and social support groups all help to overcome the negative effects of stereotyping; of course, we have other worries like we have already spoken about. We must be always vigilant since we tend to think more positively about the group we are associated with, and more negatively toward different groups. When we are in groups, our behavior tends to enhance the groups we belong. Further, sometimes members in the group will apply social pressures to others in the group to become more radical. People believe that People for the Ethical Treatment of Animals (PETA), or Antifa are terrorist organizations, or people who are in the anti-vaxxers groups are dumb. We really can categorize and label almost every association.

Gender

We can find lots of opinions on gender and stereotypes, but we want to understand where is the focus of that stereotype. Is it strictly gender (e.g., women are not representative in cybersecurity fields), or is it that women do not gear toward competencies in cybersecurity? Is it from an outward viewpoint, in that a male gender does not think that a female gender would make a good cybersecurity professional? Gender norms are very ingrained into society from the time a child is born, and these gender stereotypes are very real and make a big impact (e.g., nurse, female; car mechanic, male; pilot, male; secretary, female). These are cultural stereotypes as well and they are very hard to break. Is the stereotype an inward perspective, perhaps a female gender does not think cybersecurity is a long-lasting stable field? Notice as well, by just saying female or male, that in itself is a stereotype, and has to do more with our languages and feminine-dominant terms. In addition, given an ethnicity, Asians, Blacks, Italians, Irish, German, Latino, these feminine or dominant terms are not consistent. Therefore, it is important to understand the lens it's being placed under for observation. It could be that simply not having enough of any certain race or gender is not really stereotyping, but from a person's viewpoint and if they believe they would be stereotyped if choosing a field, that can have very real negative consequences. Perhaps it's just awareness; we touched on mere exposure effect, so perhaps the more aware cybersecurity becomes, the more the overall field will be representative of the population within. Certainly, we can see a lot of Hollywood movies that have cybersecurity tag lines and many different genders and races fill that role, and as we can now see a lot of male nurses. Examining behavior and stereotyping can impact the way behavior is being reflected, as we have seen with language and feminine-dominant terms. Raiffa (1982) examined negotiations and regarded weak negotiators as emotional, irrational, too much of trying to be a peacemaker, whereas the best negotiators terms that were described were assortative, decisive, and rational, not a peacemaker, but a deal maker. If you were to ask someone what gender do you associate with the terms emotional, irrational, peacemaker, unfortunately many will say that is of the feminine gender and their guiding behavior may reflect this thinking (i.e., she doesn't know what she's talking about, she's too irrational), or if the term associated was adolescent, we might hear, "let the grownups handle this." To have this approach in cybersecurity and not heed any advice just because of the female gender is very short-sighted and can make costly mistake. Individuals who hold these stereotypes should really look up the name Hedy Lamar, or the thousands of women code breakers during World War II. You might as well research Betty Shannon (1948), whose *A Mathematical Theory of Communication*, launched the field of information theory.

Considering that World War II ended over 70 years ago, but gender stereotypes still exist today, either we still have a long way to go, or the issue is just not understood enough, or perhaps we are still looking at it all wrong. Of course, one does not have to go back to World War II;

the Electronic Frontier Foundation's current director of cybersecurity Eva Galperin has taken a role in protecting privacy for vulnerable populations and came up with the Surveillance Self Defense, which enables users to help themselves protect their data. Another important consideration is that Galperin understands the cross-disciplinary nature of cybersecurity and mixes her technical knowledge with her political science education, a branch of knowledge that deals with systems of government and the analysis of behavior. So yes, stereotypes and gender exist and must always be taken into account.

Groupthink

Groupthink is the need for conformity in a group of people. To get along, to harmonize, to do the right thing within the group, to reach a collective consensus, even if that right thing is wrong. Even in the face of knowing this will be wrong, we will not say anything as we assume the group has already decided, and we want to belong to that group, as Solomon Asch discovered with his 1951 Asch conformity experiments. One can review history to see how often groupthink has led to countless tragedies over time; still we celebrate our own group and distrust others. There are other explanations why groupthink may exist, but in a different form. Trans-active memory (Wegner 1985) is not so much pressure from the group, but a collective wisdom of the group. Competing the individual's knowledge with that of other members that are experts of the group help to increase the knowledge held by all. Groupthink can really impact the way we understand and tackle these security problems. Groupthink can lead to negative consequences such as illusions of invulnerability, rationalizing warning signs, too much belief in the morality of the group, pressure on group members, and even self-censorship, all things that can lead to faulty assumptions and faulty behavioral actions (Graham 2011).

Stereotype Content Model

Many other aspects of stereotyping exist, and it could be that the stereotype content model can help to explain some of these issues. In this model, there are basically two dimensions we choose from, and we look at others as possible competitors to resources. We are designed evolutionary wise to look at a stranger with (1) warmth—this person or group can help us—and (2) competence—those higher in status are regarded as more competent than those of lower status. We strive to be in these groups, since we are more likely to achieve some desired end goal by our associations within these groups. Think back to the discussion on laddering we had. Groups are then measured by others on these two dimensions across four possible outcomes. There is (1) high warmth and high competence, (2) high warmth and low competence, (3) low warmth and high competence, and (4) low warmth and low competence (e.g., older retired adults may be viewed high on warmth, but low on competence), and competences are targeted (e.g., a retired person may no longer work in the IT field, and their IT skills had gotten rusty over the years), but it doesn't mean they cannot pick up and learn the skills for today. Therefore, because of the way we rate people in these groups, it will eventually dictate our behavior to people within these groups. We may choose to help someone, or deny them help, patronize them, either passively or actively. And remember, saving our cognitive energy is still key in all of this, even with stereotypes.

Everyone Stereotypes

Groupthink is a very real stereotype threat to security; just consider the many examples:

> *Ignoring Japan's attack on Hawaii in World War II.*
> *Weapons of Mass Destruction and the war on terror.*

These were groupthink related; even the US Department of Homeland Security National Commission on Terrorist Attacks argued that the greatest threat may not be from a multinational terrorist organization, but that of its collective groupthink (NCTA 2002). Now discussing cybersecurity and just some general headlines, we find:

> *Human error accounts for over 95 percent of security incidents (IBM Security Services 2014).*

Almost 90% of cyber-attacks are caused by human error or behavior (Kelly 2017).

Insider threats account for nearly 75 percent of security breach incidents (Schick 2017).

The biggest cybersecurity risk to US businesses is employee negligence (Csreinicke 2018).

Considering you are making cybersecurity decisions for your organization, and after reading these headlines, your investment decisions would be to, well, all my security problems revolve around the employee, and that probably would be one of the most unwise decisions someone can make. Is it possible for an employee, even opening up an infected e-mail cause 50 million records to be hacked? Have any of the recent breaches including point-of-sale registers or expired certificates or infected DLL files been caused by one of these employees?

Yes, employees open infected emails, and yes, employees click on links they should not have, and there are disgruntled employees, but if the collective groupthink is on employees, we end up missing some very real threats. Most of the attacks discussed in this book were not solely one person. Yes, that person may have been the catalyst that started things going, or the final straw, but there was a whole chain of events that led up to and passed that employee's actions. Review any attack mention: Target, Equifax, Marriott, Home Depot, United States Office of Personnel Management (OPM). These were not one person's fault. Did a single person at Facebook know about an expired certificate? If you are reading all these headlines and the current wisdom is that employees are my only concern, it is probably a very good chance that you are under the influence of groupthink and may miss many more potential threats. It is not the employees who suffer the stereotypes, but that of the protectors of the network. Cybersecurity professionals fall into the same traps as end users do (i.e., remind me later). In addition, why we may think it is the uneducated that tends to stereotype the most, that would be incorrect as Khazan experiments show that intelligent people can stereotype just as much.

Cybersecurity Implications and Conclusions

Stereotypes are abounded in cybersecurity, and not just from way of thinking, but from every issue we can see (e.g., gender issue). Even as we can see many instances of outreach to get women into the information technologies and cybersecurity fields, we most certainly do typecast what we think a female cybersecurity professional will look like. Do ex-military make the best cybersecurity professionals? If you say yes, that would be a typecast. Do women make the best cybersecurity professionals? Again, a typecast. Does diversity, affirmative action, or being Asian make the best, again, all typecasts? One thing we can agree on is cybersecurity is challenging, and for one to fit this role, they must love a challenge and realize that their own cognitive abilities will make or break their success in that role. This leads us into perceptions like we spoke of earlier, in both the type of person, and the perceptions they view as threats. Since the data shows the skewed differences in the population makeup and those represented by cybersecurity professionals, do we look at traits? We can't label this as there have been trailblazers in cybersecurity regardless of race, gender, or religion, but are they any traits worth examining? However, in this chapter I am not discussing any of those. I am not discussing someone's abilities to see if they are a good fit for cybersecurity. I am advocating looking at your own cybersecurity talents and your stereotypes that you hold in regards to your behavior. Do you think Windows is better than Unix? Do you think hash values are much better than encryption algorithms? Do you think steganography is enough? Do you belong to a Windows working group? Do you belong to a hash value working group, or a steganography working group? Do you think you are more intelligent than the end user? In all of these instances, the groupthink phenomenon and stereotype content model may hold influence on your cognitive thinking, and eventually guide your behavior. Ever notice all the different names for those who try to compromise systems—we have the black hat, those for personal gain, and search on the name, and you guess it, there will be some guy holding or standing over a computer wearing a black hat. Then we have the white hat, same exact picture, just the guy is wearing a white hat and I am left wondering if I am watching reruns of the *Lone Ranger*, but our cognitive economy works well here, after all, a woman would never seek to compromise a computer system, right? Then, as always, we have the middle-of-the-road hacker, the gray hat, this is the gray area, well, it's not technically illegal, yet, or is it? Why stop at these three colors? Why not have more? How about the red hat? Red hats are usually signified of social groups, like religious organizations, so red hat attackers are those who try to compromise systems but only on morally social grounds, as they would believe. Wait, we have red hats, so what about red and white mixed hats. We can then have the purple hat hackers, which was to signify vintage times, jewelry, tea, indulges, bravery, spirituality, so perhaps they are the ones who attack systems in the name of justice. Is there a purple hat yet? We have the yellow, brown, and green hats. De Bono (1985) classified six different kinds of thinking hats: (1) white, all about information, the kinds, types, quality; (2) red, emotional ties; (3) black, negative, caution awareness; (4) yellow, sunshine, look on the bright side; (5) green, new, innovative ideas; and (6) blue, this is how the thinking process is controlled.

At this rate we are going to run out of hat colors.

These are all stereotypes, and while they may help us see these different attackers in our own minds, they can direct behavior and cause all kinds of problems for us.

CHAPTER 10

Fight or Flight

Introduction

Cannon in 1915 argued that fight or flight is a hyperarousal to some danger, whether that threat is real or perceived. It is followed by rapid heartbeats, dilated pupils, or a sharp pain in the stomach; some people think they are having a heart attack. It can come on very sudden, even without warning. While people often associated it with some kind of real threat, other things like phobias, fear of public speaking, and even knowing you are about to get fired from a job can all bring on fight or flight.

Fight-or-flight sensations engage stressors within the body, which can guide our eventual behavior. These stressors are abundant (e.g., hunger, cold, danger, even a visit to a doctor's office), and the list goes on. However, there is a trigger mechanism that will take fight or flight to dangerous levels. Cannon termed the notion of the stability of our inner world as homeostasis (i.e., our pulse or blood pressures, the body's temperature). When internal or external factors threatened them, the body reacts by engaging the hormone and nervous systems, which is the attempt by the human body to revert back to homeostasis. In addition, Cannon identified the sympathico-adrenal system, which is used to maintain the body's homeostasis. It's like a circle; fight-or-flight feeling engages the adrenal system, which increases the level of your fight-or-flight response and which engages even more adrenal to counter. Eventually, your body does correct itself to bring in back to homeostasis, but the outcome is not always positive; blackouts, heart-attacks, panic attacks are all possible.

Emergencies engage these systems and will bring around changes to the body that are manifested in psychological and behavioral aspects such as releasing adrenaline. This adrenaline is released during times of stress, real or imaginary (e.g., someone experiencing low blood sugar).

This is a connection between a physical condition of low blood sugar, and the imaginary threat of an impending attack. Someone about to get laid off can feel the same way and pass out. The fight-or-flight release of adrenaline builds up in the bodies muscular and skeleton systems, constricts blood flows, and releases glucose into the blood stream. All these stressors can hurt us in the long term and can hurt others as well, if the reaction of the person under stress impacts others (e.g., your stressing out impacts the driver of a car). There has been a lot of research on stress. Some researchers argue it should be the leading cause of death due to all the serious side effects it can cause (Schneiderman, Ironson, and Siegel 2005; Khansari, Murgo, and Faith 1990; Koolhaas et al. 2011). Fight or flight also has very real cognitive negative conditions, and in some cases, it can cause a freeze reaction. Fight or flight can also cause cognitive content specificity.

It can be a never-ending circle; I am stressed about always being in stress.

Minimizing Stress

To help minimize stress, researchers have looked at and studied various programs, and they did note one thing that helps us during these times of stress is to give us control over things. Researchers who have studied stress in animals have suggested that maybe way to reduce stress is to know when the stress was about to be triggered. Several conclusions that were drawn from a large part of stress research came from the unpredictability of not knowing. When you are stuck in an airport waiting for your late flight, are you more stressed that the flight is late, or not knowing why it's late? Ever scream into a phone when a call center operator puts on hold, especially when you are calling a company's support help line? Now, many of these recordings tell you that your wait time might be 10 minutes, and some will even allow you to leave a number so they will call you back and you don't lose your place in the queue. In a traffic jam with bumper-to-bumper traffic, why are we not moving, but then you might see an accident up ahead. You now see the cause of the delay, and you begin to calm down; until you finally pass the accident, your stress is relieved. Just the act of seeing that accident reduces your stress level. It does not get you by that accident any quicker, just now you know why things are the way they are. Some foreknowledge is very helpful; even predicting foreknowledge can be helpful. Whenever I fly with connecting flights, I just know one of the flights is going to be delayed and I may even miss one. Whether or not that eventually happens, I understand I can be late, but when on time, I am happy. Some people say bad things happen in three; I assume three is being modest, and I think bad things happen in at least four or five, so when I get to the third bad thing happening, I start to feel good; it's almost over and something good is bound to happen. Some people would say this is an irrational way of looking at things:

I would agree, but it's better than screaming at the sky why the car in front of me is not moving!

Some researchers call this cognitive reappraisal (Lazarus and Folkman 1984). This is not all bad news, as at times stress helps us make better decisions. Research has shown that stressful situations could actually improve the decision-making action of individuals. A trigger was noticed depending on how the stressful situation was explained. An incoming stressful situation was better handled if the outcome has clear results vs. a possible stressful situation where negative results were conveyed (Sharot 2020). This research could have potential positive benefits for cybersecurity professionals, that instead of focusing on the negative results in security incidents, focus on the positive benefits in solving that security incident and prepare for the next one.

Cognitive Reappraisal

There are well documented ways to reduce stress, and all work to varying degrees (e.g., mediation, exercise, humor, social support). It's a coping mechanism that we design to help us get through stressful situations, like my own coping skills with traffic and delayed flights. Many people believe their religious faith can reduce stress; of course, there is debate if their religious faith can actually cure stress. If their religious faith does not relieve the stress, they become more stressful about their religious faith and the issue that got them stressed in the first place—a double-stress implication. There is research that does suggest that our beliefs about pills can work wonders on our health. While the cognitive belief does not seem to bode well for curing, the actual physical pill does. So definitely more research is needed in this area. Could this reinforce the notion of top-down associations on physical well-being (i.e., how strongly do you want to believe in that association)? Was that religious top-down association strong enough that this pill or special new type of care will cure you? Could it have been that ever since you were a child and you went to the doctor, the doctor may have given you some medicine to make you better, and you got well? This reinforces the doctor–cure association we have.

What about the placebo effect? Which one worked: the placebo or the real pill? Which of the two had the stronger association? Placeboes are not supposed to have an effect, but sometimes they have a positive effect. There have been experiments with groups of people who were paid to get drunk. Some drank alcohol and got drunk, some had something that tasted like alcohol, but contained no alcohol, yet they still exhibited the same characteristics of someone who was drunk. Perhaps to a point it depends on what you think and the association.

Procrastination

An often-overlooked area of understanding in cybersecurity is procrastination. Face it, we just don't want to do things, our taxes, our homework, writing another article, and yes, responding to an attack after it's over.

Why should we? It's over.

It just feels so good to have stopped the attack and move on. Well, we talked about that, it's homeostasis. Our bodies seek steady state, an area where everything is in equilibrium. Once the issue that drove our adrenaline to kick into overdrive comes back down, the last thing we want to do is to activate it again. We do not procrastinate just for the sake of procrastinating, we use logic. Such as:

> *We deny the events. Well, it really wasn't a big deal, it was so minor.*
> *We avoid the events; I better not walk that way again.*
> *We blame the events; it may have been a bad for me, but you should have seen what it did to her.*

We seek distraction; we have other more important things to do.

Going back to the Zeigarnik effect, the attack is over, it's closed, and I am at peace. I do not want to now go back and open it all up again. During the attack, fight or flight, fix the problem, but once the event is passed, and we seek to understand the actions that led to that event, we might have a briefing on the matter, a new management directive will go out thinking that will solve the problem, and if like so many other things I've witnessed, it will be ignored or adopted grudgingly. Until the next event, and the cycle repeats. To understand procrastination and that it is just one of the many coping mechanisms we use, which sometimes is perfectly acceptable. It is not a biological fault, it's not about poor time management or will power, it's just how our brains and emotions work together. Wohl, Bennett, and Pychyl (2010) did some very interesting research, suggesting students who forgave themselves for procrastinating study for one exam actually were less likely to procrastinate for their next exam. When you procrastinate, deep down you know you shouldn't. You should be doing something for the future, and that future will be brighter, hopefully for you if you do those things. Yes, I am procrastinating doing my taxes if I owe money, but if I don't, I will still owe that money and maybe a penalty as well. With procrastination, I know my future net value will be more, but I still accept my present value. It could very well just be like goals we have talked about earlier; the future value I cannot see from my present value, so maybe then break down those goals. Just don't let it get the best, and in some cases, it's okay to accept procrastination. Admit it, you procrastinated, it's okay, and just move on. It does seem that stress is unavoidable, no one is immune, and it is critical to understand and for management as well, and we use many coping strategies to minimize stress, and get back into balance (i.e., homeostasis), and one of the coping mechanisms we use is procrastination. The National Security Agency (NSA) conducted a stress survey using two self-reported instruments (Ziadeh 2018). The Samn-Perelli Fatigue Scale, which is a self-reported tool, is designed to measure fatigue in pilots, such as fatigue, tiredness, sleepiness, and has a definite impact on cognitive and physical capabilities. Fatigue is a serious problem affecting pilots and believed to be a contributing factor to almost 10 percent of airplane accidents. The second instrument they used was the NASA Task Load Index (NASA-TLX), which is designed to measure a range of factors, mental and physical demands, temporal demands, effort, performance and frustration levels on perceived workloads. The NSA results were as expected, and some very interesting results as well. The cognitive workload factors were analyzed and as expected linked (i.e., the mental, physical, temporal, effort, and frustration levels) rose or fell together, but the performance levels did not seem to be a factor. There was some correlation to performance and frustration, which can make sense; since if I am frustrated at work, I may also articulate that yes, my performance is suffering. So according to the study, all the factors measured seem to be causing cybersecurity operators cognitive discord, but not affecting their performance.

But the question is how would you know?

Remember, cybersecurity has no an immediate return on investment, so if a cybersecurity professional is suffering from fatigue or burnout, what will be the results three, four, or six months from now. In many examples of security breaches, suspicion is aroused, some unusual activity is spotted, an investigation is started, and in many cases, there is trail going on for months. Now the company is in a dilemma—do we report the breaches, how do we report the breaches, to who, what data do we share?

Chain of Events for Equifax

The Equifax attack was, well, remarkably simple. A simple reconnaissance of websites allowed hackers to identify a potential vulnerability in the Apache Struts vulnerability, which further allowed the exploit to occur. This exploit, known for at least two months prior from May 2017 to July 2017, allowed hackers to gain credentials and with those credentials access 48 internal servers (Ng 2018). It is interesting to note that this was not a one-short deal. The attackers spent 76 days inside Equifax before detection, and like many other attackers, they moved slowly so as not to be detected.

So, disregarding the patch that would have prevented this. Why?

Why were the alerts and signals not acted upon? Since the Internal Revenue Service (IRS), Social Security Administration (SSA), and US

Postal Service (USPS) all use Equifax identity verification services, the Government Accountability Office (GAO) conducted an investigation into this breach. In the timeline of events, Equifax admitted that there was unusual scanning activity on their systems on March 10, 2017; two days prior a release had been reported by the United States Computer Emergency Readiness Team, that the Apache Struts Web Framework was vulnerable. Equifax acknowledges even with the scan, no data was taken. On May 13, 2017, attackers gained entry, and by using encryption, were allowed to blend in as normal traffic. It was on July 29, 2017 that Equifax became aware of this ongoing attack and began to stop the damage. It was also reported that during a routine check, an IT administrator identified an error in equipment configuration; an expired certificate, which allowed the theft of data without detection, and finally on July 30, 2017, the systems were taken off-line, and the problem corrected. What happened then?

According to Equifax, they had notified system administrators throughout the company that a vulnerability existed for Apache Struts, but the distribution list was out-of-date and those responsible for the vulnerable portal were not notified. They further indicated that they did do a complete scan a week later, and the scan did not result in the detection of this vulnerability. So there are two problems here:

Out-of-date distribution list
A faulty scanning methodology, or application since the vulnerability still existed, yet was not identified.

An expired digital certificate allowed the attackers to penetrate further into the company and avoid detection. Equifax did have a tool running that would detect for unusual traffic, but somehow the expired certificate prevented that detection. This is the third problem:

Expired certificates

There was a lack of segmentation, meaning multiple databases are separated by, for example, their own networks to stop the spread; think of multiple dams stopping the flow of rivers to prevent downstream flooding.

Segmentation, or lack of

There was a lack of governance of the data, meaning there were not strong limits of attackers getting information like usernames and passwords, and these credentials were not encrypted.

Lack of strong authorization controls

Finally, query control. Attackers were allowed to conduct thousands of queries on data, when in normal business operations, maybe hundreds might be needed.

Weak database controls

Equifax's response to this is normal, and that of more control and monitoring, for network access, control queries, and governance and the rest of the report discusses follow-up actions and what federal agencies were planning to do next. So, in this chain of events we had:

- Out-of-date distribution list
- A faulty scanning methodology
- Expired certificates
- Segmentation, or lack of
- Lack of strong authorization controls
- Weak database controls

We could then think of hundreds of questions to ask, such as:

- Who would be in charge of applying that patch?
- Who would have been in charge of keeping the distribution list updated?
- Who would have been in charge of those expired certificates?
- Who was in charge of network segmentation?
- Who was in charge of strong authorization controls?
- Who was in charge of the database controls?

Using the psychology of blame, one would assign blame to each one of these questions, or another person would look at this and think, was only one person in charge of patch control, or is there a whole team of administrators and managers? Would not the same apply to database controls and governance controls? Chain of events are very real; this was not a weak link in a chain, but a chain of weak links. Does anyone really believe this is the only chain, for Equifax, or any company? We know how the attack was successful, but we don't know mentally why, and this was a golden opportunity to uncover the reasons. Why was the patch not applied? Was it an individual who just had too much work to do, or was it against company policy to install a patch without an official meeting? Was this a case of compliance? Who was in charge of the distribution list? Was it one person or a group? Were they just assuming they knew the distribution list was valid?

What about the culture then? George Town University (2017) suggests that culture at Equifax could have been a big part of the problem as well. To consider the culture, we want to understand what Equifax does, and who are its customers. Even though the data they control is on individuals, these very same individuals are not Equifax customers. Companies such as loan institutions are Equifax customers, and perhaps with the amount of data points, selling these data points were more important. In fight or flight, like we have seen many times before, there were probably warnings. People may have brought the issue up, but stay and do your job, or tomorrow you will not have a job. To say this only happened at Equifax would be to forget Wells Fargo's massive problems with fraudulent opening of accounts (McLean 2017). There will be no doubt be more chain of events and fight-or-flight responses. Perhaps next time a company can delve deeper and uncover the reasons, to reduce the likelihood of future chains, as it could very well be that these two are related, and in the face of fight or flight, we allow these chains to build until the inevitable.

Cybersecurity Implications and Conclusions

I've seen a lot of stress in cybersecurity professionals, way too much stress actually. Perhaps we need a new cognitive economy term, maybe cyber stress. Cybersecurity professionals have to deal day-in and day-out with threats, they have to safeguard systems, implement protocols, design new architectures, usually under a way too short deadline, appease management, and deal with other issues like disruptions to current systems. In addition, since some problems are just end-user-behavior initiated, they are also spending time helping internal employees. When a legitimate external attack does occur, they are now working as hard as possible controlling the external attack and the internal problem. I have seen firsthand during a major attack the management wanted a status report every 20 minutes. The information systems cybersecurity professionals had to use passwords stored on a web page that was accessible for only 10 minutes till it timed out and disappeared. If you had to log into another system, you had to call that web page back up, another system, call the web page back up, and so on, and to write any password down meant immediate dismissal. I did not even mention that they are usually on call 24 hours a day. Many have missed and cut vacations; this cuts into family time and just adds more stress. A thing about the fight-or-flight response is that in addition to releasing chemicals into the body, it can also cause emotional cognitive responses such as immobilizing terror, hopeless defeat, aggressive attacks, emotional fainting, and other biochemical patterns, just as they would in any external appearance or behavior. Stress increases the fight-or-flight response, which in turn increases stress, which again can increase the fight-or-flight response, a circle. I want a status update every 20 minutes, fix these systems, and good luck remembering passwords from a web page that keeps disappearing—think any of this would lead to fight or flight? I worked in another institution where management did not trust anyone, and we were asked to implement a Web monitoring system as management was so concerned people were goofing off at work. After installation and a trial run, we were called in to report our results. After management's tirade about employees goofing off, and yes, a number did look at sports websites, or news sites, but over 90 percent of the websites visited were Monster.com and Dice.com. Seems like everyone was on flight to leave the organization. Perhaps then fight or flight is a phenomenon in more ways than one. This is not to say that all stress is bad, on the contrary, some stress is good, and actually helps you make better decisions. It depends on the context and the message being conveyed. A kind of switch in the brain helps to release dopamine and interacts with another molecule called the corticotropin-releasing factor. Sharot (2020) reported this with firefighters and other dangerous positions that a perceived threat could trigger a stressful situation that helps with processing information and make better decisions.

There is a real shortage of cybersecurity professionals, so why not make them more stressed out, even worse, quit. It is gotten so bad that in a career path where there is a negative unemployment rate, people who may have the skills, traits, and demeanor to become a good cybersecurity professional pass on the opportunity. An interesting thing about cybersecurity professionals and programmers that I've noticed is that they think very protective (i.e., maybe my own stereotype). They want to own this little piece, it's theirs, a new subroutine, a new interface, an encryption implementation, a roll of out-edge computing, and so on, but if these things that they own get taken away or managed by someone else, what will happen to their stress levels and their motivations? Attackers are not just simply compromising a computer system, sending an infected e-mail, they are attacking this nation's energy grids, stealing health records, using public-key cryptography in ransomware attacks, moving to the Dark Web and bitcoin. With all these things happening now and more on the horizon, do we really want cybersecurity professionals stressed out? We may further push these cybersecurity professionals in threat rigidity, whereby fatigue develops within the organization and professionals and stifles further innovation (Weeks 2017). In cybersecurity, as new threats are developed and new evolutions of threats come to surface, the last thing needed is a rigid cybersecurity professional. A cybersecurity professional needs to know the technical aspects, but also have a creative nature to think, okay, what's coming at me tomorrow.

This reminds me of the 1980s NBC comedy show *Seinfeld*, where the character Frank Costanza, played by Jerry Stiller, was trying to keep his blood pressure under control and would walk around and say:

Serenity now, serenity now.

Unfortunately, we cannot have cybersecurity professionals do this, especially since serenity now turned out to be a hoax, it forces you to bottle up emotion, and the end result is:

Serenity now, insanity later.

CHAPTER 11

Language

Introduction

Even though language is universally used for communications, unfortunately many times language is misunderstood. The actual words are not misunderstood, but the meaning conveyed is often misunderstood. For the most part of any communications stream, we only pick up bits and pieces of the actual communications, and we are left to fill in the gaps, so we look for subtle cues, like body or eye movement. Language is just not often that clear, which leads to a whole host of problems, and there are several reasons why language, even the verbal form of communication, is often misunderstood.

Ambiguous

Language is often ambiguous in that it can be figurative or literal; he can just be as high as the roof, or he is standing on ladder that is as high as the roof. That cat is crazy cool, as in a great jazz player or just crazy (i.e., even crazy is ambiguous). It is also lexical in that there are just too many associated meanings (e.g., time is flying by); really? so where is its destination? It is phonetic: to, too, two, or hair or hare. It can be structural as *I slept like a bug in a rug on a cold winter's night.* Perhaps I killed a bug in my underwear last night, so was the bug actually in my underwear, or was the bug on the wall and you just happened to be in your underwear at the time. The introduction of the lexical hypothesis helps us understand each other, in that over time a language will accumulate a vocabulary to describe the culture in which it resides. Commonly observed traits will be created to explain personality types. It's a main reason why in one language there may not a word that can be easily translated to another language. Even with this limitation, each culture does have similar traits and similar lexicons in their own language; it's just not to the degree always found in other languages. In a paper presented by Schmitt, Allik, McCrae, and Benet-Martinez et al. (2007), Asians scored the lowest on the scale of extroversion. This could make sense as the Asian culture seems to center on society as a whole, where the highest score on the extroversion scale was North American, where there is more emphasis on doing one's own thing.

Since we have these times when people really don't mean what they say, (e.g., *I am going to beat you silly, I'm going to pop you upside the head)*, or perhaps being sarcastic or obtuse (*he's not the sharpest tool in the shed*), we then have to decipher these meanings. But in order to decipher what someone else is saying given the so many possible combinations, we look to the one thing we possess to help us make sense of things, and that is our neural network associations. We have our neural network associations, and they are being recalled in the context we find ourselves (i.e., the context of association). We listen to the words, and then try to place them in context. He jumped so high that he almost hit the roof. It is not just the words we are hearing, but our neural networks jumping into action, and with our billions of associations we know that person cannot jump as high as the roof, so there would likely be an association with someone jumping very high who plays sports.

We hear these words, and for the most part, we understand their meanings. Then our networks of associations kick in to understand the intended meaning given the context. While this helps us to narrow down what exactly does hit the roof mean, it's not always reliable and can cause us problems, as I gave the poor old lady some dog food, for who, the old lady or her dog. Since everything and everyone is confusing, and since language is ambiguous, we also use other coping strategies.

Such as:

If you catch my meaning.
You have a green light. To what, hit the gas pedal, or start on that work project.

Pragmatics Competence

Assumptions about the intent of the communication: what do you think their goals were when they made that comment? We use pragmatics competence suggested by Kim and Hall (2002) and Gazdar (1979) to interpret what people say. Then we use the context and then associate the context to what the words actually mean, kind of what's the secret code behind those words. Since we use cognitive economy in many areas, we also use it here to help:

- Quality—we assume people are telling us the truth, except when they are lying of course, but is there a truth-value to the words being heard.
- Relation—we assume the conversation is making sense, but really, we fill in the gaps since conversations rarely make sense.
- Quantity—we assume the right amount, but which is never enough, it's too much, or too little, but really, it's never the right amount.
- Manner—we assume clarity, but if we sense ambiguity, what's the motive, are they lying, what are they hiding.

The same things happen to us when we try to talk and communicate. While we are engaged in some group communications and talking, how close were we listening and guessing what the others are saying; so we fill in the blanks, we try to reach and understand whatever it is they really want to get across, all the while our neural network associations are going crazy trying to juggle this mess. Have you ever been talking with someone, then you hear someone in the background talking to someone else, and it's like your radar goes off? You are still engaged in your first conversation, but now you begin to pay more attention to that other conversation and listen more intensively. So now, you are engaged in two communication streams, and not really effective in either. So, how do we handle these conflicts with language? Researchers suggest that it is one of two ways:

1. Nature—we just have an innate ability and we think we were born with some gift, or,
2. Nurture—we learn as we go and we have been taught this all our lives.

It appears that since language is very difficult, we tend to learn by focusing on some of the words themselves, and typically not all the words, just some of them. Many times, we just look at the flow of words, and many times we even ignore how they are spelled since our neural network's associations are telling us how it is going to end anyway, so we need to save cognitive energy.

Statistical Regularities

What syllables do we hear? What syllables do those syllables that we have heard lead or follow the first set of syllables we heard? Looking at the distribution of the English language: the vowels are most common or remember back in grade school, it was *I before E accept after C*, and these are some of the ways we have been taught. So even if we don't see or hear the *I*, we are going to guess if we see that *E*, there was an *I* before. We also listen to the strongest syllables in the hope that we can guess correctly what the complete word will be. If we do not hear the word completely, we guess at what the word was, instead of asking for clarification. These associations are placed in our neural networks and form some very strong associations. Ever meet someone and you call him Fred. His name is really Mike, but when you meet him, and you don't know why, you always call him Fred; well, there's an association going on somewhere. They lead to the word we hear even if we don't hear it clearly. Words catch up with each other and placed in our neural networks and what is known as statistical inference.

Statistical Inference

Statistical inference is one part of the broader picture of statistical analysis. In descriptive statistics, we summarize data, with pictures, charts, the means, modes, averages, and so on. This is where you hear the terms

hypothesis, correlation, prediction, relationships, and so on; we are looking at a set of data and trying to understand the underlying meaning of
that data. As a research example. does this new drug help to lower the
risk of cancer? Normally medical researchers would start these trials using
laboratory rodents. No conclusions are drawn, this is what we have, and
this is what we see, that's all. Statistical inference, or inference statistical
gives us some room to now generate some movement about that data.
Yes, this drug does slow the levels of cancer in white rats three months
old, and then we might be able to generalize it to all white rats that are
three months old. Statistical inference is drawing a conclusion about a
whole population (i.e., the population of white rats three months old)
based upon some sample we use (e.g., if we use 12 white rats that were
three months old, scientific analysis gives us ways to be able to generalize
this to the whole population). This is not just for drugs that might fight
cancer, it's the basis for scientific research for centuries, and has been used
researching sounds, words, and even syllables. It's what we expect to happen: we expect words to follow a pattern and it's a logical conclusion by
knowing the beginning. Some researchers suggest that babies only really
start out with about 200 words, but from that, learn every other word in
their vocabulary, all from statistical inference.:

Perhaps babies really do understand that the ga-ga comes after the goo-goo.

Linguistic Relativity

Benjamin Whorf and Edward Sapir suggested that it was the structure
of a language that shaped someone's cognitive view of that language,
often referred to as the Sapir–Whorf hypothesis. These researchers did
not develop categories of linguistic relativity, or set up the hypothesis, so
in some circles this is considered a misnomer (Koerner 1992). There are
different versions of this hypothesis, such as the strong version, which says
that it is the language that determines thought and helps to determine and
place limits on cognitive categories. There is the weak version that suggests that the linguistic categories only help to influence thought. It helps
the way we speak influences the way we think about reality. The language
of a culture helps to shape culture and will have an impact and eventual

determination of the categories used in that culture. It is very noteworthy to note that later researchers have looked at linguistic categorization on cognition and have noted differences in left-brain and right-brain determinations due to spatial and color perceptions. Even some may argue the sexist language influences these languages, for example the words "fireman" or "policeman," or a "schoolteacher" or "nurse." While these have developed and changed over the years, they still exist very strongly in some cultures. It is interesting to note how language can shape the way culture develops, or how we may eventually behave. For example, some studies have suggested the people cannot see color if there isn't a word for color. Words do mean a lot—mention freedom to those who had to have actually fought for freedoms. When you shop online, what word do you normally think of? Many may think of the Internet portal Amazon; here is an example of a company changing culture and language. We engage in contentious arguments; we are so mad that we don't even know how to describe how mad we are. Different languages use words in different ways to describe masculine or feminine meanings. Genders in the words matching the person's gender influenced their descriptions, good or bad, and not just a translation, but a loss in translation. This also means that it's fluid, it changes, new ones are added, and can be corrected if needed. Language may frame your thought, perception, impact your cognitive categories, and eventually your behavior. We use top-down reasoning, pragmatics, and statistical inference to determine what is being said, and with that it influences our interpretation of everything we encounter, and eventually guides our behavior.

Language Formats

This is a practice we have to give restaurants a lot of credit, and marketers have learned that our own language is not even the same in the way it's presented. What do you think costs more? A sandwich for:

- *$12.00*
- *12*
- *Twelve dollars*
- *12.00*

It turns out where prices were written using words like twelve dollars, or one dollar twenty-five cents, people would spend more money (Yang, Kimes, and Sessarego 2009).

Another example on a menu, for example:

- a Reuben sandwich costing $12.00 (but in 16-point font) or
- a Reuben costing fifteen dollars (in a 10-point font)

People seem to choose the $15.00 Reuben sandwich; it's the size of the font factor. The bigger picture here for cyber security professionals is not the actual cost, but the different formats in which something is presented: attacks, technical solutions, prices, data points, security bulletins, and so on. All the different formats impact what we absorb and thereby possibly impact our cognitive reasoning.

Let's consider another formatting example:

Aoccdrnig to a rscheearch at Cmabrigde Uinervtisy, it deosn't mttaer in waht oredr the ltteers in a wrod are, the olny iprmoetnt tihng is taht the frist and lsat ltteer be at the rghit pclae. The rset can be a toatl mses and you can sitll raed it wouthit porbelm. Tihs is bcuseae the huamn mnid deos not raed ervey lteter by istlef, but the wrod as a wlohe.
So how far did you get reading the above paragraph?

In your mind did you think something was not right, but you could read the words, so you kept going, even to end of the paragraph? This is an excellent example of how the brain processes information. The above example has been passed around since 2003, and the original origins are difficult to trace, but this particular instance seems to be from Cambridge University (https://mrc-cbu.cam.ac.uk/personal/matt.davis/Cmabrigde/).

Ever write something down, come back to review it later, and wonder why you cannot spell. Just how dumb am I, or how did I not catch this the first time around? It's a process called generalization; we get the general meaning but miss the details. Interesting in that we discussed this earlier where the brain only gets bits and pieces and encodes the complete message with what it thinks is right. Dr. Sachs of Duke Law School in

Durham, North Carolina, wrote a little scrambler (http://stevesachs.com/jumbler.cgi) that highlights any text, for example the above paragraph becomes:

Eevr wtrie smheinotg, cmoe bcak to riveew it ltaer, and wednor why you cnnoat slpel. How did you not ccath tihs the fsirt tmie aunord. It%E2%80%99s a psceors cealld gzoaareentiiln, we get the gaernel mnaieng, but msis the dietals. Ineirstnteg in taht we descsuisd tihs eaerilr whree the bairn olny gtes btis and peices and endeocs the ceomptle mesagse wtih waht it thnigs is rghit

This is a process of random letter positioning and it does not seem to interfere with word recognition. Much of this could have to do with statistical inference, whereas words like to, be, and, never really change and even if a letter was moved, two and three letters words are easy to distinguish.

Overall, the words are in order, but the letters inside these words are out of order, consider the two examples:

1. it deosn't mttaer in waht oredr the ltteers in a wrod are
2. matter it what in are in order word doesn't the a letters

The complete sentence reads:

it doesn't matter in what order the letters in a word are.

I am sure that the first sentence was easier to understand, even though the letters were scrambled inside the words. For example, a contraction *doesn't* may normally be found in front of a noun, matter, or the preposition *in* is normally found preceding a noun. Statistical inference and statistical regularities allowed you to read the sentence. Psycholinguistics, the psychology of language, helps us understand the psychological and neurobiological factors that help humans acquire and use language to communicate with each other. It may help to explain the lexical hypothesis and how we develop language to explain in some ways our culture. We have seen several instances in this chapter of any language and its peculiarities that often arise, but we have to deal with them. Messy thinking, faulty definitions, sloppy language like jargon and colloquiums, assumptions and yes, stereotypes. Even terminology plays a big role; ever notice so many terms in cybersecurity are medical related, bugs, viruses, infections, immunity, and so on. How did so many medical terms get into technology? Should then we change terminology to cyber disease prevention? Would more people now understand? Many of these issues can be helped by the read, pause, and reflect technique. It's a technique I used with my mentees. Read some material, pause of the material, and reflect, possibly in your writing on the material, then repeat with newer material, and never re-read the same material twice while it's still in your short-term memory. This may seem to actually increase time, but the reverse is often time, as the first cycle may take a while, the second a little less, the third even less time. The result would be that in the end, less overall time is spent on a project. This issue with generalization is a real one; it can make us miss a lot of important details, and in addition, just reviewing something twice, can introduce generalization.

Where Did the Nigerian Prince Go?

Gone are the simpler days, you know, the Nigerian prince wanting to send you a million U.S. dollars in exchange for our username and password. Now, it's Mike from Tribeca Consolidated Networks, who is working with John McCullough from your public relations department on a new project, needs to know who is in charge of production. Then, it becomes Lisa who is writing to that person in charge of the production company, who now claims that she and John McCullough are working on a pilot and need you to examine if the specifications are okay. The head of production logs into the website and gets a 404 Web page not found.

Our eyes caught John McCullough, and guess what, well we trust John, and in our busy day, we ignore most of the other words like Lisa and Mike, whomever they may be, and may explain why we may not fall for the Nigerian prince scam, but the Tribeca Consolidated Networks phishing e-mail. Impersonation e-mail attacks are leading the rise in phishing types of attacks. One factor is the target of the attack. We can probably see that jim.bean@iibm.com is a forgery of someone named Jim Bean and IIBM, but we have a real issue with Jim.bean@theytookourjobs.com and jim.bean@theytookoursjob.com *theytookourjobs* is a real domain, whereas *theytookour* (s) jobs is not. *theytookourjobs* is a cute SouthPark meme from the creators of Comedy Central.

It seems people will trust jim.bean@theytookoursjob.com more than they do jim.bean@iibm.com and why the FBI has said over five billion accounts have been stolen in 2017 alone in e-mail impersonation attacks (https://ic3.gov/media/2017/170504.aspx).

Remember, earlier we said:

it deosn't mttaer in waht oredr the ltteers in a wrod are

So, *theytookourjobs.com* and *theytookour*sjobs.com look identical.

Impersonation, sextortion, and phishing are now and will always be dangerous even cute kittens' memes. Language and the way people approach language must be accounted for, and when developing technical products, take language into account. There are countless stories of miscommunications like when NASA lost their satellite when one team was calculating force in pounds (i.e., the English standard), and another team calculating force in newton (i.e., the metric standard). To this day, this miscommunication has repeated itself in many other industries like construction and medicine.

Cybersecurity Implications and Conclusions

If you were to search on language and cybersecurity, you would undoubtedly find thousands of links, all relating to what is the best programming language for cybersecurity professionals. This is so important for two reasons: (1) this is not what this chapter is about, and (2) it is a perfect example of the difficulty of language. This is example of statistical inference, but from a computer's point of view. Placing language and cybersecurity together as a search term comes back with results that are significance to technology. I am not discussing different speaking languages in the realm of cybersecurity (i.e., someone who speaks Spanish and someone who speaks Italian trying to converse in cybersecurity topics). I am talking the issues of language itself on the shared understanding of several cybersecurity professionals talking together in the same language. It's more of a pronounced problem when you are also dealing with non-cybersecurity management and end users. When you go to a doctor, he or she may speak of medical terms, and you may or may not understand them. For the most part, you do not need to, after your visit you go on your way and really never have to think of those terms. Now, imagine you're a cybersecurity doctor and you have to deal with end users, you begin to explain to them about social engineering or phishing attacks, or so many other negative cybersecurity terms, what do you think goes through their mind? Explain to them about ransomware and you've lost them, not in the understanding of ransomware, but what comes after that. Explain to an end user the threat of taking over their computer what races through their mind. Your language is not their language. If you think horrific consequences cannot occur due to incorrect translations, one of the most dangerous erroneous communications was in 1956, at the height of the US–Russia cold war, Soviet leader Nikita Khrushchev made the comment "*My vas pokhoronim*" when speaking to Western reporters. Six years later, the Cuban missile crisis happened. The error in language was in the English translation of *My vas pokhoronim*, which was "we will outlast you." Khrushchev was trying to say communism will outlast democracy, but others took it as Russia would outlast in case of a nuclear war. There is a lot of work in cybersecurity translations from English into many other languages. Countries all over the world are preparing themselves for increased cybersecurity threats, and using the English language as a base (Kaufman 2017). A lot more work is being done with artificial computer translations, for example, a ransomware virus written in Chinese and believed to be of someone fluent in Chinese turns out to be a computer input system due to certain miscues of Chinese grammar (Mastrocola 2017). This could be a double-edged sword: (1) work on artificial language translations could help us pinpoint the area of the attacker or (2) relying too heavily on AI, we may overlook things, and slang is not often taken literally. They are also doing a lot of work in translating the Danish language, as it seems Denmark is experiencing a lot of growth in cyberattacks, and that another area it seems that 38 percent of phishing attacks seem to be coming from the Netherlands.

In a later chapter, we will discuss the Feynman technique. Feynman is the American theoretical physicist who did pioneering work in quantum mechanics. The best way to teach someone is to teach it to a child, and while he did not teach quantum mechanics to a toddler, his technique is used in many applications by thousands today. There is no clear thinking on a group level, but there is on probably individual levels, but in order for cybersecurity to be effective, we do need a collective understanding and agreement, just not to the point where we fall into the trap of groupthink.

CHAPTER 12

Differences in Opinion

Introduction

Predicting one's actions and behaviors have taken large strides forward in their understandings. At the start of this book, it was mentioned that there are centuries of research to draw upon to try and identify why people behave the way they do. For a large cause of behaviors among people, it seems like we just don't agree with each other, but is that really a surprise? Modern societies argue that if you do bad things you will be punished, but it has been shown that people still do bad things. Why exactly, perhaps they get joy, and that joy overshadows any negative consequences they may think they will face. Perhaps it's fear, anger, frustration, destituteness, and the negative consequences they may experience that do not seem concerning at the moment and remember, it's in the context, think out-of-control road rage. Behaviorists see personality, a product of conditioning, is something that can be conditioned and predicted. Psychoanalysis sees personality as past unconscious memories that will help to explain behavior and eventually used for future prediction. We have seen how rewarding someone with incentives sometimes works out, but sometimes it doesn't and sometimes it just stops as there is no more motivation left. Parents can attest to this by paying kids for chores, but then after weeks, or months, the motivation for a momentary reward for a chore is not enticing as when first offered. Is it the environment, social connections, philosophical roots, genetic traits, or some disorder someone could be afflicted with? There is a whole body of literature on development psychology and our behaviors that come from our upbringings. Different researchers, different opinions: some of them are very good, some not so good, and others still being examined, but it is clear that no one branch of science can explain our behavior. All is unknown, and it is still a frontier, but like it was mentioned at the beginning of the book, we may not change that diet, but perhaps there are things we can do to eat better, and perhaps there are some commonalities across all sciences.

Feelings

Feelings help us interpret emotions. Frijda (2007) suggests we may be subconsciously unaware and make these decisions based on this unconscious process that in some event could be cause of our neural associations. Unfortunately, others cannot understand our feelings and have to fill in some blanks to understand the reasoning. Much like the example earlier in the book, where we see a speeding driver going over 100 mph, is he joy riding, or taking a sick relative to the hospital? Feelings are purely idiosyncratic, and as we say to each his own, they may lie somewhere between the biological and cognitive processes. Are they conscious or subconscious? For example, do we get really scared, and jump, right after we see the snake, or jump when seeing the snake, and then we get really scared? They also prepare us for action, flight or fight, or sometimes you say:

I have a gut feeling about this,

but feelings themselves cannot predict or dictate all behavior.

Intelligence

Intelligence is vast field and many researchers have tried to predict and to some extent measure intelligence. Some of the earliest research in intelligence and development of intelligence tests are over 100 years. One of these earliest was created by Binet (1905) who created the Binet Intelligence Scale, which tried to measure attention and memory. Binet's intent was just to measure students who might need some extra attention. Unfortunately, others used the test to identify weak and feeble minds and it was espoused during the eugenics movement.

Guilford (1967) argued that a true measure of intelligence has two parts. The first part is problem solving, which is the nuts and bolts of solving a problem, and for the most part this has been accepted into the mainstream for measuring intelligence. Guilford argues however that intelligent tests are missing a very important second part, that of divergent thinking, the creative part; think back if you ever took a writing class in school called creative writing. It is this creative part of modern intelligence tests that is missing. To truly measure a person's intelligence, Guilford states a test must measure both.

For example, think of the numbers: three, four, and 17. How many combinations can you make with these numbers using the four normal algebraic functions of add, subtract, multiply, and divide. Given some time, you would probably be able to account for all variations like three times four, 17 plus three, four times three plus 17 divided by three times four, and so on. But now think of a pentagon-shaped box, a wet suit that an underwater scuba diver would wear, a 56 Chevy Bel Air with a dual four-barrel carb with a 411 engine, and a can of soda. How many combinations can you come up with? This is the creative part. How many things can you imagine and create with these four items? So, Guilford's position was that you needed both to measure intelligence. Arguing against Guilford's position and as we have seen, that perhaps while intelligence is a good indicator of what a person might do in certain situations, we have learned that with the power of persuasion and stereotyping, even intelligence cannot predict or dictate all behavior. When looking at the intelligent scores of large populations, we notice many people fall on the intelligent side of the scale and the reason for that was that it was it was designed that way. The average is 100, and the intelligence curve is based on 100. It was designed that way and will stay that way, so perhaps depending on how we are feeling on any certain day:

We could be considered another Einstein or just dumb as a rock.

Cattell (1941) also suggested that intelligence is made up of two parts: (i) fluid intelligence, which is reason, thinking, abstract logic, and (ii) crystallized intelligence, which consists of facts and figures. He divided these two parts from the G concept, created earlier by Spearman (1904). Fluid intelligence is a genetic trait as it differs from one person to the next, whereas crystallized intelligence comes from our learning and past experiences, possible top-down processing. These two parts are independent of each other, but work together. Reasoning and higher level of fluid intelligence would lead to a subsequent higher level of crystallized intelligence, which would lead to a higher level of overall intelligence.

The Dunning–Kruger (Kruger and Dunning 1999) effect really impacts this area. The Dunning–Kruger effect basically says, those who seem to have high IQs, measured over time, actually underestimate their own intelligence, whereas those usually measuring under 100 on the scale overestimate their intelligence. This by itself would not be an issue, but many of these on the lower end of the scale have a noted ability to persuade others just the opposite, and they hold a high IQ. So, Guilford could be somewhat correct as this persuasion factor is the creative intelligence part influencing others. While the Dunning–Kruger effect was coined in 1999, previous research led up to the phrase, and unfortunately it is still very real today. A study in 2019 by Fernbach et al. showed that those individuals who were the biggest opponents of genetically modified food knew the least about the subject. Additionally, they suggested that we do not think alone, in that, what others say have an impact on what we truly believe. Instead of having one individual incorrect, we can have whole societies incorrect. Indeed, as Bertrand Russell said in 1933:

The triumph of stupidity is upon us.

Ever notice you feel your intelligence changes from Monday to Friday, or from when you are full or hungry. Why does my intelligence change when I have nothing to worry about, to times you are worried about something? If you had to measure your intelligence with things in the background like my car payment is due, am I getting laid off, is my child sick, all these external factors would impact how you preform. How many times have you heard or said,

Quiet, I can't hear myself think.

Humor on Intelligence

Are people with a good sense of humor more intelligent than people without one? There is a large body of research that suggests that is the case. A classic experience is when Albert Einstein was asked to pose for a picture, and the renowned scientist stuck out his tongue. Einstein often credited his child-like sense of humor for his intelligence. In what category are we assuming this laughter hypothesis? In Guilford's argument, there are two parts to intelligence: the knowing, and the creativity part. It is the sum of both these parts that leads to a higher overall intelligence. Looking at some famous scientists who exhibited both, here are some of their famous quotes:

> *Stephen Hawking: I have no idea.*
> *Albert Einstein: I have no special talents.*
> *Ivan Sutherland: I didn't know it was so hard.*
> *Sigmund Freud: If you want your wife to listen to you, talk to another woman.*

There are also different types of humor styles, and we discussed some of them earlier. Some seem to suggest that it's the dark sense of humor more associated with intelligence. Dry jokes, morbid jokes, and so on, and this agrees with Sigmund Freud's position back in 1905 proposing humor as an outlet. Dark humor is often associated with pain, aggression, and death. But in safe environments, researchers have noted that those who employ dark humor were typically better educated, had lower aggression levels, and less mood disturbances. Dark humor, with its more aggressive tendencies, is enjoyed by those with less aggressive tendencies. Perhaps it's the opposite thing of attraction. I am so opposed to aggression, and it somehow attracts me. Some researchers suggest it's more of an outlet; at times the majority of us will experience pent-up frustration, and perhaps dark humor serves as a release outlet. It is a very interesting viewpoint that dark humor is associated with stable personality, high self-esteem, emotional ability, and even to enhance relationships. Dark humor, however, is not negative humor, such as those who engage in putdowns of others, sarcasm, and some self-defeating humor is not negative. These types seem to alienate people and cause increased depressions and aggression in those who engage in negative humor traits.

You may notice that in this book I make many attempts at humor, so then I must be intelligent, but that would be open for debate. My children are very much into social media like any teenager, so I asked them to set up a social media account for me and make it look professional. For my profile picture, they used a picture of a Niagara Stealth. Do a search for a Niagara Stealth, and you will know why I was not very intelligent to trust them. Niagara Stealth is a fantastic piece of technology; it's just not me. I do believe in neural network associations, and if a particular humorous example or story increases neural network associations and improves recall, then it is something that should be practiced.

Personality

Personality is formed from our multiple traits. This is not that we have multiple personalities, just that all our individual traits make up our own unique personality. Allport (1961) believed that we all have at least a set of common traits that are common among the majority of people. Some common traits include things like honesty, caring, anger, and so on. Then we have the secondary traits that we exhibit at different times (e.g., we may get nervous if asked to speak to a group of people or some people giggle in certain situations). Fleeson (2001) termed the phrase density distributions, in that personality traits don't change, but they fluctuate throughout the day, and that people are more tuned to exhibit multiple types of traits the more they are accustomed to repeating these patterns of modifying traits.

There are the cardinal traits. These traits are often unique and often times referred to an individual that is symbolic to these traits: Einstein, genius; Hitler, evil; Machiavelli, ruthlessness; George Washington, founding father of America. Allport like other researchers believed that these traits are often reflected even in our language. Allport took the English language that was current in his lifetime and identified 18,000 unique words to describe personality. He narrowed this down to about 4,500 words, and out of these, narrowed those further into categories. Then divided these into two main groups: (i) genotypes, the internal forces that help us relate to the world, and (ii) phenotypes, those external forces placed upon us and how we accept these forces that may guide our behavior. Allport was trying to examine if traits can be connected to behavior and was a sort after goal. Allport used as an example, the fictional tale of Robinson Crusoe. Robinson had some very strict traits, but after saving and teaching Friday, his other traits surfaced due to their relationship and time.

Ever hear *flattery will get you everywhere?*

You may have heard this phrase, and indeed flattery does, and it can really impact what we believe our personality to be. Stagner (1958) conducted a research study asking managers to participate on a personality test. After the results, Stagner then shared the results with the managers. However, he did not give the managers the real results, but he gave them feedback based on horoscopes and other analysis. Then, he asked the managers if they agreed with the results and they all agreed. Forer (1949) conducted another study with psychology students. Similar to Stagner's approach, he gave a test, scored the results, but did not share the real results, instead shared only positive results, like *you have a good sense of humor, you care about security, you can be critical of yourself*, and so on. Again, the psychology students agreed almost five out of five on the scale. Even the phrase you can be critical of yourself is not negative in nature, but a positive indication that you know you can be unbiased, when, in reality all these statements were biased and had nothing to do with the student's answers. People will believe the positive and neglect the negative.

Temperament

Eysenck (1967) was trained as a biologist and looked at temperament as the physiological factor that contributed to one's personality and could possibly explain behavior. He suggested that if someone were an over-inclusive thinker and had a very high IQ of more than 165, he or she could be considered a genius. However, if the same person who was an over-inclusive thinker had some psychotic symptoms, they could be insane.

Therefore, Eysenck's conclusion is, are we all sane or insane; is there really any difference?

Earlier work by early Greek physician Galen (129 AD) divided temperament into four categories: (1) sanguine, (2) choleric, (3) phlegmatic, and (4) melancholic (Stelmack and Stalikas 1991) all relating to some ailment of physical proportions. Eysenck took these four categories and laid them out between two dimensions: (1) the scale of someone being an introvert to an extrovert, and (2) the scale of someone being a neurotic to having emotional stability. Within this circle, habits are reflected (e.g., someone who is an introvert and high on emotional stability could be characterized as being calm, or peaceful, whereas someone who is considered an extrovert and high on neuroticism could be considered impatient, fidgety, aggressive, etc.). He did a number of tests on this model, had some good results, and a lot of inconclusive results, but later he was ridiculed by his peers for this belief that empirical evidence leads one to believe in paranormal activity.

Well, who could have predicted that behavior?

Motivation

We discussed motivation earlier, and that there are some researchers who believe if you know what makes someone motivated, you will then be able to predict their behavior. And while motivation is a key component, as for example in job performance, McClelland (1987) suggested you cannot always rely on people to tell you what motivates them, since motivations are largely unconscious. He suggested there were three classifications of motivation: (1) achievements, (2) power, and (3) affiliation. Achievement is an internal drive for results, to excel, to improve, to reach a goal. Power is the power over others to influence and manage (but not in the sense of cruelty, although some may have that, it's the power given by an organization) and affiliation, part of a group working toward the same goal. These three motivations are oftentimes unconscious. We may say what motivates us, but since motivations are subconscious, how can we trust what someone says. He developed the Thematic Apperception Test (TAT), which helps to reveal the subconscious and show true motivations. His test did not work in the business world, but his ideas of motivations are still important, but still not enough to predict behavior.

Mental Disorders

At first, this seemed to be an easy concept to understand for early researchers. Mental disorders are seen through the underlying symptoms someone exhibits. People's behavior is the result of some earlier mental disorder and judged accordingly. However, Rosenhan (1973), in a series of experiments, showed this judgment can be wrong. He conducted a series of experiments in a psychiatric hospital, and derived results using the same group of people. Recording the judgment of others, on the first trial, people were judged insane, whereas in the second trial, they were judged sane. Therefore, mental disorders can be diagnosed through symptoms. His conclusion was that psychiatric diagnoses are not objective, and probably the worst place to see this is in an actual psychiatric hospital. If we cannot get the right diagnosis, even in a hospital with specialists designed to treat mental illnesses, how could we ever expect to predict future behavior. The above discussion shows some attempts over the years have been made to understand why people behave the way they do, and eventually can behavior be predicted, but the results are not promising.

As I am writing this book, I am eating a donut. However, it's only the one donut that I had all week, so I didn't change my diet, but I did modify my diet limiting to one donut. It's one of those low-sugar donuts; it says so on the box, so I am persuaded to eat the donut, and I found a link for healthy banana donuts with chocolate glaze, and even a skinny donut at 60 calories (i.e., my confirmation bias), so perhaps I will have two then. Therefore, if we cannot predict whether I will have one or two donuts, we cannot predict behavior of an attacker. We could then have problems modifying our own behavior guarding against these cyber attacks. However, if we can understand why things get in the way of our thinking, and subsequent behaviors, then possibly at times (e.g., creating a cybersecurity solution), we can make better products and services, implement them better, and not worry about the attacker's behavior, for now anyway.

When I Want Your Opinion, I'll Give It to You

I think everyone has heard the above phrase:

Merriam-Webster's online dictionary (2019) describes opinion as:
An Opinion: a view, judgment, or appraisal formed in the mind about a particular matter.

Common synonyms: belief, conviction, eye, feeling, judgment, mind, notion, persuasion, sentiment, verdict, view. A view, judgment, formed about a matter, conviction, notion. Basically, anything can that be formed, changed, modified in a setting. So, we read about loss of millions of personal data from the US Federal Government's Office of Personnel Management (OPM), Equifax, Target, Facebook, Yahoo, eBay, TJX, Capital One, Marriott Hotels, Adult Friend Finder, Uber, JP Morgan, Sony, and the countless others.

Then we see stories like:

Workers are the biggest insider threat.
Employees are the weakest link.
Ninety-five percent of attacks are due to employees.
Insider threat, the biggest threat.

I am often left to wonder after reviewing the root causes of hundreds of security attacks, employees are never mentioned in the actual attack itself. Some trusted relationship got compromised, an infected .dll was loaded during a patch upgrade, e-mail retention policies, and other items that employees would have no power to interact with anyway.

Therefore, whose opinion is it that the employees are always at fault?

We have to be careful here that we don't fall into the illusion of control (Langer 1975). My opinion as a cybersecurity expert is better than that of an end-user employee, and certainly better than management. My expectancy of success in implementing security solutions is inappropriately higher than probability would dictate. Therefore, my prediction is better on any solution I implement since I have more control over that implementation. This illusion of control grows as my familiarity of the solution I am implementing, my choice of the solution, and my experiences. It's the same way that I go to a store, see 50 different lotteries tickets, and I buy four tickets. I then rationalize I will have more success with the four that I choose, then just asking the clerk to give me four random tickets. So, on it goes, and end-employees will blame the security administrators, management will blame the end users, security administrators blame both, after all it's

The Psychology of Blame—just working overtime.

Cybersecurity Implications and Conclusions

At the outset of writing this book, I assumed there would be more than enough literature to motivate what drives someone's behavior.

To that end, there is a lot; it's just that no one agrees.

What motivates our behavior? Well, it seems there are a lot of factors that motivate our behavior, and as in other research fields I am sure over time we will refine and rethink these knowledge areas, and hopefully being closer to predict behavior a little better. In cybersecurity, Iulia, Reeder, and Consolvo (2015) examined the differences in good cybersecurity practices from security experts and nonsecurity experts. As usual there were differences in any subject; if you walk into a room with 20 cybersecurity experts and ask them the best way to safeguard an organization, expect 20 answers; all good actually. If you want to get into a heated argument, attend an information technology conference. I attended a conference about a decade ago, and the topic was, "Should we call it information technology or information systems?" The argument got so heated I thought a fight was about to break out. Fast forward to the present, should we call it information security, information assurance, network security, operations security, cybersecurity? Get ready for the sparks to fly. In Iulia, Reeder, and Consolvo's work, it wasn't that the nonexpert practiced bad security habits, they just did not practice the same habits as security experts would recommend. For example, nonexperts practiced changing passwords, strong passwords, using antivirus software as best security practices, and security experts said using multifactor authentication was the best practice.

Were they both correct? Absolutely!

It's just a difference of opinion whose is best—one set of neural networks tells one group something is best, while another set of neural networks tells a different group something else is better. Given their understanding of the concept of security and their perceptions of threats they faced, both groups applied the most appropriate security measures. One result that was suggested was that some nonexperts do not install updates due to the lack of awareness of how effective updates are, which was their perception. They also noted on additional responses that non-experts said they were not sure if always updating software is safe, and given that at times, updating patches something caused unexpected consequences, again, their perceptions could be influencing their behavior at both extremes. These results might give emphasis that cybersecurity experts should try to help those who do not understand or perceive threats accurately, as we have written about earlier, not in an authoritative way, but by building a relationship. This may motivate them to practice stronger security practices, away from well the company is forcing me to, and combined with the social learning we looked at earlier may encourage even more participation of stronger security practices. We have seen it's almost impossible to predict behavior; the further out we go, how one behaves today will not be the same way they behave tomorrow, in a week, in a month, in a year, or in a decade. Therefore, we can't change someone's else's behavior outright, but we can modify ours to help them modify theirs. I've pointed out in this book so many ways we harm ourselves, like the saying goes:

We are our own worst enemy.

It's true that our own cognitive abilities, thinking, neural network associations, stereotypes, everything has an impact on our decisions, and ultimately our behavior. If we can spot these and understand why these things happen, then perhaps we can all make cybersecurity decisions, like the saying goes life does get in the way.

CHAPTER 13

Cyber Maturity and Ethics

Introduction

While this book is not focused on cyber maturity it's more focused on understanding psychology and behavior. Psychology, behavior, and maturity have crossed research paths. All of these literature streams have taken steps to look at maturity factors that might lead us into bad behaviors. Therefore, perhaps we can look at these behaviors that result from maturity levels that lead us to make bad decisions, and maybe we could then turn them into good decisions, which is probably a good idea, and if we could, could we then generalize that to better cybersecurity decisions?

Cyber Maturity

Cyber maturity seems to have a lot of basis in models that cover broad ranges of categories. Many models touch on both policy and human aspects and cover major areas such as risk, business continuity, governance, feasibility, human resource, and so on. There are many more, and it's not our goal to evaluate them, just make note they exist. There are those models that are aligned with federal standards, such as the National Institute of Standards and Technology cybersecurity framework (NIST CSF) (NIST 2019) and the cybersecurity capability maturity model (C2M2) (U.S. Department of Energy 2014). The C2M2 model was developed by power and utility companies to help measure the maturity of the overall security models. The domains include (1) risk management, (2) asset, change, and configuration management, (3) identity and access management, (4) threat and vulnerability management, (5) situational awareness, (6) information sharing and communication, (7) event and incident response, and continuity of operations (8) supply chain and external dependencies management, (9) workforce management, and (10) cybersecurity program management. Each one of these domains is then measured against a maturity indicator level MILO through MIL3. The NIST CSF may not be considered a maturity model by the NIST, but it does offer in a sense similar to other models that there are progressive tiers that make the more automated structure of many models (e.g., from reactive to proactive in nature to threats).

Models can be very helpful in measuring and adjusting a robust cyber protection system for any organization, but not in measuring the maturity of any cyber program. This might be why many cyber security certifications are lacking any robust discussion of any theoretical bodies of knowledge on human behavior. If you think about cybersecurity, attention always turns to the human element, but in most models and certifications, there is no mention or domain that covers the human element. We have discussed a number of ways how human behavior is impacted (e.g., conditioned response, behaviorism, psychoanalytical reasoning, stereotyping, the structure of language), but when was the last time you took a security certification that you have to answer a question on conditioned response?

In addition, while it is usually reported that the vast majority of incidents are caused by human behavior, the vast amount of cyber solutions are of a technical nature, and these two do simply not match, so perhaps cyber maturity, like many other metrics evaluation systems are not measuring what is needed to be measured. For example, can you measure attacks not successful? Can you measure employees that open an infected e-mail, but for whatever reasons, did not propagate on the network? How can you measure something that has not happened? If we hire a penetration testing outfit to test our environment and the results are good, does this mean our entire cyber environment is good overall? This was a one-shot test in a particular area, but even if it was a multishot test, will we believe and introduce the Dunning–Kruger effect? Will we begin to overestimate our abilities and believe we have created an even better cyber protections solution. From the daily security incidents we hear and read about, where are the weaknesses? Many penetration testers will tell you they are much better at defending their own network and then hacking into someone's else's network. On the surface, this makes sense as you have the keys to your system, all the passwords, you know where every-thing is, and have access to everything. Whereas with another network you have to guess, explore, and conduct reconnaissance. So, you may begin to feel strongly about your own abilities, but with that of which you know, or are familiar with, or the Dunning–Kruger effect:

You overestimate your ability to protect your own network.
You underestimate your ability to compromise someone's else network.

Cyber Ethics

Think of any association, such as medical, legal, project management, or accounting, there is always a code of ethics. Even in cybersecurity, there is a code of ethics. Sometimes they are called a code of conduct, and some organizations even have preamble to their code of ethics. Code of ethics, from the top management view on ethics, centers on leadership, but as for the code of conduct, it directs employees' actions and their behavior with an organization or association. The preamble would describe the ethical principles about to be laid out for members of an organization. Then in this context code of conduct would be more appropriate.

"Cyber ethics" is the term coined for individuals who use computer systems (e.g., do not send threatening e-mails), which many of us have seen and heard before. It also goes into copyright, as many like to believe that information should be free, sharing a digitally downloaded song or movie would be against cyber ethics, not forgetting it could also be very illegal. Peer-to-peer and torrent sharing and their users have come under some very heavy legal fines for sharing copyrighted material.

However, is free speech against cybernetical behavior?

If I researched a new technology device, and discovered how to circumvent the encryption protection, and then decided to share that knowledge with the research community, am I guilty of violating some cyber ethical code of conduct? Good question, it could be the association you are affiliated yet, but it could also be illegal, as the 1998 Digital Mil-lennium Copyright Act (DMCA) (U.S. Copyright Office 1998) has some very strong legal cases on both sides. For the most part, I would argue cyber ethics are good, and needed, as most ethics and laws are based upon a collective society decision on what's good or bad (e.g., revenge porn was not illegal for many years, but was it unethical), if not for an ethical standard that existed. Looking back to one of our earlier chapters, our language (Chapter 11) helps us to shape out reality. So that leads us to a code of conduct for hackers:

Hacker's Code of Conduct:

These are indeed very interesting, since some of these codes of conduct will compete with each other and the codes of conduct we just mentioned above.

The Hackers Freedom Code of Conduct

It's from the Free Software Foundation (Stallman 2012) (i.e., try before you buy). Remember shareware, which is a very good motto for most things. You try some software, or like test driving a car, if you like the software (if you like that car), you would buy that product. However, as we see in the press, peer-to-peer networks and torrents do not always abide by this creed. It seems most of this hacker ethics philosophy goes to Steven Levy (1984) who published the book *Hackers: Heroes of the Computer Revolution* in 1984, and governed three areas: (1) access—if something can teach you to learn and build upon knowledge, it should be available to everyone, (2) freedom of information—all information should be free to help build on and make those things better for all mankind, and (3) improvements in life—computers and technology can help improve human lives and everyone should have equal footing to enjoy these benefits. All of these do seem to be very noble. However, like the above freedom creed, take some software and freeing it does not really seem ethical, especially if it eventually leads to people losing their jobs because their companies are losing money on pirated software. However, like most things, they can be used for good and bad. For example, a piece of software was shared, which was a small piece of code that is used in medical machines to monitor and regulate heart beats. The software was shared, reverse engineered, found out to be defective but people already died because the company did not notify authorities. Definitely an ethical situation somewhere here. No matter what one might think of cyber ethics or hacker ethics, whether they are effective or not, they work the same, and you even agree with all of them, but they do have the result of reinforcing our neural network strengths.

Training reinforces neural networks associations that we know. The more association we have, the quicker the recall. Many companies do make an effect to train employees, but to push that further, more neural network associations are needed. The way to do this is to share what happens when an attack is successful, barring any undisclosed information on how to duplicate the attack, include employees and end users on how a successful attack occurred, how it was targeted, what steps were involved, and what happened, and what were the consequences. Was money lost, accounts hacked, personal data taken? The more associations that can be activated, the quicker the recall will be, and the better off for the organization.

Cybersecurity Implications and Conclusions

As we look back at this chapter, and again distinguish that while this book is not on cyber maturity, as there are enough books on the subject, perhaps maturity then has an impact on behavior. Considering the amount of security breaches we read about on a daily basis, could some of us be overestimating our ability to protect own network? Otherwise we would have so many successful breaches. Therefore, could the Dunning–Kruger effect be somewhat responsible for some of these breaches, and would someone at a certain maturity level correlate to this effect, it's certainly a possible research area. If you think about cybersecurity, it really is a game of cat and mouse, but in this case, the mouse adapts to outwit the cat. The cat reacts, stops the mouse (i.e., the threat), and the game is reset, only to be repeated again after the mouse has adapted a new line of attack.

Reminds me of the Roadrunner, always adapting and never quite getting caught.

I would like to see a cyber maturity model based on the sanity–insanity scale, because every time I talk to someone about cybersecurity, and the different threats and attack vectors, hacker motives, government and state players,, to someone who is not well versed in the terminology, they look at me and say, wow, you're crazy. It must be how my eyes light up when I talk about the different attacks.

I like to look at hacking and the protection from hacking analogs to a builder building a house. Each one requires a set of steps and anywhere along the lines you can weaken the steps, for example, an attack vector methodology could consist of:

- Reconnaissance
- Footprinting
- Enumeration
- Escalation of privileges
- Movement
- Maintaining access
- Covering your tracks

Comparing that to a home builder, and some of the steps would be:

- Blueprints
- Foundation
- Shell
- Dry-in
- Rough-in
- Mechanicals
- Finished work

But the one thing building a house and attack vectors do not have is checks and stops, in a real building, what we really have is:

- Blueprints, permits, and inspections
- Foundation, permits, and inspections
- Shell, permits, and inspections
- Rough-in, permits, and inspections
- Mechanicals, permits, and inspections
- Finished work, permits, and inspections

A permit in home building is an indication to go on; things are set with some minimum set of standards that others could proceed successfully. The only way a hacker could be successful if their permits were valid, as in:

- Reconnaissance, inspections, success, data obtained
- Footprinting, inspections, success, data obtained
- Enumeration, inspections, success, data obtained
- Escalation of privileges, inspections, success, data obtained
- Maintaining access, inspections, success, data obtained
- Covering your tracks, inspections, success, data obtained

How would a hacker get permits for reconnaissance? Simple, by finding out what information is out there, government records, Internet searchers, Domain Name Server lookups, and so on. If an attacker could not get a permit for this reconnaissance information, most likely they would abandon their pursuit. Movement—very few models have this. Ever watch a Hollywood spy movie, and you see some computer graphics on the screen, and it's trying to show on someone or a program is jumping from one point to the next. In movement, attackers get into a system and then look for another system to compromise. In the event they get locked out of one system, they have access to another system. Many companies log when people and even applications log onto a system, but they do not analyze the logs across all systems.

The trusted relationship is not normally part of penetration testing, but I think it should, or least at a much more emphasis added somewhere. If I were going to break into any big company that had a lot of money and resources, I wouldn't. I would simply break into a supplier of theirs, exploit a trusted relationship, and then exploit that connection. Examine some of the security breaches you have heard about lately and see if it was the company which was exploited, or some system, application, or something that they used from a trusted host. Therefore, a good penetration testing service would be tests against two companies: the main company and one of its vendors. Working collaboratively between the two companies and a penetration outfit might help shine some light on why trusted hosts are often compromised.

With social media, we are all connected, so too are businesses connected. If I am at any retailer, think of all those scanners on the checkout aisle. I doubt very much it was the retailer that also developed those scanners. So, if I wanted to hack into a major retailer, I would find out who made those scanners and start my reconnaissance there, and look at all the public information that is on that scanner manufacturer. It's the same thing with any technology really; pick any automobile, do you think the car manufacturer makes the radio or computer in your car? Start there. Follow the chain of events; if we have chain of custody, we might want to consider chain of events. It is not like this isn't available, it's simply the supply chain. Therefore, instead of a company jumping to technical solutions, turn to search solutions, and find out exactly what it is that is out there about your company and what publicly available information can be used. I guarantee many hackers look at copyrights, trademarks, and patents for information. Why would a company go for a copyright, trademark, or a patent? Maybe a new idea coming out soon, a new domain name registration to follow, a new website to be added, and it's always best to break into a site when its first coming online, during the early phases. Most other phases have similar components, so while technical solutions are indeed critical, you have to examine how someone thinks.

There are many hackers who really have limited technical skills, but have great research skills, and being part of a team, each hacker plays their part. If you think hackers do not work in teams, look up Anonymous, Syrian electronic army, 414s, Legions of Doom, and so on. There are probably thousands of hacking groups. The U.S. government and many governments worldwide use hacking groups.

I do wish some the hacking groups would change their name. They are so dreadful. How about

- Mary's pumpkin patch.
- Peaches and cream.
- Floppy ears.
- I stubbed my toe.

It would be interesting to see how someone reacts when they find out floppy ears has broken into their company's computer systems. First, how will they react, will they lessen their guard, slow down, and think more rationally. For hackers, many people may not even pay attention so much, and really good hackers want to be silent and unknown.

Well, that does seem to be changing.

Hackers had always been attuned to privacy. Go to any cybersecurity conference, and you will see hackers of all kinds gladly giving out autographs, signing books, and giving lectures. One big reason is corporate sponsorship and a chance to be seen and accepted as a good, no, a great cybersecurity individual. Hackers are indeed hired by many companies, and many governments, and it's kind of difficult to put on one's resume: I hacked into three companies last week, stole some corporate secrets, hacked into a major medical organization, found some medical information, and so on. And why would companies hire hackers? A hacker who can develop a cybersecurity solution that can guard against the same very hack he or she has developed and can make a company million in royalties. Perhaps, hackers are getting older; in some research we discussed in this book, many hackers are around 19 to 39 years, so possibly as they get older, they decide it's time to make a career with what they are good at and legally (i.e., does maturity come with age?). So, there are many reasons for their change, and there is a whole chapter on motivation, so perhaps cyber maturity should also look at age and other factors and gauge where cyber maturity really sits on the scale.

CHAPTER 14

Theory of Cybersecurity

Introduction

Is There a Theory of Cybersecurity?

Well, there isn't any.

If you think about marketing, a body of literature exists going back a century, but there is no accepted theory of marketing. There are many models you may have examined from your early college days like the 4P's (Price, Promotion, Product, Placement) or perhaps channel marketing, or Porter's five forces, or even the well-known Strengths, Weaknesses, Opportunities and Threats (SWOT) analysis. The Balanced Scorecard, the Marketing Mix, and even Maslow's hierarchy of needs as being used marketing theories. However, there is still not an accepted universal marketing theory. Information technology and the scholarly body of literature started in the late 1960s and early 1970s, and technology has been around for centuries, but from the academic perspective, many journals and associations started in the late 1990s with some exceptions (e.g., the Association for Computing Machinery was founded in 1947).

That brings us to the world of cybersecurity or even security, which has been used since the start of mankind, I am sure:

Even caveman worried about becoming lunch.

When did this academic body of security knowledge begin? It is hard to pinpoint a date since so many things use the word security, and I think until we agree on a common name (i.e., security, information security, information assurance, operations security, network security, information assurance and security, and the latest being cybersecurity). I doubt we can agree on a common definition of a cybersecurity theory. However, like marketing, there are models and proposals for cybersecurity, and perhaps one day one of these will be eventually accepted. There are many models: ISO, NIST, DHS, NSA, IEEE, and so on. They are all very good and they all cover a lot of areas in security but are not classified as a theory of cybersecurity. We also have theories that have been used in cybersecurity research (e.g., protection motivation theory (PMT), game theory, adoption theory, neutralization, and warfare theory), but none of them are called specifically a cybersecurity theory.

Theories to Borrow: Gregor

Since we have many models of security, and many theories that have been borrowed from other bodies of literature in security research, let's examine some of those. Perhaps we can extend what we currently have to see if a theory of cybersecurity could emerge. Since cybersecurity is a relatively new term, and cybersecurity theory is unknown, let's borrow what we have already. We find many proposals that we might use to begin to develop a cybersecurity theory. The foundation then perhaps this will lead to an actual cybersecurity theory we could test. Since there is no theory, we need to start from the fundamental components of developing theory, and Gregor (2006) is a good starting place, as his work on information systems is probably a novel way to examine cybersecurity in terms of other research approaches. Gregor starts by asking what should we examine. These are the domains in a discipline that are encouraged to be explored and Gregor identified four critical areas:

1. The domain question: what is the phenomena, the problem, the topic of interest, why are we even interested?
2. The ontological questions: the meaning of theory, what questions are asked in theory, and how is theory composed?
3. The epistemological questions: how can scientific knowledge be created and how would the theory be tested?
4. The socio-political understanding: who are the stakeholders and how are they involved, what has been developed, are there agreed upon theories, and is there knowledge and has it been applied?

Gregor makes the claim that although each of these areas have received attention, it is the second area, that of the ontological questions, that is lacking. As a practical example, for the first area and in the discipline of information systems, researchers have examined the content of information systems and information technology, such as management information systems. There is an argument, however, that information technology is the same or different from information systems. We can see the same issues now when we examine cybersecurity: is it operations security, network security, or even information security? The epistemological area has also received considerable attention since the field of information systems now has a few decades of research under its knowledge belt. There are several hundred academic journals, and research in both quantitative and qualitative research studies are presented. We do see cybersecurity growing, especially during the last decade, and we also see a very wide range of disciplines under security (e.g., network protection, cryptography, forensics, policy, etc.). The socio-political understanding is a discipline approach that has been grounded in historical developments, and its integration to enhance humans and be embraced by humans for their end goals. Cybersecurity seems to be the reverse, in that, much more practical human involvement is being used to answer these socio-political understandings (e.g., we know end users are sometimes careless with e-mails, but now we seek to examine and research the reasons behind their behavior). For the ontological concerns, Gregor argues that the theory of information systems is scattered. It could be the language that is missing, as we can recall in an earlier chapter when we discussed the issue of language and how a culture can be shaped by that language. In the field of information systems, theory is often not used but models are discussed, and a very similar mode is followed in cybersecurity today. As the beginning of this chapter points out, there are many models but no theory. In a review of the information systems literature, many more articles discussed what a theory is, rather than proposing a theory. Gregor presents a view on theory. One can read the research, but what is important to remember is about theory that can explain or predict (i.e., what we have been discussing in this book).

Can we explain someone's behavior?
Can we predict someone's behavior?

There are many ways to approach theory development, but all scientific theories must be universally accepted and open to refinement. We must have knowledge about these scientific theories, a consensus, and a language that comprises scientific understandings. Another important factor is generalization (i.e., given a sample, can we generalize it to a larger population?). If I can uncover knowledge that sheds light on the reasons why someone engages in hacking, can I then generalize that knowledge to all hackers, or at least a very large population of hackers? If not, then my current knowledge could be faulty, or needs refinement. For example, in scientific research, are we considering cause and effect, or correlation? These are different, and while many times cause and effect can show correlation, it cannot be said the reverse is true. With the examination of theory, Gregor (2006) starts to examine information system theories using four primary goals: (1) analysis and description—what the phenomena is and how to analyze the phenomena, (2) explanation—the how, why, and where things happen, (3) prediction, future looking, (4) explanation and prediction—the how, why, where, and what will happen, and (5) design and action—says how something should be done, a model, technique, a relationship, and so on (see Figure 14.1). A theory does not exist in the real world unless a human creates a model.

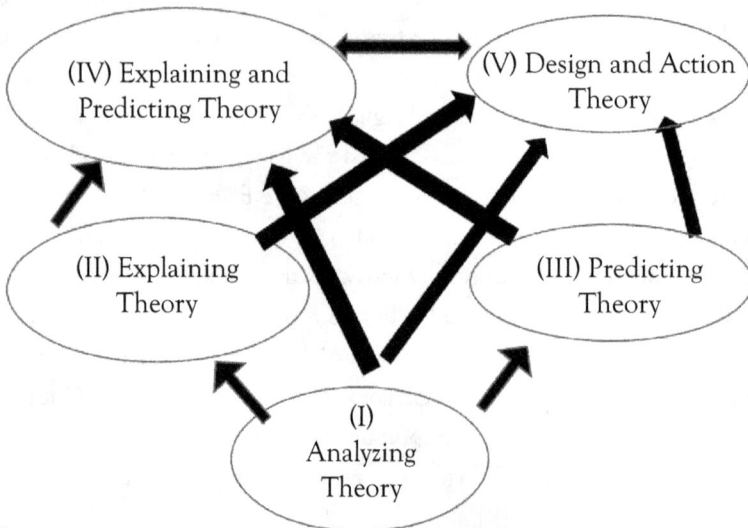

Figure 14.1 The Nature of Theory in Information Systems: Adapted from: Gregor, S. 2006. "The Nature of Theory in Information Systems." MIS Quarterly 30, no. 3, pp. 611-642.

As we look to expand on Gregor's work and search for a model, we might consider a model for analyzing and description in Iivari, Hirschheim, and Klein's (2000) framework, which was a method to compare similarities and differences among different information system approaches. One model that could be used for explaining would be Orlikowski's (1992) model, which suggests technology is also combined with human practice. Giddens's (1984) structuration theory and Latour's (1987) and Latour and Woolgar's (1986) actor-network theory help explain reciprocal relationships. A theory that could be used for predicting. Moore's (1965) model predicted that the number of transistors would keep doubling every two years; however, Moore's law is unique in that information systems are lacking in predictive models. Explanation and prediction could be gleaned from general systems theory (von Bertalanffy 1969) and the technology acceptance model (TAM) (Davis et al. 1989); for design and action, Markus et al.'s (2002) design theory and Turban and Aronson's (2001) decision support models can be employed. Gregor (2006) suggests there is a relationship and taxonomy among these five areas of theory development and a theory development could be consistent with these five areas, and he shows the interrelationships among the different classes of theory. However, not all theories will fit all five categories, and not all five categories have to be present in all theories. There are problems in any class of theories such as causality, cause and effect, assumptions, and so on, but in meta-analysis of 50 research articles, some of these areas were presented. Therefore, this could be a good starting point for a cybersecurity theory.

A Theory for Information Security

In 2016, researchers Horne, Ahmad, and Maynard proposed an examination of theory on information security (see Figure 14.2). It is not a theory per se, but it lays the groundwork to continue examining a basis to create future cybersecurity theory and builds upon Gregor's (2006) early work. There are reasons to understand this new area as cybersecurity theory is lacking. They bridge existing factors and develop several factors and relationships to create a base for theory development for information security. They build on Gregor's (2006) different approaches to theory including the ontological, epistemological, and socio-political approaches. They examined how information security has been defined, as in most models of security we might come across the confidentiality, integrity, availability (CIA) triad, which has been now expanded to include other aspects such as non-repudiation, accountability, authorization, authenticity, and more recently being expanded with the concepts of privacy and trust. They agree with the view that although information security and cybersecurity are used interchangeably, there are some subtle differences that should be understood (i.e., cyber adds in the human element). There are four proposed constructs to this schematic theory that consist of controls, threats, resources, and information. Information is what can be seen, touched, felt, experienced, stored consciously, and subconsciously. However, information is not data, so I can see a binary pattern stored in my mind, but I cannot see how that binary pattern makes me feel. Controls are countermeasures; physical, administrative, operational all are controls. Regulations and standards also are pseudo-controls since they will direct us to implement other controls, like Sarbanes–Oxley (SOX), the Health Insurance Portability and Accountability Act (HIPAA), or the Family Educational Rights and Privacy Act (FERPA). Threats are those that seek to interrupt our use of resources by making them unavailable and through modifications, and other means. Resources are the inputs, the units of analysis. These are the things that are going to be measured (e.g., a unit of analysis of a survey might be the one taking that survey).

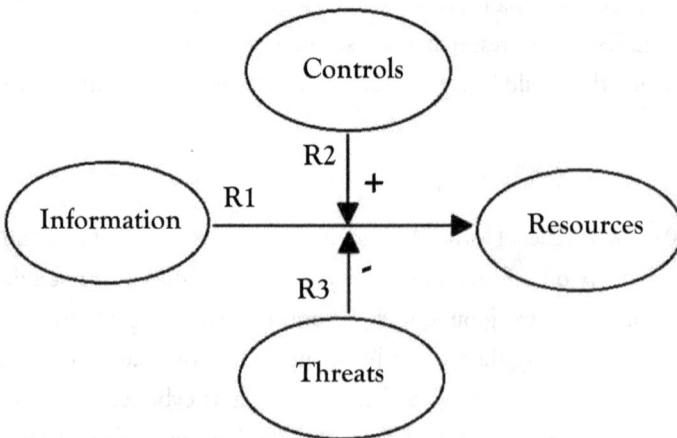

Figure 14.2 A Theory on Information Security. Adapted from: Horne, C., Ahmad, A., & Maynard, S. 2016. "A Theory on Information Security." The 27th Australasian Conference on Information Systems, At Wollongong, Australia

Horne, Ahmad, and Maynard's (2016) *Schematic of Theory on Information Security* examines the relationship between information and resources. If I seek to access some resource, what is the control that allows or prohibits that access. The relationship between controls and information—what types of controls are allowing or curtailing access to this information. This includes both hard-coded media like data on a hard drive and memory in our cognitive hard drive (e.g., secret government employees with information to classified data may have to take periodic lie detector tests). The relationship between threats and information—what threats do we know about, how can they change, evolve, what do we know, what we don't know, and how will the controls react to threats we do not understand. They do admit that in their model, some things normally associated with research are absent such as causal explanations but argue that there are four types of causal analysis that can be applied. Since this is not an applied theory, but more of a framework, hypothesis would not be appropriate given the context, and a prediction and prescriptive narrative is not followed. However, this is a good viewpoint of the conceptually viewing information security and coupled with Gregor's (2006) different approaches could lead the way to an eventual cybersecurity theory.

Von Solms and Van Niekerk (2013) suggested that cybersecurity also needs the human element and moves away from previous information security knowledge that did not include this dimension. They argue like other researchers that the normal cognitive thinking of cybersecurity of the generally accepted models of confidentiality, integrity, and availability are too much of an overlap to information security and do not reflect the new boundaries of cybersecurity. They suggest that security is not a thing, but a process, and as this book has shown chain of events and cognitive emotions are indeed not a thing, but a flow of events. They do make the argument that if cybersecurity is too closely aligned with information security, and lack the human component, for example, what category would cyber bullying fall under? Or perhaps sexting? social engineering? cyber terrorism? All human, not technology, aspects of security. Much in the way that peer-to-peer is technology, and while that technology itself may fall under information security, the motives to engage may not. Their model is one of an overlap between information security and cybersecurity and good for discussion.

Game Theory for Cybersecurity

Earlier we discussed game theory and behavioral game theory. Shiva, Roy, and Dasgupta (2010) proposed extending and using game theory as a basis for cybersecurity. It is a holistic security approach consisting of examining the whole picture of security. Their approach includes a central component of hardware and software surrounded by cascading layers of self-checking modules. As the layers work outward, and just like peeling an onion, we would have the traditional security infrastructure protection measures such as cryptography. Going further out there would be a list of secure applications. Each of these levels would have self-checking security measures. The outer layer would consist of the game theoretic decision modeling. If you are familiar with the famous standard Open System Interconnection (OSI), which has been used decades now in networking, this does not compete with that model, but rather works within the model. The purpose of the addition of the game theory would be to assist the inner layers to make the best decisions with regards to security in terms of cost, benefits, and so on. This game theory approach could be used with the deployment of a semiautonomous defense architecture that could react when cyber defenses are needed. A distributed architecture is also used along with a set of game agents that will detect and respond to threats. A honeypot could also be used to help force and redirect threats. While not necessarily a security theory, it's another good model from which theory could be developed.

Theory of Cybersecurity

In examining any theory, we need to build upon previous work. Therefore could what we have just discussed lead us to develop a cybersecurity theory? While there is no current accepted theory in marketing, or computer forensics, the research continues, so it will be with cybersecurity. Over time these models and frameworks will move in the direction where an eventual theory will be developed, so this will be just a start.

We can continue with Gregor's (2006) work, which could be a very good place to start, since if we agree with the dimensions of how theory is developed, we might be able to develop constructs within those confines.

1. In analyzing what is the phenomena under consideration? Is it the loss of information, the loss of a system resources, the loss of personnel? It seems that loss is a core component. And cybersecurity has moved away from just information security to include the technical and human components.

2. In explanation, what are we trying to explain? Why hackers break into systems? Why companies do not insist on secure hashes while storing personal data? Why seems like a human behavioral trait we should seek to address? Could distributed cognitive theory help to explain some areas here? Cognitive experiences and differences help to explain a person's motives, so perhaps will help to explain why patches are not done correctly.

3. In prediction, are we looking at someone's future behavior, or the number of attacks a company faces? Since the chain of events are many times the result of human action, is it possible again? We are looking at predicting human behavior (e.g., why was not the correct patch applied or what were the decisions to store data in clear text?). We have seen that social activity plays a lot in someone's perceptions, so perhaps we could borrow from activity theory that helps to explain how humans seek to accomplish tasks with resources, in this case, technology.

4. In explanation and prediction, we probably have half of this already. We do not store the correct patch and store data in clear text. We can predict what will most likely happen. Could we borrow from management and organizational theories? We have seen the psychology of blame and stress levels attributed to cybersecurity professionals. Could pressure from management of the organization culture contribute to not using the stronger, most available technologies?

5. In design and action, we probably have more than enough models we can take from, and possibly replace constructs most likely aligned with a cybersecurity focus. Therefore, by starting with Gregor's (2006) explanation of theory development, and examining current theories that have been used in cybersecurity research, we may eventually come up with a cybersecurity theory. We have many of these; most of cybersecurity research uses already established models, like the technology acceptance model of Davis (1985).

While examining the development of cybersecurity theory, the first dimension—analyzing—still needs to be researched, which makes sense since we still call it security or information assurance or information security and now cybersecurity, so are we sure of what we are protecting? Perhaps we don't even know what we are protecting. But what is the real phenomena? When asked to give what we believe is cybersecurity, we typically refer to specific individuals' items, such as computer systems, networks, passwords, viruses, and phishing, but this is not theory. These would more be aligned with concepts and constructs of a theory.

In all of these specific areas, they all point to one thing, and that is data, or even more appropriately information. Cybersecurity is protecting information, anywhere, anytime. Even a person, in the general sense, is information for what they know. That is why when we calculate risk, we do not look at the time value of data, but the time value of information. Companies spend millions protecting their chief executives than they would a random employee. Nations spend millions more protecting their presidents than the average civilian. So what are they protecting? The person, the data, or the information the person has? Therefore, even a person can be summed up in a common denominator along with technology in that it's the information we are protecting, and not just the information, but the entropy of that information.

What about information theory then?

Shannon's (1948) proposed information theory looked into quantification, storage, and communication of information. His approach was a more practical one and studies the communications of information over a noisy channel and is widely used today in fields such as artificial intelligence, cybernetics, machine learning, and adaptive systems. What is interesting about information theory is that it examined entropy (i.e., the amount on uncertainty of a random process). Entropy is used in a wide range of fields, and perhaps it could help us to try and solve Gregor's (2006) area of analyzing. We seek to protect information, either by someone's else eyes, or when they seek to deny our use of this information. The riskier that we wish to protect has much greater uncertainty given the information (e.g., it is much riskier to protect this nation's nuclear stockpiles than my login and password to a social networking site). So perhaps, in analyzing we can use entropy, in that the phenomena we are trying to investigate is the entropy of the information we are trying to protect. We now have several parts that are needed in a model for a theory of cybersecurity.

Figure 14.3 illustrates a conceptual theory of cybersecurity based upon entropy of information. In any theory, we need dependent and independent variables. Since entropy is a condition of the unpredictability of the state, and in this case information, we could set this as a continuous dependent variable (i.e., the rate of information that could become stolen could depend on the entropy of that data), that is, how effectively is that data protected and label it information entropy. Then borrowing from Gregor's (2006) work, it is possible that other areas are cause for that information entropy, which could be termed dependent causes. While much more research is certainly needed, it is probably prudent in any cybersecurity theory that we examine the entropy of the information, since any security endeavor is the protection of that information, whether in a hard drive, the cloud, or a person's brain.

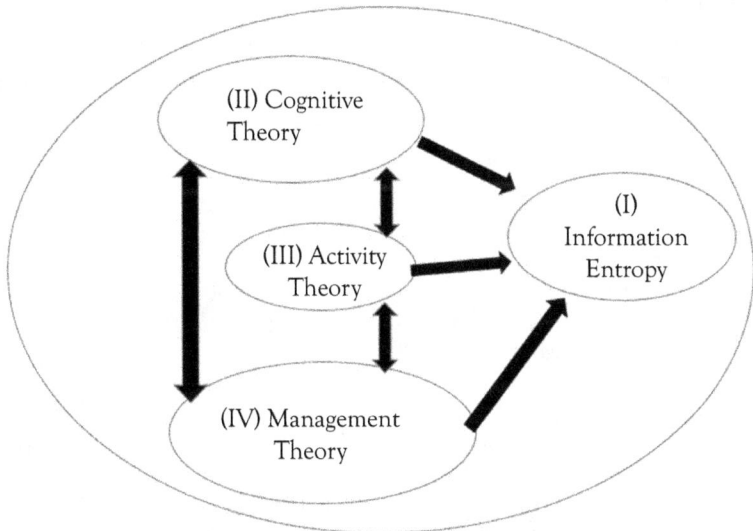

Figure 14.3 A theory of cybersecurity

Cybersecurity Implications and Conclusions

In this model of cybersecurity we examined, the theory is cybersecurity information entropy. The entropy of information is dependent on multiple factors, which taken together will impact the entropy of that information. As the entropy increases, the more chance that the information will become compromised. As we have seen throughout this text, human behavior and perceptions motivate behavior. The more we understand this, the more we can take better protection measures. The lower the entropy will become, the safer the information.

In our theory, for all the factors that impact our cognitive abilities, social activity behaviors, and management, organizational culture could help to shed light on how variable information within our organization will become. The model is viewed within the context of the various information systems models we have now, for example, in cognitive theory, we would want to examine constructs from the relevant literature like game theory. In activity theory, we would examine constructs possibly from the social engineering literature. This model emphasizes the human behavior more closely than other models but is grounded in the literature pertaining to cybersecurity and other technology-based literature and so on. Since it was stated earlier that behavior follows perceptions, within a given stimuli, in a particular circumstance, perhaps we can use these concepts as starting points to Gregor's dimensions, and from a cybersecurity viewpoint.

CHAPTER 15

Future

Introduction

As with most research, we uncover new and interesting areas of future study and hope that further research will lead to more knowledge in that area of study. As in many of this book's examples, perhaps there are also future areas we could consider to make us become better cybersecurity professionals. Therefore, in this last chapter, we are just going to touch on some of these areas, and perhaps we may see there are indeed new and possible future areas to explore.

Single-Cell Solution

Could a single-cell solution solve complex problems in cybersecurity? There exists the salesman's paradox that has bothered mathematicians for decades. In this paradox, as a salesman with multiple customers with multiple routes, how does that salesman make the most efficient use of their time in traveling those routes? If that salesperson can find shortest overall time, the more opportunities that salesman will have at selling more products and services, and the more potential for earnings. There is the shortest path formula (i.e., calculate the shortest paths among routes) and create the route. It works perfectly with only a few destinations; if the salesman has only four cities to worry about, the maximum number of routes possible is six. However, if the salesman has ten cities, just six more, the number of routes shoots up to over 180,000, an incredible increase in computations. Now, think of public key cryptography. Each user generates their own public–private key pair. In order to communicate with any other user, they must have their own pair. For a third user, another pair is needed. As users grow, keys grow but not in a linear format. The number of users of 10 to the 3rd power will need many keys less than compared to 10 to the 9th power.

Take a look at this table—unfortunately I don't have the link anymore

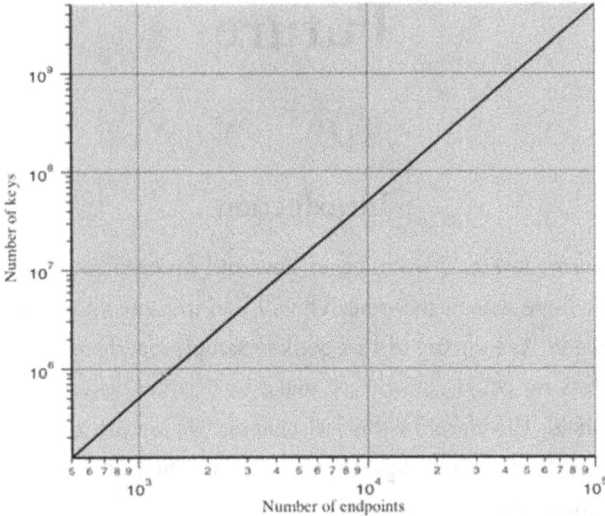

If I have 10 x 4th number or endpoints or people—I need almost 10 x 7.6 number of keys, so If I have a million people communicating with each other, I might need 7 or 8 million keys. Its not a linear growth.

Compare this to the typical network with users, routers, switches, mobile devices, physical barriers, and so on, and each new entry into this environment does not grow by the addition of one, but by the addition of $n + 1/2$ factorial. Each new addition must be secured by means to, and away from the n devices on the network. The dilemma is how can a cybersecurity expert protect all these new routes in their network. It may not just be identifying the shortest route, but all routes. Researchers at Tokyo's Keio University have been using an amoeba to solve the traveling salesman problem (Zhu, Song-Ju, Hara, and Aono 2018). The concept is using slime mold, which walks toward food and away from light. The amoeba instinct knows how to create this travel path in the least amount of time by lights that go on and off depending on the distance to the next path. Expanding this to public urban planning, as more cities are added, the process is not changed, and the shortest path is still detected. Extending this to a cybersecurity simulation of a network, as more nodes are added and the scenario with amoeba are run, it could highlight and show all potential vulnerable points of entry. An example could be of a guest account or adding a vendor account. Many times, these accounts are left active, even after there is no longer need for these accounts. This potential technology could help to highlight them more frequently.

Threat Modeling with Single-Cell Solution

In threat modeling, considering multiple attackers and multiple attack vectors, questions like where is the organization most vulnerable, where are the most important assets, where are the points of entry that must be identified are of critical importance. There are many threat modeling models: visual, agile, and simple threat modeling (VAST), trike risk methodology (TRIKE), operationally critical threat, asset, and vulnerability evaluation (OCTAVE), and others that look at the totality of the environment (think Gestalt). Look at and prioritize the risks, protect against the high-profile ones, and guard against any residual ones left. However, many risk models fail to guard against all threats not because they do not understand threats, but it's a matter of finding them. Perhaps in the case of a single-cell solution, all threats could be identified, resources applied appropriately, and have enough resources left over for the residual risks usually not guarded.

Security Intelligence

There is new term in the literature lately called security intelligence. Is it that we are becoming more intelligent in understanding security, or is it that security itself is becoming alive with its own intelligence? Perhaps within the realm of artificial intelligence it very well could be in the future. As data grows, as more data is pushed to the edge, the cloud, more devices, data analytics, and interpreting and acting on that data perhaps will make security more intelligent. It could also get to the point where we just give up and admit failure. From earlier readings, we have discussed human intelligence, human behavior, human motivations, human shortcomings, and if we never address these to our satisfaction, I am not sure how we can address cybersecurity to the point where we feel safe.

We've looked at a lot of the research on intelligence and current research dictates there are two parts: (1) the knowhow (i.e., the numbers, facts, figures, etc.), and (2) the creative piece. Considering we have so much data as there are so many attacks that we can easily extrapolate the first part from data, so we probably need to focus more on the second part.

Knowledge

There are basically two types of knowledge: one is the knowing the name of something and the second is the knowing of something; these are completely different. Feynman (1994) understood these two types and developed a way to be able to teach complicated subject matter to a layman. Most of the information you may locate on Feynman would mention toddler, but I doubt many toddlers would ever understand Feynman's work in quantum mechanics. However, the point of the toddler is a very good one: how would you explain quantum mechanics to a toddler? Who has a very limited vocabulary of only two to four letters? What Feynman's technique does is to remove all your own biases and force you to concentrate on the receiver of the message, not you, the sender. When I discuss some cybersecurity topics with my doctoral mentees, I often ask them, what does your wife do, what does your husband do, what does your 12-year-old child like to do. They will often come back with a number of different topics, none of which are focused on cybersecurity. I tell them, okay, now go to them and explain your topic of your research, and when they understand that topic, let's talk again. This technique is really not for the wife, the husband, or the child, but for the mentee. The world of cybersecurity and dissertation research is very complicated. There are many avenues of conflicting data and ideas that are often jumbled together, and this technique helps them to clarify ideas in their own minds. You have no choice but to clarify ideas when only using three- and four-letter words. Therefore, while we have two forms of knowledge— knowing the name of something, and knowing something—a third form could be the knowing of something we think we know. Knowing the name is something is easy, knowing something is easy too, after a bit of knowing that something, but remember if we think we know, we may be overestimating our own judgments. Knowing of something we think we know really stands out when you ask someone to explain that something to you, as they jump from from point to point, not detailing a clear picture. They may think they know something, but in the back of their own minds, they know they are confused. To combat this problem, and as an example, I asked my mentees to address the following questions at the beginning of their dissertation:

- Write a simple paragraph as if you are explaining this research to your friend, in a short page.
- Who is the researcher or researchers that report this as an issue, and who identified it as a gap that needs to be studied?
- For a quantitative study, what are the dependent variables (DVs) and what are the independent variables (IVs)?
- What analysis method are you using—correlation, regression, sum of least square?
- For a qualitative study, what is the model or framework are you using? What are the concepts you want to measure?
- Write your research questions, and they must line up with your variables or constructs.
- Name your population. Are you talking about security administrators, IT workers, IT managers, help desk, and IT people?
- What is your problem statement in 10 words or less and cite this?
- What is your purpose statement?
- What do you expect to find?

But before sending me the above assignment, I ask them to teach someone what they are doing. Get that 12-year-old or significant other to understand the above questions, and when you can do that, you understand it yourself. If you think you can't get a 12-year-old to understand correlation, tell them that the number of ice cream cones sold goes up with the number of toilet flushes.

They will get that; kids always like bathroom humor.

Once they understand, that means you have it explained it to a toddler, like Feynman's approach, but more importantly it's clear in your head, that is why number one is so important. The first point is the most important step here, and you cannot achieve the first step until you go through all the other steps. I sometimes refer it to as an articulated mess or an unarticulated mess. I can fix an articulated mess (e.g., if they mention surveys but say they are doing qualitative research). If they say correlation but using sum of least squares, that I can correct. However, I cannot correct an unarticulated mess (i.e., they want to talk about privacy but using a theory on satisfaction). So, in cybersecurity, there exists a need to be clear—clear in your head and clear in everyone's else's head. Because it turns out if it's not clear in someone else's head, it wasn't clear in your head to begin with. The reason for the exercise is just all the things we have been discussing—assumptions, ambiguity, clarity, and stereotyping. I believe if cybersecurity education begins to look at this as complete process that takes into account its dynamic nature with the interactions among many different players, rather than a one-off technical solution, we can gain a lot more knowledge in this area.

Nutrition

Why would food even be considered a topic in cybersecurity? During the writing of this book we've discussed many different facets of the human behavior—why humans are motivated, what compels them to behave in a certain way, and we always come back to neural network associations. These associations help to inform us and help us make decisions, and even though we will sometimes do something completely different than what our neural networks associations are telling us (i.e., cognitive dissonance); they are nevertheless still informing us.

The phrase *you are what you eat* is true. Food quality directly affects your brain. Gómez-Pinilla (2008) did a 160 meta-study analysis illustrating the importance of good nutrition on cognitive abilities, and several researchers have suggested that the smartest neural networks compete for food in an evolutionary battle. Human beings want to remain in homeostasis, but as Ruffin, Salameh, Boron, and Parker (2014) point out that there may be a link between a person's potential hydrogen (pH) and the increase of neuronal excitability inside a person's brain. Since nutrition effects pH and can have devastating effects on neural transporters, leading to such ailments as Alzheimer's and Parkinson's, could it also have an effect on our neural network associations even if not so drastic? Another positive effect of proper nutrition is reduced inflammation. Healthy diets are linked to positive effects in the brain (Lassale et al. 2019; Foster and Neufield 2013; Ramsey 2016). Molecules in the brain are impacted by the quality of food. They can reduce depression, reduce inflammation, and help you live longer. This is not to imply to never eat another donut or fast food burger again, or that a capsule would suffice, but it does raise the possibility that if the correct nutrition was identified, and since our cybersecurity neural network associations are active and competing for food resources, could we somehow in the future make these associations stronger and more productive. If food can give us all kinds of bad ailments, like cholesterol and diabetes, could it also give us targeted benefits, and if it can help us to increase recall of neural network associations in cybersecurity, wouldn't that be a benefit?

Music

Can music possibly help cybersecurity?

In the same way nutrition might, and probably even more so since music is actually stimuli, in that it stimulates all the senses—touch, feel, sound, and vision—and induces life-long physical changes to the brain. In the event that someone lacks the ability of any of those senses, the other senses work harder. Neuroscientists have suggested one possible explanation that music has connection to emotions on brain activity. Neuroscientists have shown repeatedly shown that music changes the brain structure (e.g., both left and right sides of the brain are connected). However, the corpus callosum, which connects the two sides, are notably larger in musicians. Costandi (2016) reports that the brain areas that are responsible for movement, hearing, and visuo-spatial abilities are larger as well, and music helps to reach areas of the brain other techniques like brain games cannot. A very positive benefit is that it is not just the long-term musicians who can benefit, but short-term music can help stimulate the brain's neural connections. Schlaugh, Norton, Overy, and Winner (2006) have reported results showing that certain areas of the brain are larger depending on the instrument played. During MRI scans, they reported finding significant changes in just one year of music training. While their research did not examine other factors such as intensity of training, length of practice sessions, musical notation, and so on, they do find changes in brain structure, which could increase neural network communications. Chan, Ho, and Cheung (1998) have found that music training increases the left planum temporal region of the brain, which can increase the cognitive functions of the left side of the brain that includes verbal memory. So, while being a musician will not make one a better cybersecurity expert, the increased and larger connections of the different parts of the brain may help neural network associations, improve cognitive abilities overall, and improve recall, which is critical for cybersecurity experts.

And, if music can soothe the savage beast, why can't music soothe the savage cybersecurity expert as I have known a lot of grumpy cybersecurity professionals.

Multiple Attacks

Attacks happen more than once to the same organization. After a successful first attack, what makes a company a prime target for repeated attacks? This has shown to be indeed the case, as banks, social networking sites, online portals, payment vendors, and others get attacked again and again. There has to be a reason for this happening. Well, looking at regular household attacks, several reasons emerge, such as

1. Familiarity—I've been here before, and I know the layout.
2. Less effort—I know my way around already.
3. Entry and exit points identified—I know how to get in, what worked, and where to leave.
4. Weaknesses known—I know what works and what doesn't.

Therefore, if your company has been hacked, be prepared that many more attempts, and some may be successful again. Also, remember insurance; while many companies have insurance for crimes, they may be exposed to liability to losses from repeated crimes, or if they did not exercise due diligence to close off access.

Blameless Root-Cause Analysis

After reading so many security papers, we come to the conclusion that someone is to blame, someone is always to blame, so let's just blame it on the end user. Blameless root-cause analysis is the root-cause analysis simply without blame. How did an accident occur, why it happened, what led up to the accident, and how can we learn from what has happened? Yes, I am a cybersecurity expert, and yes, I opened up an infected e-mail, and why, well I was curious, the e-mail subject was interesting and I've never seen this type of e-mail before. Am I going to admit I did this? No! I will say it's a new virus. I am going to basically lie and say it's self-opening by just reading the subject line, and I hope they believe that. Now we are chasing ghosts. Instead of trying to see why this message was curious, we have to ask why our antivirus systems did not catch this, and why was this subject line so interesting (e.g., see one of the latest e-mail scams, sextortion)? Our end goal should be how did this accident occur and what conditions let up to that person opening the e-mail? When criminal justice experts interview prisoners why they robbed a certain house, prisoners often reply the windows easy to open, blocked by shrubbery, the other neighbors had a dog, and so on. When an end user opens up an infected e-mail, they usually ask someone so far removed to stop it from happening again. This is not the most effective way of troubleshooting. Cybersecurity experts should ask the users (i.e., without fear of reprisals, why did you open that e-mail).

The Multiple Causation Theory

Multiple causation theory (MCT) is very important for cybersecurity professionals to understand, as it may help us not to keep chasing ghosts. MCT builds upon domino theory from Heinrich (1931). Imagine a domino set design created and push over the first dominos, the rest will fall. This is cause and effect, and in cybersecurity it can be a lot worse. In other cases, it can lead to death and destruction.

A cause has an effect, which in turn causes another effect, which in turn causes another effect and so on, therefore it is like:

- Cause 1 causes effect 1
- Cause 2 (which is really effect 1) causes effect 2.
- Cause 3 (which is really effect 2) causes effect 3.
- and so on.

There have been many examples of this over the years (e.g., the electrical grid blackout last decade of the eastern part of the United States that put over 50 million people in the dark). Without electricity, no light, no power for water pumps, no electric transportation, and just think of all the things that use electricity were not working. Nuclear power plants have had experiences in this cause and effect, and fortunately they do build safeguards. So a lot of tragedies were averted by breaking this cause–effect cycle; however, there have also been deadly nuclear accidents.

Heinrich introduced Heinrich triangle, which shows that major incidents do not just happen. There are warnings, he argued, that in just one major incident, there were over 29 previous minor incidents and over 300 incidents overall. What led to that massive 2003 electrical blackout in the United States, and how many incidents happened? There were over 300 overall incidents, including a combination of old power lines, summer heat, overgrown trees, outdated equipment, and human error, and a software bug in the alarm system failing to tell operators that some power lines were starting to hit some tree branches, thereby disrupting the amount of electricity between supply and demand, a system tripped, the other facilities could not handle the load, they kept going off line, *cause and effect, cause and effect, cause and effect.* In cybersecurity, we need to understand this cause and effect, just like the curious end user who opened up that infected e-mail? Was this really just the one time an infected e-mail got thought the defenses? Were there others and were they ignored? Did we just not have the resources to correct a deficient system? Did we not have the political willpower? We've seen this played out time and time again, when company executives admit something should have been done earlier, and vow that it will never happen again.

Living Laboratory Framework

An interesting proposition is advocated by McNeese et al. (2013) and that of a living laboratory. Their argument is that analysts do not enjoy a comprehensive environment to deal with in order to learn (i.e., the real world is often the term used). When it comes to warfare, unless there is actual war, it's a static laboratory. Team interplay, opposing forces, all create a dynamic rich environment to grow, and while no one is calling for open conflict, maybe moving away from a static environment, it is a way to enhance this body of knowledge. A cyber operations framework living laboratory can be very beneficial. For one thing, analysts are disconnected and the cognitive representation of the open world, where cognitive factors, changing forces of play due to human emotion and behavior are intertwined and changed frequently. In typical analysis, I may see my enemy, but in a cyber analysis I am left guessing as to who is my enemy. Even in some cyber strategy games, the stage is set, and it's up to an analyst to figure out the next month. Wouldn't it be more beneficial having a real-life simulation? A living laboratory is where both sides are actively competing to reach some goal. In these cyber analysts, these reflexes are often one-dimensional (i.e., an analyst who might be good at understanding routers may not be versed in spoofing e-mails, or versed in understanding bitcoin ransoms). A troubling point these researchers point out is the nature of secrecy in cyber analysis. It is understandable for analysts in war scenario to hide what they are doing for national secrets, whereas the hotel down your block will not be engage in any war-related activities. However, the hotel may have a much higher probability of a cyber attack, especially if the hotel is located in an area where government agencies are also located, or conferences held. So, at times the secrecy that surrounds cyber analysis is not a worthwhile attribute. It is like the saying a rising tide lift all boats used in economics where more income equality is spread across all those participating, and as one rises, all will rise. This should be thought in the same context—the more one's cybersecurity knowledge rises for one, it should also rise more for all participating. Perhaps, multiple causation and domino theories can help us at least examine the weak links. Much like the electrical utility has learned, perhaps cybersecurity professionals can learn as well to identify multiple cause and effects without their realm our responsibility to develop and implement better cybersecurity solutions. Just in case that one alarm does not trip.

Artificial Intelligence, Machine Learning, Block Chain, Internet of Things, Swarm Learning, the Intelligent Edge, Massive BOT Net Attacks, Massive Computer Resource Stealing, and more etc.

Are any of these really the future? After all, these are technologies, so we can either try to protect data used by these technologies, or try to understand how we understand our own behaviors in protecting data used by these technologies. They are not some nefarious entities looking to cause havoc. They are not alive, they do not think, and it's the people using these technologies that do the thinking and are motivated to behave in a certain way.

Remember all these terms:

- In the 1990s, virtual private networks were in style.
- In the 1980s, object-oriented programming was the rage.
- In the 1970s, Client–Server technology was ruling.

Who could forget Y2K was going to cause airplanes to fall out of the sky?

Artificial intelligence has made great strides and will continue to do so, however, it has its problems resulting from the context of the message. Place a yellow school bus on the road, an AI interface will see it as a yellow school bus. Place the school bus on the side, AI will see it as a snow plow; place the AI interface underneath the school bus, it will now identify it as a garbage truck, so unless all these contexts are built into the AI, there will still be problems. With all these new terms, or technologies, what are we trying to protect and what do they all have in common? Data perhaps, information definitely. An interesting experiment done by Chu, Zhmoginov, and Sandler (2017) examined when artificial intelligence worked the way it was supposed to work. What is wrong with something working the way it was supposed to? Well, it was designed to work the correct way, but it was not expected beforehand. Researchers design a study going in; they kind of already know what the outcomes will be, or what they should be, and in this study it wasn't that the outcome was incorrect, it performed exactly the way the technology was supposed to do, but that the researchers did not understand the outcomes, which shed some fantastic results on our understanding of neural networks. It was a simple enough design—take satellite data and import it onto Google Maps, basically seeing the stars all laid out on a map. It was working very well, but something was wrong, there was more data than it appears to be. So, where did this extra data come from? Whereas the program saw this data, the researchers did not. The computer system was behaving exactly the way it was designed to, display data on a map, whereas we, humans, could not see that data. A technology works exactly the way a technology should work, just not the way we assumed it would work. It's a well-known technology issue—a 24-bit computer monitor can display over 16 million colors, whereas a human eye can sense about 7 to 10 million colors. This doesn't mean we can distinguish all those different colors, just that the brain can sense them. This goes for frequency—what we can hear versus what can be produced, touch, smell, and so on. Humans simply are not designed to comprehend this level of detail. Speech is another human characteristic that computers can mimic better than humans can. What is so interesting about this research is that it shows while the computer is accurate in what it does and can only do what we tell it to do. If the computer can show 16 million colors, and let's say we only make it identify 10 million colors (i.e., because of what we think we sense) there are now 6 million places to hide data. A vast area to hide all kinds of bad things, like viruses, trojans, and so on. We make assumptions on what it will do, look back in this book, and how many times have we mentioned that humans are always making assumptions. In cybersecurity, when we make assumptions about some technology, our assumptions better be correct, however, most of the time, our assumptions are wrong.

Deepfakes

Of course, not all our assumptions are wrong. The term Deepfakes means the combination of artificial intelligence and deep learning. It has been used in mass manipulation of the populous. Doctored videos and audios make it very hard to detect the real from the imitation. You may be witnessing a riot when none has happened, you may witness a politician speaking when it's fake, and you may witness massive amount of artificial intelligence and Internet robots (BOTs) in the next level of information warfare. In this case, our assumptions are correct, but the underlying facts are incorrect. Deepfakes is also used extensively in revenge porn (i.e., cropping someone's head onto a pornographic actor or actress), and extracting some concession from that target. It has been used in a number of past intimate relationship scandals. However, the reverse is true, given the advances in this technology and artificial intelligence, then we accept our assumptions to be wrong. Think about that again, we are basing our decisions upon our assumption, but yet we accept our assumptions are wrong? We do that now, think cognitive dissonance. So Deepfakes helps makes the case for our cognitive dissonance that much stronger. We could actually applaud research by Chu, Zhmoginov, and Sandler (2017) and others, so that future technology could make sure that everything is as it should be and that we, the human, are not responsible for accepting something as true, when it is in fact false. Making things more complicated is that Deepfakes can be very subtle. There is an amazing technology developed by the researchers at the Samsung Artificial Intelligence Center in Moscow. With just one image they can create a Deepfake image, even a movable gif that is all but undetectable to the average person (Zakharov, Shysheya, Burkov, and Lempitsky 2019). While we are on the subject of artificial intelligence, what about the concept of Extended Intelligence? Artificial intelligence is singular in nature, a programmer or programmers will create something that will take the place of a process and allow for variations to that process. Extended intelligence is augmenting a process, not necessarily replace them, so while an artificial intelligence completely developed, Deepfake may be easier to spot for some, an extended intelligence Deepfake may not be so easy to spot. We should also assume as technology gets easier and cheaper, very soon, you too will be able to make your own Deepfake video.

Crowdsourcing

Crowdsourcing is the act of a large number of groups working on a single project. There are many examples of crowdsourcing; the early ones simply started as opinion gathering, but they have moved onto collecting more information, and unfortunately, people give their data willingly. A German startup is examining how people are assigned their Schufa, similar to the FICO credit sources in the United States. Since what calculates the Schufa score is private, unlike in America where you can get a copy of your credit report each year, Germans had no idea how their Schufa was calculated. A group started a project to collect individuals' data and work on an algorithm to match that user. This is all voluntary; an individual would give over their data and their Schufa score to the group, and the group would then work on an algorithm to try and match that score, with enough data and enough correct matching, the Schufa algorithm would be determined. The problem is the data—thousands of people now have already handed over all their financial data. Therefore, one might be careful just how much of a good thing is a good thing. There are many models of the crowd model, crowd solving, crowdfunding, and crowdsources in software development, all places where vast amounts of data could be stored, stolen, and abused. Now we fast forward today and look at another country and that of China and GitHub. Griffiths (2019) reports that GitHub is a repository for code and offers tools so that large numbers of programmers can work on collaborating with each other on software fixes.

This moves us from just data (i.e., the bits and bytes) to data, to the people or programmers. GitHub is making big inroads to securing open source code and have developed Security Lab, where exists a collaborate place for researchers, programmers, developers, and so on, to work on securing open source code and offer a code analysis tool CodeQL, which helps to spot vulnerabilities. Apparently, many leading vendors in the IT industry are also interested in GitHub's effort. As GitHub became more popular, it's understandable more traffic would follow, but finally GitHub experienced a massive distributed denial-of-service attack (DDoS). Engineers at GitHub traced the problems back to Chinese hackers, but why? GitHub's members were working on some anti-Chinese projects. Normally, the Chinese government is very sensitive to projects inside their borders, or under their control, but now they are also sensitive to external pressures. What both these stories show is perceptions do not change, or they change very slowly, depending on our environment. For example, back in the early 20th century, the United States did not think much of Robert Goddard's work on rocket technology. Then the environment of war changed, so their behavior changed. The Chinese fear internal chaos and will seek to minimize that internal chaos, even if it means moving outside to stop what they perceived as a danger and that guides their behavior.

Behavioral Informatics

The interactions of applying behavior informatics means the use of computing systems to understand, learn, and predict behavior. From the informatics viewpoint, it consists of an entity (i.e., a human, a program, etc.), these are the subjects and objects, there are the operations (i.e., the actions performed by and on these subjects and objects), relationship between the actions and subjects and their properties, and these are represented by vectors. Then these techniques are applied in the hopes of changing behavior. We try to uncover how and understand why behavioral patterns are formed, how they interact in the world, and how behaviors impact decision making. The term "behavior informatics" is often used with the term "behavior computing" to identify it's used with computing resources. While behavioral informatics is used mainly in the health and human services areas (e.g., nursing, psychology, medical, etc.) to help overcome addictions, it may be helpful here to understand these techniques to learn of insights that might help cybersecurity behavior. When we examine cybersecurity investments versus the costs, studies differ greatly, we can see 76 percent, 93 percent, even larger and suggest human behavior contributes to security incidents. Not all are malicious, sometimes just opening up an infected e-mail or going to an infected website can lead to damage. However, many studies suggest that up to 90 percent of investments in cybersecurity protections is on technical solutions. Does it seem reasonable then that behavior would dictate such a large percentage of security problems, yet such a large percentage of investments to stop would be of a technical nature. Is it possible to do extraordinary things with something that is extraordinary basic? We have seen and read about so many attacks, and so many of them seemed related. How many times have companies been hacked, their personal data on their customers stolen, and yet, the conclusion is that they did not use a full-strength encryption at rest, no salt in the encrypted password file, or just stored data in plaintext. So, is the problem really a problem at all, or is it a perception of a problem that does or does not exist? If encryption at rest was used, along with a salted hash value, the exploit still would have occurred, but the data would still be computationally secure (i.e., even in our lifetime, the cost of the computers, if they exist, do not justify the return on value of that data). Anyone who works in information technology, help desk support, and any kind of troubleshooting will always tell you look at the basics, isolate the issue, and more likely than not you will find the problem. The issue usually isn't the technology, but how that technology was implemented. There is a term called "cyber hygiene," the idea that end users should practice good cyber skills instead of bad ones to better protect their company. I find that very folly way of thinking, and not because of what they will or will not do, for example, telling an accountant not to open an infected email is a good step. Telling them not to visit a bad site is much harder since just a typo in a browser will take you to fraudulent site that can infect their own website. There are two issues right here,

Bad, what exactly is bad? Bad to you is not bad to me.

Skimming—so many times our fingers are typing away on the keyboard that we simply do not look at what we are typing, and that can direct us to a fraudulent website. When we revisit history, we can see similar patterns, back to the early 1900s and Robert Goddard who was the leading pioneer in rocket research. Why is this important in a cybersecurity book? Well, look at not only what Goddard did, but who was interested in his research. In World War I, the U.S. military was not interested in Goddard's rocket technology, but another country was—Germany. They carefully studied his work, asked him for help, and reviewed his patents, which was available in the U.S. Patent office, and with over two hundred patents to his credit, Germany's scientists had a lot of research to use. However, the military did come around and saw the value in Goddard's work, and his work was credited to bring an end to the war. Of course, the tables were turned and a fascinating story is told in the *Great Patent Heist*, and those of Germany's patents.

Brainjacking

Talk about something straight out of science fiction, Brainjacking. We may have heard about brain implants, individuals for various reasons have devices implanted into their brains, often referred to as deep brain stimulation (Pugh et al. 2018). Instead of the computer–human interface, we now have the brain–computer interface (BCI). There has been wonderful research and marvelous breakthroughs in this area to treat such ailments as chronic pain, muscle spasms, Parkinson's, and a whole host of other conditions waiting to be treated. However, what if these same brain implants were now subject to compromise and hijacking?

For now, researchers worry about malicious intent to interfere with these medical devices (e.g., stopping a pacemaker), or insulin pumps (Wordsworth 2017). However, could these attacks grow to then remote control an individual, or not merely remote control, but urge someone (e.g., could a certain stimulus push a recovering addict to go back on drugs), or an ex-gambler start to gamble again? Brain implants are becoming much more common, they are getting smaller and aiming to treat a whole new host of aliments, and if not careful, we may indeed wake up one day to find there really is a Manchurian candidate.

Cybersecurity Education

It would probably be more of an occurrence to find someone who says we need more cybersecurity education than someone to say we need to right cybersecurity education. Many researchers in the field will agree that cybersecurity is both a technical issue and a people issue. Unfortunately, while we do have an abundance of education on the technical issues, we have very little in the people's part of the process. In a research study I conducted three years ago with one of my colleagues, Dr. Winfred Yaoku-mah, Department of Information Technology, Pentecost University College, Accra, Ghana, we could not find any cybersecurity certifications that included any bodies of knowledge on human behavior. I am not referring to an in-depth discussion or extensive knowledge, which is often the hallmark to achieve a certification. Just an understanding, or just an awareness that cybersecurity must include the human element. We began our research just examining theories that were used in cybersecurity research.

Activity theory	Bedney & Meister (1997) [15]
Agency theory	Eisenhardt (1989) [16]
Critical theory	Stahl et al. (2014) [17]
Deterrence theory	Huth (1999) [18]
Diffusion of innovation theory (DOI)	Stone (2004) [19]
Distributed cognition theory (DCT)	Brown et al. (1993) [20] Heylighen et al. (2003) [21]
Game theory	Myerson (1991) [22]
Psychological contract theory (PCT)	Rousseau (1989) [23] Starr (1969) [29]
Protection motivation theory	Rogers (1975) [24]
Rational choice theory (RCT)	Blume & Easley (2008) [25]
Security-related stress	D'Arcy et al. (2014) [26]
Social congnitive theory	Bandura (1986) [27]
Socio-technicla systems theory	Cooper & Foster (1971) [28]
Technology threat avoidance theory (TTAT)	Starr (1969) [29]
Technology acceptance model	Rogers (1983) [30]
Theory of reasoned action	Gillmore et al. (2002) [31]
Theory of planned bechavior	Chatterjee et al. (2015) [32]
Theory of social action (SAT)	Hedstrom et al. (2013) [33]

Figure 15.1 Theories used in security research

The numbers in brackets [ ] in Figure 15.1 Theories used in security research indicate how many times we located a theory used in cyber-security research, a researcher's name is also used as an example of that number (e.g., we found 27 instances of social cognitive theory, Bandura (1986) was one of those examples). Then we examined many of the current cybersecurity certifications and wrote down the number of times a certain area of knowledge was mentioned.

Access Control (n=8)
Application Security (n=5)
Authentication (n=3)
Business Continuity Planning (n=3)
Compliance (n=2)
Cryptography (n=5)
Department of Defense Directive (n=3)
Forensics (n=4)
Governance (n=2)
Identity Management (n=6)
Network Security (n=10)
Legal (n=2)
Physical Security (n=3)
Risk Management (n=4)
Security Operations (n=3)
Vulnerability Management (n=5)
Wireless (n=4)

Figure 15.2 Knowledge areas in security certifications

In Figure 15.2 knowledge areas in security certifications we noted that in these different cybersecurity certifications, forensics was mentioned four times as a domain of knowledge (i.e., Forensics, *n* = 4). What we did not find was any overlapping of any theory to any domain knowledge (e.g., protection motivation theory as shown in Figure 15.1). Protection motivation theory discusses fear appeals. People will base themselves on four levels: (1) perceived threat, (2) perceived probability of that threat, (3) efficacy of preventable behavior, and (4) perceived self-efficacy. It's a coping mechanism to deal with threat appraisals. If we were to examine risk management, wouldn't a coping mechanism be integrated into risk? After all, how do we cope during or after a cyber attack? How well do I cope with an attack and the threat appraisals of various attacks need to be examined under risk management? Then, would it not make sense to discuss risk management threat appraisals, in the context of the protection motivation theory. Access control is another domain knowledge. There are basically three types: (1) discretionary access control (DAC),

(2) mandatory access control (MAC), and (3) role-based access control (RBAC). Some would suggest that biometrics and multifactor authentication are other types, which is fair as this is just for an example. Access control is a fear appraisal. I want to implement some access control mechanism, and I want to make sure that only the things individuals are authorized to access, they can. I do not want to cope with individual getting additional access they are not entitled to, so therefore the following study would make sense (Figure 15.3). As Figure 15.3 illustrates, it might be helpful to combine security education and certifications with some theoretical bodies of knowledge on human behavior.

This book has touched on many topics of human behavior, and many cybersecurity experts agree we need to focus on the human part. However, these are not discussed in any cybersecurity certifications.

Isn't this a disconnect right there?

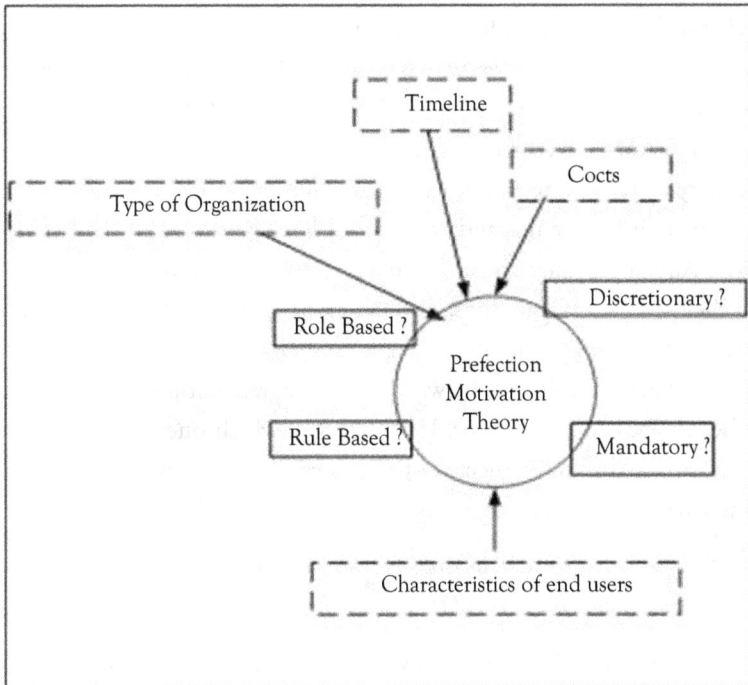

Figure 15.3 Access controls coupled with protection motivation theory

Some cybersecurity experts argue end users are to blame, some argue they don't follow protocols, and some argue it's a waste of time training them. That is a hard position to take. After all, attacks can happen to anyone, with any kind of training, and if the attack is against some strong behavioral motivations, like the sextortion attack mentioned earlier, even the best can make mistakes. Bruce Schneier has a very good quote that sums it up:

> *If you think technology can solve your security problems, then you don't understand the problem and you don't understand the technology.*

The Human Gaps in Cyber Security

During a panel discussion at the 2016 Human Factors and Ergonomics Society annual meeting, several researchers such as Vieane et al. (2016) discussed the issue with our understanding of human knowledge in cyber defense, and as we have written in this book, it's lacking still. These researchers conclude as we have been saying in this text, that yes, we do have a human gap in understanding. Vieane et al. (2016) looked at the human factors and current educational norms, and as I would agree, they are very heavy in a technical nature. In addition, that cyber defense and various training are unstandardized, which we have seen in the last section. And while they argue that novices may be at a disadvantage due to their diverse backgrounds, I would argue that what backgrounds are being referenced? If the objective is to install a firewall, and individuals have different training on firewalls, I might agree, but if we a looking at different individual behavior, I would argue which ones, since we have seen earlier, that traits such as openness can lead to positive outcomes. These researchers make a great point:

> *Cyber-security analysts at whatever level they serve, must engage in extensive attention switching (p. 772).*

This is something I would agree with. I can only relate this to the medical field in the late 18th century, where your family doctor, was also your dentist and also your veterinarian. There are just too many hats for a cybersecurity expert to wear. Social engineering attacks are still very successful and they hack the human, not the technology. The U.S. government has realized that cybersecurity, while part technical, is also part human and in the budget includes outlays for studying the human aspect. According to the U.S. Federal Cybersecurity Research and Development Strategic Plan from the National Science and Technology Council (2019), human behavior is critical to understand. That human behavior causes security accidents by accidental accidents, and it's critical that organizations understand this and create systems that do not place heavy demands on users. They argue that cybersecurity experts can create capable and secure systems, but these will fail if they do not understand how users (i.e. users, architects, criminals, adversaries) interact with these systems. It is estimated that anywhere from 80 to 90 percent of these cybersecurity failures are due to these human and organizational problems. Therefore, much more research is needed with regard to the human aspect of the cybersecurity problem. There have been areas we have covered in this book—social pressure, persuasion, stereotypes—and this human gap will continue to grow. Game theory is a good example—I will make the best moves when I know my opponent's moves, and of course, I will make rational decisions. Not so fast! We all know human beings do not make rational decisions. Several of the paradoxes we have spoken about highlight that case. We make decisions based upon on neural network associations in a given content (i.e., at a moment in time). Behavioral game theory is a much better choice since it also takes into consideration emotions, and we know emotions can drive behavior, or is it behavior that drives emotion? We examined both, and there were researchers who took both sides.

Cybersecurity Implications and Conclusions

As we look back on this book, and I think any good researcher will tell you, the more I know the less I know would be a good credo to live by. A good rule of thumb I swear by is that if you learn something, you remember 10 percent, but if you teach that something, you remember 80 percent, and if add to the body of knowledge of that something, you will reach 90 percent.

Well, before I found out my logic was faculty, but my associations, but my associations and heuristics still get the better of me, and face it, my cognitive dissonance will never allow me to let it go.

However, in my own world of learning, it may be okay, but in many other fields, it could have bad consequences. As we look back on the chapters, we can begin to draw a matrix of the various attacks vs. the behavior exhibited in the book (see Figure 15.4).

				Behavioral Reasons			
Other Attacks	Check the Box	Traits	Conditioned Response	Zeigarnik Effect	Closure	Goal Gradient Hypothesis	Other
Equifax	x	x					?
Target	x						?
DNC Hack						x	?
Home Depot				x	x		?
Panera		x	x				?
Other Attacks	?	?	?	?	?	?	?

Figure 15.4 Attacks vs. behaviors

We may begin to see some of the reasons why a particular attack occurred. We have to be careful since we can't predict behavior, we can't say there is a one for one match, but there seems to be undying nontechnical reasons why these attacks occur. This matrix might at least give us some understandings why some of the same types of attacks keep happening, and perhaps we can offer specialized training in those areas.

In another example of my keen intelligence as I wrote this book, I setup my own website. It contains decades of research I've examined and collected on behavior and cybersecurity, but this time I decided not to enlist the help of my children. Especially thinking about my top-down processing and all the help they gave me earlier; my neural rework associations were warning me like on the 1960s show *Lost in Space*: *Danger, Will Robinson, danger!*

As I started on the social media, I've posted a few early pieces on cyber behavior, and I received a text from my son, *"Dad, remove that Tweet, hurry, now."* Thinking of the current social politically correct environment we now find ourselves in, and remember our current environment can influence our behavior, I assumed I did something wrong, I insulted someone, made an off-colored joke, and so on. So, I just removed the post that was the target of his dismay. When I asked him about what was wrong with the post (i.e., and my neural network associations were firing on all cylinders telling me I did something horrible), his reply was that I did not capitalize the beginning of a sentence, and at the end of one sentence I left off the period.

He said it was so embarrassing!
And while I pondered of all the way parents can embarrass their children, I did not think grammar was anywhere near the top.

However, what this does show is that no matter how hard we try, our associations, our top-down processing, our stereotypes that we hold, and so on, are not going away, and will always be in the subconscious directing our behavior. My behavior was fear. So how would that make me react? So, while I think I am discussing some cybersecurity, I have seemed to gloss over details in grammar. I could have easily glossed over some other important detail. Who is to know which details I overlooked? Is it because you didn't patch a system really the cause of a widespread Botnet attacks and SQL attacks? During the writing of this book, a major attack hit American newspapers—WannaCry ransomware—all because of one patch missed? Therefore, when we think about cybersecurity, we should consider other viewpoints, and realize that when I design these solutions, when I implement these solutions, when I maintain these solutions, am I at my best? Am I under some influence like openness, cognitive bias, cognitive economy, and am I designing systems based on faulty and often incorrect and missing pieces? Or, as the artificial intelligence example shows, did I design a system and it works exactly the way it was supposed to, just not the way I thought it was supposed to work, meaning I did not know what was even correct. What does that tell you about our cognitive recognition of the way any technology works? A simple search on the Internet will reveal hundreds of projects that went off the trails, and we are amazed how could that have happened.

There are a number of predictions on what the future of cybersecurity will entail. Back in the 1980s when I was in college, I had a class called the physics of Star Trek, an elective that talks about those technologies from the television series *Star Trek*, and if those things could become possible. Well, if you are a fan of that show, you would have certainly seen the rise of cell phones, ray guns, black matter, even teleporting, not here quite yet, but we have teleported information.

Now I think Terminator *and wonder.*

There are two things people seem to want: information and they want it quickly, and many companies understand this and are really pushing the envelope to get you that information. Think of all the smart voice-activated devices in your home. Are they really needed for you to be able to play music? What happens with your voice patterns that are sequenced and analyzed? Have a smart television. Don't be surprised if you are talking with someone about a coat your saw someone wearing, and later start seeing commercials about that same coat staring right at you.

You are walking pass a retailer and your clothes ring; yes, your clothes start ringing. Location-based services, RFID, and other mobile technologies are really keeping a tab of you, so if you post to social media that you like red socks, and you just happen to walk pass a retailer that sells underwear, do not be surprised if your clothes call you up, and say, there is a sale going on inside with red socks. This whole book has been on cybersecurity and behavior and looked at perceptions that may influence our behavior, but really, who knows, our perceptions could be wrong, but our assumptions are usually incorrect.

One thing for sure, it will be a ride.
One last thing, what was the blurry question I asked?

Don't forget, I also led you back in Chapter 6 when I said you will probably remember this question.

References

Chapter 1

Boolos, G. 1996. "The Hardest Logic Puzzle Ever." *The Harvard Review of Philosophy* 6, pp. 62–65.

Hammack, S., M. Cooper, and K. Lezak. 2011. "Overlapping Neurobiology of Learned Helplessness and Conditioned Defeat: Implications for PTSD and Mood Disorders." *Neuropharmacology* 62, pp. 565–75. doi: 10.1016/j.neuropharm.2011.02.024

Maier, S.F., and M.E.P. Seligman. 1976. "Learned Helplessness: Theory and Evidence." *Journal of Experimental Psychology: General* 105, no. 1, pp. 3–46.

Smullyan, R.M. 1978. *What is the Name of this Book? The Riddle of Dracula and Other Logical Puzzles.* Englewood Cliffs, NJ: Prentice-Hall.

Smullyan, R.M. 1985. *To Mock a Mocking Bird and Other Logic Puzzles: Including an Amazing Adventure in Combinatory logic.* New York: Knopf.

Chapter 2

Basani, V. January 20, 2014. "'Checkbox Compliance' Won't Stop Target-Like Breaches." Retrieved from https://usatoday.com/story/cybertruth/2014/01/20/why-checkbox-compliance-wont-stop-target-like-breaches/4655859/.

Berkowitz, B. 2019. "Quest Diagnostics Says Up to 12 Million Patients May Have Had Financial, Medical, Personal Information Breached." https://nbcnewyork.com/news/local/quest-diagnostics-12-million-people-data-breach-2/1828773, (accessed December 19, 2019).

Darwin, C. 2009. "The Expression of the Emotions in Man and Animals." In *Cambridge Library Collection - Darwin, Evolution and Genetics,* ed. Darwin, F. Cambridge: Cambridge University Press. doi: 10.1017/CBO9780511694110

Elmer, R. 2015. "Check-the-Box Mentality Exposes Banks to Big Cyber Risks." *American Banker.* https://americanbanker.com/opinion/check-the-box-mentality-exposes-banks-to-big-cyber-risks, (accessed November 3, 2019).

Guthrie, E.R. 1946. "Psychological Facts and Psychological Theory." *Psychological Bulletin* 43, pp. 1–20.

Kuo, Z.Y. 1938. "Further Study of the Behavior of the Cat Toward the Rat." *Journal of Comparative Psychology* 25, no. 1, pp. 1–8.

Lashley, K.S. 1950. "In Search of the Engram." *Society of Experimental Biology Symposium* 4, pp. 454–82.

Lorenz, K. 1937. "On the formation of the Concept of Instinct." *Natural Sciences* 25, no. 19, pp. 289–300.

Miller, N.E. 1967. "Laws of Learning Relevant to its Biological Basis." *Proceedings of the American Philosophical Society* 111, pp. 315–25.

NeSmith, B. 2018. "Council Post: CEOs: The Data Breach Is Your Fault." *Forbes Magazine*, https://forbes.com/sites/forbestechcouncil/2018/06/26/ceos-the-data-breach-is-your-fault/#5189126b58b0, (accessed October 1, 2019).

Nevin, J. 1999. "Analyzing Thorndike's Law of Effect: The Question of Stimulus-response Bonds." *Journal of the Experimental Analysis of Behavior* 72, pp. 447–50. doi: 10.1901/jeab.1999.72-447

Pavlov, I.P. 1927. Conditioned Reflexes: An Investigation of the Physiological Activity of the Cerebral Cortex. Oxford, England: Oxford University Press.

Richardson, K. 2019. "It's the End of the Gene as We Know It." http://nautil.us/issue/68/context/its-the-end-of-the-gene-as-we-know-it, (accessed September 12, 2019).

Schwartz, J. 2016. "Checking the Box: Beyond Compliance Basics." https://mediapro.com/blog/checking-box-beyond-compliance-basics, (accessed December 10, 2019).

Semon, R. 1921. *The Mneme*. London: George Allen & Unwin.

Skinner, B.F. 1938. The Behavior of Organisms: An Experimental Analysis. Oxford, England: Appleton-Century.

Thorndike, E.L., E.O. Bregman, M.V. Cobb, E. Woodyard, and Inst of Educational Research Div. of Psychology, Teachers Coll, Columbia U. 1926. *The Measurement of Intelligence*. New York, NY, US: Teachers College Bureau of Publications. http://dx.doi.org/10.1037/11240-000

Tolman, E.C. (1948). Cognitive maps in rats and men. Psychological Review, 55(4), 189-208. http://dx.doi.org/10.1037/h0061626

Watson, J.B. 1913. *Psychology as the Behaviorist Views it*. Indianapolis: Bobbs-Merrill.

Chapter 3

Digman, J.M. 1989. "Five Robust Trait Dimensions: Development, Stability, and Utility." *Journal of Personality* 57, no. 2, 195–214. doi: 10.1111/j.1467-6494

Deutchman, P., and J. Sullivan. 2018. "The Dark Triad and Framing Effects Predict Selfish Behavior in a One-Shot Prisoner's Dilemma." *PloS ONE* 13, no. 9, pp. 1–15.

Egelman, S., and E. Peer. 2015. "Scaling the Security Wall: Developing a Security Behavior Intentions Scale (SeBIS)." *Proceedings of the ACM Conference on Human Factors in Computing Systems*, pp. 2873–82. Seoul.

Furnham, A., and H. Cheng. 2016. "Childhood Intelligence Predicts Adult Trait Openness: Psychological and Demographic Indicators." *Journal of Individual Differences* 37, no. 2, pp. 105–11. doi: 10.1027/1614-0001/a000194

Friedman, M., and R. Rosenman. 1959. "Association of Specific Overt Behavior Pattern with Blood and Cardiovascular Findings." *Journal of the American Medical Association* 169, no. 12, pp. 1286–96.

Galla, B.M., and A. Duckworth. 2015. "More than Resisting Temptation: Beneficial Habits Mediate the Relationship Between Self-Control and Positive Life Outcomes." *Journal of Personality and Social Psychology* 9, no. 3, pp. 508–25. doi: 10.1037/pspp0000026

Gratian, M., S. Bandi, M. Cukier, J. Dykstra, and A. Ginther. 2017. "Correlating Human Traits and Cybersecurity Behavior Intentions." *Computers & Security* 73, pp. 345–58. doi: 10.1016/j.cose.2017.11.015

Hadlington, L. 2017. "Human Factors in Cybersecurity; Examining the Link Between Internet Addiction, Impulsivity, Attitudes Towards Cybersecurity, and Risky Cybersecurity Behaviours." https://ncbi.nlm.nih.gov/pubmed/28725870 (accessed June 18, 2019).

Haney, J., and W. Lutters. 2017. "The Work of Cybersecurity Advocates." *Proceedings of the CHI Conference Extended Abstracts on Human Factors in Computing Systems*, pp. 1663–70. Denver, Colorado. doi: 10.1145/3027063.3053134

Henrich, J., S. Heine, and A. Norenzayan. 2010. "The Weirdest People in the World?" *Behavioral and Brain Sciences* 33, no. 2–3, pp. 61–83. doi: 10.1017/S0140525X0999152X

Houliham, D. 2018 "Krebs on Security." https://krebsonsecurity.com/2018/04/panerabread-com-leaks-millions-of-customer-records (accessed May 21, 2019).

Hron, M. 2018. "10 of the Biggest Data Breaches in 2018." https://avast.com/biggest-data-breaches (accessed July 21, 2019).

Landy, D., N. Silbert, and A. Goldin. 2013. "Estimating Large Numbers." *Cognitive Science* 37, no. 5, pp. 775–99. doi: 10.1111/cogs.12028

Matulessy, A., and N. Humaira. 2016. "Hacker Personality Profiles Reviewed in Terms of the Big Five Personality Traits." *Psychology and Behavioral Sciences* 5, no. 6, pp. 137–42. doi: 10.11648/j.pbs.20160506.12

Plous, S. 1993. *The Psychology of Judgment and Decision Making*. New York, NY: McGraw-Hill.

Smith, M. 2018. "Panera Bread Blew off Breach Report, Leaked 37M Customer Records." https://www.csoonline.com/article/3268025/panera-bread-blew-off-breach-report-for-8-months-leaked-millions-of-customer-records.html (accessed October 3, 2019).

Tversky, A., and D. Kahneman. 1981. "The Framing of Decisions and the Psychology of Choice." *Science* 211, no. 4481, pp. 453–58.

Mischel, W., E.B. Ebbesen, and A. Raskoff Zeiss. 1972. "Cognitive and Attentional Mechanisms in Delay of Gratification." *Journal of Personality and Social Psychology* 21, no. 2, pp. 204–18. doi: 10.1037/h0032198

Watts, T.W., G.J. Duncan, and H. Quan. 2018. "Revisiting the Marshmallow Test: A Conceptual Replication Investigating Links Between Early Delay of Gratification and Later Outcomes." *Psychological Science* 29, no. 7, pp. 1159–77. doi: 10.1177/0956797618761661

Chapter 4

Banjo, S. 2014. "Home Depot Hackers Exposed 53 Million Email Addresses." *The Wall Street Journal*. Dow Jones & Company, https://wsj.com/articles/home-depot-hackers-used-password-stolen-from-vendor-1415309282 (accessed December 5, 2019).

Chater, N. 2018. *The Mind is Flat: The Illusion of Mental Depth and the Improvised Mind*. London: Penguin Books.

Creswell, J., and N. Perlroth. 2014. "Ex-Employees Say Home Depot Left Data Vulnerable." https://nytimes.com/2014/09/20/business/ex-employees-say-home-depot-left-data-vulnerable.html (accessed May 3, 2019).

Damen, T., M. Strick, T.W. Taris, and H. Aarts. 2018. "When Conflict Influences Liking: The Case of the Stroop Task." *PloS One* 13, no. 7, e0199700. doi: 10.1371/journal.pone.0199700

Fritz, J., R. Fischer, and G. Dreisbach. 2015. "The Influence of Negative Stimulus Features on Conflict Adaption: Evidence from Fluency of Processing." *Frontiers in Psychology* 6, no. 185. doi:10.3389/fpsyg.2015.00185

Gonzalez, J.J., and A. Sawicka. 2002. "A Framework for Human Factors in Information Security." In: Proceedings of the 2002 WSEAS International Conference on Information Security (ICIS'02), Rio de Janeiro.

Huang, D., P.P. Rau, and G. Salvendy. 2010. "Perception of Information Security." *Behaviour* & IT 29, pp. 221–32.

Nacs. 2014 "Could Home Depot Have Prevented Massive Breach?" https://convenience.org/Media/Daily/ND0922141 (accessed October 8, 2019).

Stroop, J.R. 1935. "Studies of Interference in Serial Verbal Reactions." *Journal of Experimental Psychology* 18, no. 6, pp. 643–62. doi: 10.1037/h0054651

Vezzani, S, B.F. Marino, and E. Giora. 2012. "An Early History of the Gestalt Factors of Organization." *Perception* 41, no. 2, pp. 148–67. doi:10.1068/p7122

Wogalter, M.S., J.W. Brelsford, D.R. Desaulniers, and K.R. Laughery. 1991. "Consumer Product Warnings. The Role of Hazard Perception." *Journal of Safety Research* 22, no. 2, pp. 71–82. doi: 10.1016/0022-4375(91)90015-N

Zeigarnik, B. 1938. "On Finished and Unfinished Tasks." In: *A Source Book of Gestalt Psychology,* ed. W.D. Ellis, pp. 300–14. London: Kegan Paul, Trench, Trubner & Company. doi: 10.1037/11496-025.

Chapter 5

Camerer, C. 2003. *Behavioral Game Theory: Experiments in Strategic Interaction.* New York: Russell Sage Foundation.

Craik, K. 1943. The *Nature of Explanation.* Cambridge: Cambridge University Press.

Datz, T. 2019. "Higher Consumption of Sugary Beverages Linked with Increased Risk of Mortality." https://datto.com/blog/why-are-ransomware-attacks-like-wannacry-so-effective (accessed July 27, 2019).

Forrester, J.W. 1971. "Counterintuitive Behavior of Social Systems." *Technological Forecasting and Social Change* 3, 1–22. doi.org/10.1016/S0040-1625(71)80001-X

Greenbergm, A. 2015. "Hackers Remotely Kill a Jeep on the Highway—With Me in It." https://wired.com/2015/07/hackers-remotely-kill-jeep-highway (accessed May 3, 2019).

Hietaranta, P. 2015. "Cognitive Economy and Mental Worlds: How Much can They Account for Errors in Translation?" *Conference: Translation in Transition II,* Germersheim: Germany.

Holscher, C., S. Büchner, M. Brösamle, T. Meilinger, and G. Strube. 2007. "Signs and Maps: Cognitive Economy in the Use of External Aids for Indoor Navigation." *Proceedings of the Annual Meeting of the Cognitive Science Society* 29, pp. 377–82.

Kahneman, D., and A. Tversky. 1973. "On the Psychology of Prediction." *Psychological Review* 80, no. 4, pp. 237–51. doi:10.1037/h0034747

Langde, R. 2017. "WannaCry Ransomware: A Detailed Analysis of the Attack." https://datto.com/blog/why-are-ransomware-attacks-like-wannacry-so-effective (accessed October 12, 2019).

Lemos, R. 2013. "Five Habits of Highly Successful Malware." https://darkreading.com/vulnerabilities---threats/five-habits-of-highly-successful-malware/d/d-id/1139668 (accessed September 3, 2019).

Lupyan, G. 2013. "The Difficulties of Executing Simple Algorithms: Why Brains Make Mistakes Computers Don't." *Cognition* 129, no. 3. pp. 615–36.

Michaelidis. G. 2018. "The Road to Cybersecurity is Paved with Extraordinarily Basic Things." *Behavioral Scientist.* http://behavioralscientist.org/the-road-to-cybersecurity-is-paved-with-extraordinarily-basic-things (accessed May 7, 2019).

Munger, C. 1994. "A Lesson on Elementary, Worldly Wisdom as It Relates to Investment Management & Business." USC Business School, https://old. ycombinator.com/munger.html (accessed August 3, 2019).

Nash, J. 1949. "Equilibrium Points in n-Person Games." *Proceedings of the National Academy of Sciences of the United States of America* 36, no. 1, pp. 48–49.

National Safety Council 2019. "Motor Vehicle Deaths Estimated to Have Dropped 2% in 2019." https://nsc.org/road-safety/safety-topics/fatality-estimates (accessed October 21, 2019).

Nicas, J., N. Kitroeff, D. Gelles, and J. Glanz. 2019. "Boeing Built Deadly Assumptions Into 737 Max, Blind to a Late Design Change." https:// nytimes.com/2019/06/01/business/boeing-737-max-crash.html?utm_source=pocket-newtab (accessed October 12, 2019).

Pinker, S. 1999. *How the Mind Works*. New York: W.W. Norton.

Shostack, A. 2017. In *Hacking the hacker: Learn from the Experts Who Take Down Hackers,* ed. Grimes, R.A. Indianapolis: Wiley.

Siwicki, B. 2017. Cybercriminals Deploy Malware for Half of Successful Cyberattacks, IBM Study Finds." https://healthcareitnews.com/news/ cybercriminals-deploy-malware-half-successful-cyberattacks-ibm-study-finds (accessed December 19, 2018).

Tversky, A., and D. Kahneman. 1974. "Judgment Under Uncertainty: Heuristics and Biases." *Science* 185, no. 4157, pp. 1124–31. doi:10.1126/ science.185.4157.1124

Von Neumann, J., and M. Oskar. 1944. *Theory of Games and Economic Behavior*. Princeton, NJ: University Press.

Washburn, H. 2019. "Why Are Ransomware Attacks Like WannaCry So Effective?" https://datto.com/blog/why-are-ransomware-attacks-like-wannacry-so-effective (accessed January 7, 2020).

Chapter 6

Baddeley, A.D. 1986. *Working Memory*. Oxford, England: Oxford University Press.

Brown, R., and J. Kulik. 1977. "Flashbulb Memories." *Cognition* 5, no. 1, pp. 73–99.

Dale, E. 1946. *Audio-Visual Methods in Teaching*. New York: Dryden Press.

Davis, R.L. 2011. "Traces of Drosophila Memory." *Neuron* 70, pp. 8–19.

Dawkins, R. 1976. *The Selfish Gene*. Oxford University Press.

Dresler, M., S. William, K. Boris, M. Nils, W. Isabella, F. Guillén, C. Michael, and G. Michael. 2017. "Mnemonic Training Reshapes Brain Networks to Support Superior Memory." *Neuron* 93, doi: 10.1016/j.neuron.2017.02.003

Ebbinghaus, H. 1913. In *Memory: A Contribution to Experimental Psychology,* Trans. Ruger, H.A. and Bussenius, C.E. New York, NY: Teachers College Press. doi: 10.1037/10011-000

Hardt, O., K. Nader, and Y.T. Wang. 2013. "GluA2-Dependent AMPA Receptor Endocytosis and the Decay of Early and Late Long-Term Potentiation: Possible Mechanisms for Forgetting of Short- and Long-Term Memories." *Philosophical Transactions of the Royal Society of London. Series B, Biological Sciences* 369, no. p. 1633, 20130141. doi: 10.1098/rstb.2013.0141

Johns Hopkins Medicine. 2016. "Want to Learn a New Skill? Faster? Change up your Practice Sessions." *ScienceDaily.* https://hopkinsmedicine.org/news/media/releases/want_to_learn_a_new_skil_faster_change_up_your_practice_sessions (accessed December 10, 2019).

Long, J., Q. Xie, Q. Ma, M.A. Urbin, L. Liu, L. Weng, X. Huang, R. Yu, Y. Li, and R. Huang. 2016. "Distinct Interactions between Fronto-Parietal and Default Mode Networks in Impaired Consciousness." *Scientific Reports* 6, no. 38866, doi: 10.1038/srep38866

Kaufman, M. 2018. "Facebook and WhatsApp Malware Attack is yet Another Stark Reminder: Be Wary of Links." https://mashable.com/2018/01/19/dark-caracal-hackers-phish-whatsapp-and-facebook-accounts/#purdns_UzSqp (accessed November 11, 2019).

Miller, N.E. 1967. "Laws of Learning Relevant to its Biological Basis." *Proceedings of the American Philosophical Society* 111, pp. 315–25.

Oppenheimer, D., C. Diemand-Yauman, and E. Vaughan. 2012. "Hard-to-Read Fonts Promote Better Recall." *Harvard Business Review* 90, pp. 32–33.

Pageaux, B., R. Lepers, K.C. Dietz, and S.M. Marcora. 2014. "Response Inhibition Impairs Subsequent Self-Paced Endurance Performance." *European Journal of Applied Physiology* 114, no. 5, pp. 1095–1105. doi: 10.1007/s00421-014-2838-5

Pageaux, B., S.M. Marcora, V. Rozand, and R. Lepers. 2015. "Mental Fatigue Induced by Prolonged Self-Regulation does not Exacerbate Central Fatigue During Subsequent Whole-Body Endurance Exercise." *Frontiers in Human Neuroscience* 9, no. 67. doi: 10.3389/fnhum.2015.00067

Pastuzyn, E.D., C.E. Day,, R.B. Kearns, M. Kyrke-Smith, A.V. Taibi, J. McCormick, N. Yoder, D.M. Belnap, S. Erlendsson, D.R. Morado, J.A. Briggs, C. Feschotte, and J.D. Shepherd. 2017. "The Neuronal Gene Arc Encodes a Repurposed Retrotransposon Gag Protein that Mediates Intercellular RNA Transfer." *Elsevier* 172, no, 1, pp. 275–88, doi: 10.1016/j.cell.2017.12.024

Perry, S. 2001. *Writing in Flow: Keys to Enhanced Creativity.* Writer's Digest Books.

Reinhart, R., and J.A. Nguyen. 2019. "Working Memory Revived in Older Adults by Synchronizing Rhythmic Brain Circuits." *Nature Neuroscience* 22, pp. 820–27. doi: 10.1038/s41593-019-0371-x

Richards, B.A., and P.W. Frankland. 2017. "The Persistence and Transience of Memory." *Neuron* 94, no. 6, pp. 1071–84, doi: 10.1016/j.neuron.2017.04.037

Rogowsky, B.A., B.M. Calhoun, and P. Tallal. 2020. "Providing Instruction Based on Students' Learning Style Preferences Does Not Improve Learning." *Frontiers in Psychology* 11, pp. 1–7. doi 10.3389/fpsyg.2020.00164

Shibata, K., Y. Sasaki, J.W. Bang, E.G. Walsh, M.G., Machizawa, M. Tamaki, . . . and T. Watanabe. 2017. "Overlearning Hyperstabilizes a Skill by Rapidly Making Neurochemical Processing Inhibitory-Dominant." *Nature Neuroscience* 20, pp. 470–75. doi: 10.1038/nn.4490

Willingham, D., E. Hughes, and D. Dobolyi. 2015. "The Scientific Status of Learning Styles Theories." *Teaching of Psychology* 42, pp. 266–71. doi: 10.1177/0098628315589505

Chapter 7

Brown, A., D. Ash, M. Rutherford, A. Nakagawa, A. Gordon, and J. Campione. 1993. "Distributed Expertise in the Classroom." In *Distributed Cognitions Psychological and Educational Considerations,* Gavriel S, ed. (pp. 188–228). New York: Cambridge University Press.

Gutman, J. 1982. "A Means-End Chain Model Based on Consumer Categorization Processes." *Journal of Marketing* 46, no. 2, pp. 60–72.

Gutman, J. 1997. "Means-End Chains as Goal Hierarchies." *Psychology & Marketing* 14, pp. 545–60.

Hull, C.L. 1932. "The Goal-Gradient Hypothesis and Maze Learning." *Psychological Review* 39, no. 1, pp. 25–43, doi: 10.1037/h0072640

Landsberger, H. 1958. *Hawthorne Revisited.* Ithaca, NY: Cornell University.

Lipton, E., D.E. Sanger, and S. Shane. 2016. "The Perfect Weapon: How Russian Cyberpower Invaded the U.S." https://nytimes.com/2016/12/13/us/politics/russia-hack-election-dnc.html (accessed October 27, 2019).

Locke, E., and G. Latham. 2002. "Building a Practically Useful Theory of Goal Setting and Task Motivation. A 35-Year Odyssey." *Am Psychol.* 57, no. 9, pp. 705–17. doi: 10.1037//0003-066x.57.9.705

Maslow, A.H. 1943. "A Theory of Human Motivation." *Psychological Review* 50, no. 4, pp. 370–396.

Nunes, J., and X. Drze. 2006. "The Endowed Progress Effect: How Artificial Advancement Increases Effort." *Journal of Consumer Research* 32, pp. 504–12, doi: 10.1086/500480

Wingfield, J.C., D.L. Maney, C. Breuner, and J. Jacobs. 1998. "Ecological Bases of Hormone–Behavior Interactions: The 'Emergency Life History Stage.'" *American. Zoologist* 38, pp. 191–206. doi: 10.1093/icb/38.1.191

Woody, E.Z., and H. Szechtman. 2013. "A Biological Security Motivation System for Potential Threats: are there Implications for Policy-Making?" *Frontiers in Human Neuroscience* 7, no. 556. doi: 10.3389/fnhum.2013.00556

Chapter 8

Alicke, M.D. 2000. "Culpable Control and the Psychology of Blame." *Psychological Bulletin* 126, no. 4, pp. 556–74. doi 10.1037/0033-2909.126.4.556

Aronson, E. 1972. *The Social Animal*. New York: Viking Press.

Artic Wolf Networks. 2016. Cybersecurity dissonance. https://arcticwolf.com/cybersecuritydissonance (accessed October 2, 2019).

Asch, S.E. 1951. "Effects of Group Pressure on the Modification and Distortion of Judgments." In *Groups, Leadership and Men*, ed. H. Guetzkow, pp. 177–90. Pittsburgh, PA: Carnegie Press.

Burger, J.M. 1981. "Motivational Biases in the Attribution of Responsibility for an Accident: A Meta-Analysis of the Defensive Attribution Hypothesis." *Psychological Bulletin* 90, pp. 496–512.

Cialdini, R.B. 1984. *Influence: The Psychology of Persuasion*. New York: William Morrow e Company.

Coronel, J.C., S. Poulsen, and M.D. Sweitzer. 2020. "Investigating the Generation and Spread of Numerical Misinformation: A Combined Eye Movement Monitoring and Social Transmission Approach." *Human Communication Research* 46, no. 1, pp. 25–54, doi: 10.1093/hcr/hqz012

Goffman, E. 1959. *The Presentation of Self in Everyday Life*. Garden City, NY: Doubleday & Company.

Fazzini, K. 2020. "Ashley Madison Cyber-Breach: 5 Years Later, Users are Being Targeted with 'Sextortion' Scams." https://cnbc.com/2020/01/31/ashley-madison-breach-from-2015-being-used-in-sextortion-scams.html (accessed February 2, 2020).

Festinger, L., and J.M. Carlsmith. 1959. "Cognitive Consequences of Forced Compliance." *The Journal of Abnormal and Social Psychology* 58, no. 2, pp. 203–10.

Glasser, W. 1998. *Choice Theory: a New Psychology of Personal Freedom*. 1st Harper Perennial ed. New York: Harper Perennial.

Haney, C., W.C. Banks, and P.G. Zimbardo. 1973. "A Study of Prisoners and Guards in a Simulated Prison." *Naval Research Review* 30, pp. 4–17.

Jones, E.E., and V.A. Harris. 1967. "The Attribution of Attitudes." *Journal of Experimental Social Psychology* 3, no. 1, pp. 1–24.

Lerner, M.J., and C.H. Simmons. 1966. "Observer's Reaction to the 'Innocent Victim': Compassion or Rejection?" *Journal of Personality and Social Psychology* 4, no. 2, pp. 203–10. doi 10.1037/h0023562

Lewin, K. 1951. *Field Theory in Social Science.* In *Selected Theoretical Papers,* ed. Dorwin Cartwright, Oxford, England: Harpers.

Peterson, A. 2019. "Adult FriendFinder Hit with One of the Biggest Data Breaches Ever." Report Says. https://washingtonpost.com/news/the-switch/wp/2016/11/14/adult-friendfinder-hit-with-one-of-the-biggest-data-breaches-ever-report-says/ (accessed October 19, 2019).

Ragan, S. 2015. "Adult FriendFinder Confirms Data Breach 3.5 Million Records Exposed." http://csoonline.com/article/2925833/data-breach/adult-friend-finder-confirms-data-breach-3-5-million-records-exposed.html (accessed October 29, 2019).

Staff, D.R. 2016. "412 Million Users Exposed in Adult FriendFinder." Penthouse Breach. https://darkreading.com/attacks-breaches/412-million-users-exposed-in-adult-friend-finder-penthouse-breach--/d/d-id/1327478 (accessed November 4, 2019).

Milgram, S. 1963. "Behavioral Study of Obedience." *The Journal of Abnormal and Social Psychology* 67, no. 4, pp. 371–78.

Moscovici, S. 2000. *Social Representations: Explorations in Social Psychology.* New York: New York University Press.

Shaver, K.G. 1970. "Defensive Attribution: Effects of Severity and Relevance on the Responsibility Assigned for an Accident." *Journal of Personality and Social Psychology* 14, pp. 101–13.

Tetri, P., and J. Vuorinen. 2013. "Dissecting Social Engineering." *Behaviour & Information Technology* 32, no. 10, pp. 1014–23.

vpnMentor. 2020. "Report: Adult Site Leaks Extremely Sensitive Data." https://vpnmentor.com/blog/report-pussycash-leak (accessed February 2, 2020).

Whittaker, Z. 2016. "Adult FriendFinder Network Hack Exposes 412 Million Accounts." https://zdnet.com/article/adultfriendfinder-network-hack-exposes-secrets-of-412-million-users (accessed November 19, 2019).

Zajonc, R.B. 1980. "Feeling and Thinking: Preferences Need no Inferences." *American Psychologist* 35, no. 2, pp. 151–75. doi: 10.1037/0003-066x.35.2.151

Chapter 9

Csreinicke. R. 2018. "The Biggest Cybersecurity Risk to US Businesses is Employee Negligence, Study Says." https://cnbc.com/2018/06/21/the-biggest-cybersecurity-risk-to-us-businesses-is-employee-negligence-study-says.html, (accessed December 5, 2019).

De Bono, E. 1985. *Six Thinking Hats.* Boston: Little, Brown.

Graham, R. 2011. "No, It Really is "Groupthink."" https://blog.erratasec. com/2011/04/no-it-really-is-groupthink.html#.XFoL6FxKiUk (accessed December 11, 2019).

IBM Security Services. 2014. "IBM Security Services 2014 Cyber Security Intelligence Index. IBM Global Security Services, Research Report." https:// ibm.com/developerworks/library/se-cyberindex2014/index.html (accessed October 2, 2019).

Kelly, R. 2017. "Almost 90% of Cyber Attacks are Caused by Human Error or Behavior." https://chiefexecutive.net/almost-90-cyber-attacks-caused-human-error-behavior (accessed July 3, 2019).

NCTA. 2002. "The National Commission on Terrorist Attacks Upon the United States." https://chiefexecutive.net/almost-90-cyber-attacks-caused-human-error-behavior (accessed May 21, 2019).

Raiffa, H. 1982. *The Art and Science of Negotiation*. Harvard: Harvard University Press.

Schick, S. 2017. "Insider Threats Account for Nearly 75 Percent of Security Breach Incidents." https://securityintelligence.com/news/insider-threats-account-for-nearly-75-percent-of-security-breach-incidents (accessed March 2, 2019).

Schrader, T., and W.M. Hall. 2014. "Stereotype Threat in School and at Work: Putting Science into Practice." *Behavioral and Brain Sciences* 1, no. 1, pp. 30–37. doi: 10.1177/2372732214548861

Wegner, D.M. 1995. "A Computer Network Model of Human Transactive Memory." *Social Cognition* 13, no. 3, pp. 1–21. doi: 10.1521/soco.1995.13.3.319.

Chapter 10

Cannon, W.B. 1915. *Bodily Changes in Pain, Hunger, Fear, and Rage*. New York: Appleton-Century-Crofts.

George Town University. 2017. "How to Explain the Equifax Breach? Start with the Culture." https://scs.georgetown.edu/news-and-events/article/6646/how-explain-equifax-breach-start-culture, (accessed August 3, 2019).

Lazarus, R.S., and S. Folkman. 1984. *Stress, Appraisal, and Coping*. New York: Springer.

Khansari, D., A. Murgo. and R. Faith. 1990. "Effects of Stress on the Immune System." *Immunology Today* 11, no. 5, pp. 170–75.

Koolhaas, J., A. Bartolomucci, B. Buwalda, S.F. de Boer, G. Flügge, S.M. Korte, P. Meerlo, R Murison, B. Olivier, P. Palanza, G. Richter-Levin, A. Sgoifo, T. Steimer, O. Stiedl, G., van Dijk, M. Wöhr, and E. Fuchs. 2011. "Stress Revisited: A Critical Evaluation of the Stress Concept." *Neuroscience and Biobehavioral Reviews* 35, no. 5, pp. 1291–1301.

McLean, B. 2017. "How Wells Fargo's Cutthroat Corporate Culture Allegedly Drove Bankers to Fraud." https://vanityfair.com/news/2017/05/wells-fargo-corporate-culture-fraud (accessed March 25, 2019).

Ng, A. 2018. "How the Equifax Hack Happened, and What Still Needs to be Done." https://cnet.com/news/equifaxs-hack-one-year-later-a-look-back-at-how-it-happened-and-whats-changed, (accessed September 29, 2019).

Schneiderman, N., G. Ironson, and S.D. Siegel. 2005. "Stress and Health: Psychological, Behavioral, and Biological Determinants." *Annual Review of Clinical Psychology* 1, pp. 607–28.

Sharot, T. and University College London. 2020. "How Your Mind Gets Better at Processing Bad News - Aeon." https://getpocket.com/explore/item/how-your-mind-gets-better-at-processing-bad-news?utm_source=pocket-newtab, (accessed January 7, 2020).

Weeks, M. 2017. "Threat Rigidity in Cybersecurity." https://sans.org/reading-room/whitepapers/critical/paper/38135 (accessed October 7, 2019).

Wohl, M.A., T.H. Pychyl, and S. Bennett. 2010. "I Forgive Myself, Now I Can Study: How Self-Forgiveness for Procrastinating can Reduce Future Procrastination." *Personality and Individual Differences* 48, pp. 803–08. doi: 10.1016/j.paid.2010.01.029

Ziadeh, Z. 2018. "NSA Cybersecurity Operators Fight Through Stress for National Security, But at What Cost?" https://governmentciomedia.com/nsa-cybersecurity-operators-fight-through-stress-national-security-what-cost (accessed March 22, 2019).

Chapter 11

Gazdar, G. 1979. *Pragmatics: Implicature, Presupposition, and Logical Form.* Academic Press: New York.

Kim, D. and J.K. Hall. 2002. "The Role of an Interactive Book Reading Program in the Development of Second Language Pragmatic Competence." *The Modern Language Journal* 86, pp. 332–48. doi: 10.1111/1540-4781.00153

Kaufman, Y. 2017. "One Hour Translation: 280% Surge in Cyber-Security Translations From English In The First Half Of 2017." https://informationsecuritybuzz.com/study-research/one-hour-translation-280-surge-cyber-security-translations-english-first-half-2017, (accessed August 8, 2019).

Koerner, E.F.K. 1992, "The Sapir-Whorf Hypothesis: A Preliminary History and a Bibliographical Essay." *Journal of Linguistic Anthropology* 2, no. 2, pp. 173–98.

Schmitt, D., J. Allik, R. McCrae, V. Benet, L. Alcalay, L. Ault, I. Austers, K. Bennett, G. Bianchi, F. Boholst, C. Ann Borg, J.G. Braeckman, E. Brainerd, L. Caral, G. Caron, C. Martina, M. Cunningham, I. Daibo, C. De backer, and A. Zupanèiè. 2007. "The Geographic Distribution of Big Five Personality Traits: Patterns and Profiles of Human Self-Description Across 56 Nations." *Journal of Cross-Cultural Psychology* 38, pp. 173–212.

Mastrocola, C. 2017. "Are Your Translations Exposing You to Risk?" https://linguist.com/2017/09/translation-risks, (accessed July 3, 2019).

Yang, S.S., S.E. Kimes, and M.M. Sessarego. 2009. "$ or Dollars: Effects of Menu-Price Formats on Restaurant Checks." *Cornell Hospitality Report* 9, no. 8, pp. 6–11.

Chapter 12

Allport, G.W. 1961. *Pattern and Growth in Personality*. New York: Holt, Rinehart and Winston.

Bertrand, R. 1933. "The Triumph of Stupidity." https://russell-j.com/0583TS.HTM, (accessed November 7, 2019).

Binet, A. 2004. *L'étude expérimentale de l'intelligence (1903)*. Paris: L'Harmattan.

Cattell, R.B. 1941. "Some Theoretical Issues in Adult Intelligence Testing." *Psychological Bulletin* 38, p. 592.

Eysenck, H.J. 1967. *The Biological Basis of Personality*. Thomas: Spring-field, Ill.

Fernbach, P.M., N. Light, S.E. Scott, Y. Inbar, and M.P. Rozin. 2019. "Extreme Opponents of Genetically Modified Foods Know the Least But Think They Know the Most." *Nature Human Behavior* 3, no. 3, pp. 251–56. doi: 10.1038/s41562-018-0520-3

Fleeson, W. 2001. "Toward a Structure and Process Integrated View of Personality Traits as Density Distribution of States." *Journal of Personality and Social Psychology* 80, no. 6, pp. 1011–27.

Forer, B.R. 1949. "The Fallacy of Personal Validation: A Classroom Demonstration of Gullibility." *Journal of Abnormal and Social Psychology* 44, no. 1, 118–23. doi: 10.1037/h005

Frijda, N.H. 2007. *The Laws of Emotion*. Mahwah, NJ: Lawrence Erlbaum Associates Publishers.

Guilford, J.P. 1967. "Creativity: Yesterday, Today, and Tomorrow." *The Journal of Creative Behavior* 1, no. 1, pp. 3–14. doi: 10.1002/j.2162-6057.1967.tb00002.x

Iulia, I., R. Reeder, and S. Consolvo. 2015. "... No One Can Hack My Mind: Comparing Expert and Non-Expert Security Practices." In *Proceedings of the Symposium on Usable Privacy and Security* (SOUPS'15), pp. 327–46.

Kruger, J., and D. Dunning. 1999. "Unskilled and Unaware of It: How Difficulties in Recognizing One's Own Incompetence Lead to Inflated Self-Assessments." *Journal of Personality and Social Psychology. American Psychological Association* 77, no. 6, pp. 1121–34.

Langer, E.J. 1975. "The Illusion of Control." *Journal of Personality and Social Psychology* 32, no. 2, pp. 311–28. doi: 10.1037/0022-3514.32.2.311

McClelland, D.C. 1987. *Human Motivation*. New York: University of Cambridge.

Rosenhan, D.L. 1973. "On Being Sane in Insane Places." *Science* 179, pp. 250–58. doi: 10.1126/science.179.4070.250

Spearman, C. 1904. ""General Intelligence," Objectively Determined and Measured." *The American Journal of Psychology* 15, no. 2, pp. 201–92. doi: 10.2307/1412107

Stagner, R. 1958. "The Gullibility of Personnel Managers." *Personnel Psychology* 11, no. 3, pp. 347–52. doi: 10.1111/j.1744-6570.1958.tb00022.x

Stelmack, R.M., and A. Stalikas. 1991. "Galen and the Humour Theory of Temperament." *Personality and Individual Differences* 12, no. 3, pp. 255–63, doi: 10.1016/0191-8869(91)90111-N

Chapter 13

Levy, S. 1984. *Hackers: Heroes of the Computer Revolution*. Garden City, NY: Anchor Press/Doubleday.

Stallman, R. 2012. "The Hacker Community and Ethics: An Interview with Richard M." https://gnu.org/philosophy/rms-hack.en.html (accessed April 3, 2019).

U.S. Copyright Office. 1998. "The Digital Millennium Copyright Act of 1998." https://copyright.gov/legislation/dmca.pdf (accessed June 02, 2019).

U.S. Department of Energy. 2014. Cybersecurity Capability Maturity Model," https://energy.gov/sites/prod/files/2014/03/f13/C2M2-v1-1_cor.pdf (accessed July 24, 2019).

Chapter 14

Davis, F.D., R.P. Bagozzi, and P.R. Warshaw. 1989. "User Acceptance of Computer Technology: A Comparison of Two Theoretical Models." *Management Science* 35, no. 8, pp. 982–1003. doi: 10.1287/mnsc.35.8.982

Davis, F.D. 1985. "A Technology Acceptance Model for Empirically Testing New End-User Information Systems: Theory and Results." Massachusetts Institute of Technology. http://hdl.handle.net/1721.1/15192

Giddens, A. 1984. *The Constitution of Society*. Polity Press: Cambridge, UK.

Gregor, S. 2006. "The Nature of Theory in Information Systems." *MIS Quarterly* 30, no. 3, pp. 611–42. doi: 10.2307/25148742

Horne, C., A. Ahmad, and S. Maynard. 2016. "A Theory on Information Security." The 27th Australasian Conference on Information Systems. At Wollongong, Australia.

Iivari, J., R. Hirschheim, and H.K. Klein. 2000. "A Dynamic Framework for Classifying Information Systems Development Methodologies and Approaches." *Journal of Management Information Systems* 17, no. 3, pp. 179–218.

Latour, B., and S. Woolgar. 1986. *Laboratory Life: The Construction of Scientific Facts*. Princeton, NJ: Princeton University Press.

Latour, B. 1987. *Science in Action: How to Follow Scientists and Engineers through Society*. Cambridge, MA: Harvard University Press.

Markus, M., L.A. Majchrzak, and L. Gasser. 2002. "A Design Theory for Systems that Support Emergent Knowledge Processes." *MIS Quarterly* 26, no. 3, pp. 179–212.

Moore, G.E. 1965. "Cramming More Components onto Integrated Circuits." *Electronics* 38, no. 8, pp. 114–17.

Orlikowski, W.J. 1992. "The Duality of Technology: Rethinking the Concept of Technology in Organizations." *Organization Science* 3, no. 3, pp. 398–427.

Shannon, C.E. 1948, "A Mathematical Theory of Communication." Bell *System Technical Journal* 27, pp. 379–423 and 623–56.

Shiva, S., S. Roy, and D. Dasgupta. 2010. "Game Theory for Cyber Security." CSIIRW 10: Proceedings of the Sixth Annual Workshop on Cyber Security and Information Intelligence Research. Oak Ridge: Tennessee. doi: 10.1145/1852666.1852704

Turban, E., and J. Aronson. 2001. *Decision Support Systems and Intelligent Systems*. Prentice-Hall: Upper Saddle River, NJ.

Von Bertalanffy, L. 1969. *General System Theory: Foundations, Development, Applications*. New York: George Braziller.

Von Solms, R., and J. van Niekerk. 2013. "From Information Security to Cyber Security." *Computers & Security* 38, 97–102. doi: 10.1016/j.cose.2013.04.004

Chapter 15

Bandura, A. 1986. *Social Foundations of thought and Action: A Social cognitive theory*. Englewood Cliffs, N.J.: Prentice-Hall.

Chan, A.S., Y.C. Ho, and M.C. Cheung. 1998. "Music Training Improves Verbal Memory." *Nature* 396, no. 6707, p. 128. doi: 10.1038/24075

Chu, C., A. Zhmoginov, and M. Sandler. 2017. "CycleGAN, a Master of Steganography." ArXiv abs/1712.02950

Costandi, M. 2016. "Want to 'Train Your Brain'? Forget Apps, Learn a Musical Instrument." http://getpocket.com/explore/item/want-to-train-your-brain-forget-apps-learn-a-musical-instrument (accessed September 19, 2019).

Foster, J.A., and K.A. Neufeld. 2013. "Gut–Brain Axis: How the Microbiome Influences Anxiety and Depression." *Trends in Neurosciences* 36, pp. 305–12.

Gómez-Pinilla, F. 2008. "Brain Foods: The Effects of Nutrients on Brain Function." *Neuroscience* 9, no. 7, pp. 568–78.

Griffiths, J. 2019. "When Chinese Hackers Declared War on the Rest of Us." https://technologyreview.com/s/612638/when-chinese-hackers-declared-war-on-the-rest-of-us (accessed December 5, 2019).

Heinrich, H.W. 1931. *Industrial Accident Prevention: A Scientific Approach.* McGraw-Hill. OCLC 571338960.

Lassale, C., G.D. Batty, A. Baghdadli, F. Jacks, A. Sanchez-Villegas, M. Kivimaki, and T. Akbarely. 2019. "Healthy Dietary Indices and Risk of Depressive Outcomes: a Systematic Review and Meta-Analysis of Observational Studies." *Molecular Psychiatry* 24, pp. 965–86. doi: 10.1038/s41380-018-0237-8

McNeese, M., V. Mancuso, N. McNeese, T. Endsley, and P. Forster. 2013. "Using the Living Laboratory Framework as a Basis for Understanding Next-Generation Analyst Work." The International Society for Optical Engineering, Baltimore, Maryland. doi: 10.1117/12.2016514

Pugh, J., L. Pycroft, A. Sandberg, T. Aziz, and J. Savulescu. 2018. "Brainjacking in Deep Brain Stimulation and Autonomy." https://ncbi.nlm.nih.gov/pubmed/30595661 (accessed December 17, 2019).

Ramsey, D. 2016. *Eat complete: The 21 Nutrients that Fuel Brainpower, Boost Weight Loss, and Transform Your Health.* New York: Harper Wave.

Feynman, R. 1994. *Six Easy Pieces: Essentials of Physics Explained by Its Most Brilliant Teacher.* Basic Books.

Ruffin, V.A., A.I. Salameh, W.F. Boron, and M.D. Parker. 2014. "Intracellular pH Regulation by Acid-Base Transporters in Mammalian Neurons." *Frontiers in Physiology* 5, no. 43. doi: 10.3389/fphys.2014.00043

Schlaug, G., A. Norton, K. Overy, and E. Winner. 2006. "Effects of Music Training on The Child's Brain and Cognitive Development." *Annals of the New York Academy of Sciences* 1060, pp. 219–30. doi: 10.1196/annals.1360.015

Vieane, A., G. Funke, R. Gutzwiller, V. Mancuso, B. Sawyer, and C. Wickens. 2016. "Addressing Human Factors Gaps in Cyber Defense." *Proceedings of the Human Factors and Ergonomics Society* 60, pp. 770–73. doi: 10.1177/1541931213601176

Wordsworth, R. 2017. "Brainjacking: Are Medical Implants the Next Target for Hackers?" https://wired.co.uk/article/brainjacking-are-medical-implants-the-next-target-of-hackers, (accessed October 2, 2019).

Zakharov, E., A. Shysheya, E. Burkov, and V. Lempitsky. 2019. "Few-Shot Adversarial Learning of Realistic Neural Talking Head Models." *IEEE/CVF International Conference on Computer Vision (ICCV) (2019): 9458–9467.*

Zhu, L., S. Kim, M. Hara, and M. Aono. 2018. "Remarkable Problem-Solving Ability of Unicellular Amoeboid Organism and its Mechanism." *Royal Society Open Science* 5, no. 180396. doi: 10.1098/rsos.180396

National Science and Technology Council. 2019. "Federal Cybersecurity Research and Development Strategic Plan." http://nitrd.gov/pubs/Federal-Cybersecurity-RD-Strategic-Plan-2019.pdf (accessed January 3, 2020).

About the Author

Dr. Brown is the Director of the University of the Cumberlands' Ph.D. program in Information Technology. The University has grown from its private Christian, Appalachian roots to a global University that provides opportunities for personal and professional growth with particular emphasis on meeting the educational and professional needs of diverse populations through a range of professional programs designed for success.

In addition to developing an innovative, advanced curriculum and recruiting highly qualified faculty, and his publications and presentations, Dr. Brown has mentored numerous dissertations in information technology, cybersecurity, networking, forensics, management, and so on., even in music. His philosophy is that it is essential to expand knowledge in multiple research areas to improve one's unique area of expertise.

Dr. Brown's leadership and scholarship draw on a deep and diverse set of experiences acquired in decades developing Cybersecurity Masters/Doctoral programs, participation in many governmental standard bodies such as the National Security Agency (NSA/DHS) Center of Academic Excellence in Information Assurance (CAEs) and National Initiative for Cybersecurity Education (NICE). He is also developing the CERTIFIED CYBERSECURITY BEHAVIORAL PROFESSIONAL (CCSPB) certification (ccsbp.org).

Dr. Brown's current book presents a fresh perspective incorporating the latest research on the combination of cybersecurity and behavior, where the new cybersecurity challenge is not just to understand cybercriminals' behavior, but our behavior, and to realize that some of our behaviors could lead us to make ineffective cybersecurity decisions. When not working, Dr. Brown enjoys time with family, friends, and practicing Krav Maga at home in North Carolina.

Index

OTHER TITLES IN THE BUSINESS LAW AND CORPORATE RISK MANAGEMENT COLLECTION

John Wood, Econautics Sustainability Institute, Editor

- *Artificial Intelligence Design and Solution for Risk and Security* by Archie Addo and Muthu Shanmugam
- *Artificial Intelligence for Security* by Archie Addo and Muthu Shanmugam
- *Artificial Intelligence for Risk Management* by Archie Addo and Srini Centhala
- *The Business-Minded CISCO* by Bryan C. Kissinger
- *Getting the Best Equipment Lease Deal* by Richard M. Contino
- *Equipment Leasing and Financing* by Richard M. Contino
- *AI Concepts for Business Applications* by Nelson E. Brestoff
- *How New Risk Management Helps Leaders Master Uncertainty* by Robert B. Pojasek
- *Understanding Cyberrisks in IoT* by Carolina A. Adaros Boye
- *The Business of Cybersecurity* by Ashwini Sathnur
- *Conversations in Cyberspace* by Giulio D'Agostino

Concise and Applied Business Books

The Collection listed above is one of 30 business subject collections that Business Expert Press has grown to make BEP a premiere publisher of print and digital books. Our concise and applied books are for...

- Professionals and Practitioners
- Faculty who adopt our books for courses
- Librarians who know that BEP's Digital Libraries are a unique way to offer students ebooks to download, not restricted with any digital rights management
- Executive Training Course Leaders
- Business Seminar Organizers

Business Expert Press books are for anyone who needs to dig deeper on business ideas, goals, and solutions to everyday problems. Whether one print book, one ebook, or buying a digital library of 110 ebooks, we remain the affordable and smart way to be business smart. For more information, please visit www.businessexpertpress.com, or contact sales@businessexpertpress.com.

www.ingramcontent.com/pod-product-compliance
Lightning Source LLC
Chambersburg PA
CBHW061143220326
41599CB00025B/4336